Reactive Programming for .NET Developers

Get up and running with reactive programming paradigms to build fast, concurrent, and powerful applications

Antonio Esposito
Michael Ciceri

BIRMINGHAM - MUMBAI

Reactive Programming for .NET Developers

First published: July 2016

Production reference: 1150716

Published by Packt Publishing Ltd.

Livery Place

35 Livery Street

Birmingham

B3 2PB, UK.

ISBN 978-1-78588-288-3

www.packtpub.com

Credits

Authors
Antonio Esposito
Michael Ciceri

Reviewer

Uladzimir Kazakevich

Commissioning Editor

Amarabha Banerjee

Acquisition Editor

Larissa Pinto

Content Development Editor

Arun Nadar

Technical Editor

Sachit Bedi

Copy Editors
Akshata Lobo

Project Coordinator

Ritika Manoj

Proofreader

Safis Editing

Indexer

Rekha Nair

Graphics

Jason Monteiro

Production Coordinator

Aparna Bhagat

About the Authors

Antonio Esposito is a Microsoft Certified Trainer, software architect, father, son, and lover of cooking and eating. He has been addicted to computer programming from age 8, a developer since 2002, and a speaker from 2010. He has moved across Europe in the last fifteen years working as freelance consultant or speaker for companies such as UniCredit Bank, Ferrari F1 Racing Team, Microsoft Italy, IBM, and many others. He actively attends as a speaker at a lot of conferences, such as MCT Summit and WPC Italy. He is already an author for Packt with Learning .NET High Performance Programming in 2014.

To my children Tommaso and Matteo, and my lovely wife Giusy, who supported me during my many and many nights of writing.

Michael Ciceri is a technology consultant in .NET Framework and Microsoft. He is a functional programming, mathematics, technology, psychology, and science enthusiast. He started as an autodidact and passionately became an analyst and software developer in several areas, such as image processing, banking ATM services security, intranet back end, app monetizing. Recently, he has been working on the analysis and development of functions in the core application to solve problems or improve capabilities.

About the Reviewer

Uladzimir Kazakevich has been writing code for as long as he can remember. He is a developer, consultant, and solution architect. With over 15 years of experience in delivering solutions across industry sectors, such as social media, education, e-commerce and finance, he specializes in technologies, such as Microsoft .NET, WebAPI, Windows Communication Foundation, MSSQL, Microsoft Azure, scalable and high-performant infrastructure. He is certified by SEI as Software Architecture Professional and is TOGAF 9-certified.

Uladzimir serves as Head of EPAM Microsoft Competency Center with focus on Solution Architecture. His key focus is to harness, develop, and scale innovative technologies and engineering methodologies in the company, competency center and successfully apply them in client engagements.

When he codes for fun, he spends his time using Arduinos, sensors, Raspberry Pis, and Azure Machine Learning to build own house automation system. He is also the organizer of local TechTalks and SETCON conferences; he is also an active speaker at such events.

Uladzimir lives in Brest, Belarus, with his wonderful wife Alena and their awesome little girl Nika.

www.PacktPub.com

For support files and downloads related to your book, please visit www.PacktPub.com.

Did you know that Packt offers eBook versions of every book published, with PDF and ePub files available? You can upgrade to the eBook version at www.PacktPub.com and as a print book customer, you are entitled to a discount on the eBook copy. Get in touch with us at service@packtpub.com for more details.

At www.PacktPub.com, you can also read a collection of free technical articles, sign up for a range of free newsletters and receive exclusive discounts and offers on Packt books and eBooks.

https://www2.packtpub.com/books/subscription/packtlib

Do you need instant solutions to your IT questions? PacktLib is Packt's online digital book library. Here, you can search, access, and read Packt's entire library of books.

Why subscribe?

- Fully searchable across every book published by Packt
- Copy and paste, print, and bookmark content
- On demand and accessible via a web browser

Free access for Packt account holders

If you have an account with Packt at www.PacktPub.com, you can use this to access PacktLib today and view 9 entirely free books. Simply use your login credentials for immediate access.

Table of Contents

Preface	1
Chapter 1: First Steps Toward Reactive Programming	7
Programming paradigms	8
Dataflow programming	11
Statelessness	13
The data-driven approach	14
Data streams	14
Observer pattern	15
Functional programming	16
Reactive programming	20
Reactive manifesto	21
The programming experience	22
Change propagation and cancellation	23
Linguistic characteristics	24
Programming languages and frameworks	25
Reactive programming approaches	26
Further reading	27
Summary	27
Chapter 2: Reactive Programming with C#	29
IObserver interface	29
IObservable interface	33
Subscription life cycle	38
Sourcing events	42
Filtering events	44
Correlating events	47
Sourcing from CLR streams	52
Sourcing from CLR enumerables	55
Changeable collections	56
Infinite collections	59
Summary	62
Chapter 3: Reactive Extension Programming	63
Setting up Rx.NET	63
Marble diagrams	65

Subjects   66
   ReplaySubject   67
   BehaviorSubject   68
   AsyncSubject   69
   Custom subjects   69
   Subject from IObservable/IObserver   72
   Transforming operators   73
      Delay   73
      Map   74
      Scan   74
      Debounce   75
      Amb   77

Combining operators   78
   Combine latest   78
   Concat   79
   Merge   81
   Sample   82
   StartWith   83
   Zip   84

Filtering operators   85
   Filter   85
   Distinct   86
   DistinctUntilChanged   87
   ElementAt   88
   Skip   89
   Take   90

Mathematical operators   90
   Min/Max/Avg/Sum/Count   91

Logic operators   91
   Every/Some/Includes   91
   SequenceEqual   92

References   94
Summary   94

Chapter 4: Observable Sequence Programming   95

Sequence creation basics   95
   Empty/Never   96
   Return   96
   Throw   97
   Create   97

Range   99
Generate   100
Time-based sequence creation   100
Interval   100
Timer   101
Timeout   102
TimeInterval/Timestamp   104
Sequence manipulation and filtering   105
Where   105
Join   106
If   107
TakeUntil/TakeWhile/SkipUntil/SkipWhile   108
TakeLast/SkipLast   109
Sequence partitioning   110
GroupBy   110
Aggregate   111
MaxBy/MinBy   112
Advanced operators   113
IgnoreElements   114
Repeat   114
Publish/Connect   115
RefCount   116
PublishLast   117
Replay   118
Multicast   119
Summary   120
Chapter 5: Debugging Reactive Extensions   121
Tracing sequences   121
Materialize   121
Dematerialize   123
TimeInterval   124
Do   125
Inspecting sequences   127
Contains   127
Any   128
All   128
SequenceEqual   129
Exception handling   130
Catch   130

OnErrorResumeNext	132
Finally	132
Retry	134
Summary	135
Chapter 6: CLR Integration and Scheduling	137
Sourcing from CLR events	137
FromEventPattern	138
FromEvent	143
ToEvent	145
Threading integration	145
Sourcing from a Task	146
Task cancellation	146
Scheduling	147
Default schedulers	150
SubscribeOn/ObserveOn	151
Injecting schedulers	153
Custom scheduling	154
Future scheduling	155
Virtual time	156
Testing schedulers	159
Historical records	161
Summary	164
Chapter 7: Advanced Techniques	165
Designing a custom operator	165
Designing the AsObservable operator	166
Designing the AcceptObservableClient operator	168
Case study – writing a reactive socket server	170
Disposing Create	173
Designing a custom provider	176
Designing a custom scheduler	177
Dealing with the scheduler state	179
Creating Pattern	181
Implementing event sourcing with Rx	183
Creating and validating an invoice	184
Event sourcing an invoice creation	188
Creating Interactive Extensions (Ix) operators	190
Summary	192
Chapter 8: F# and Functional Reactive Programming	193

F# – first time	193
Introduction to F# and FRP	194
The immutable and deduce type	195
Type inference	196
Functions as first class values	197
Using the Type function for object-oriented programming	199
Collection – The heart of F#	201
F# – how to use it	**211**
Pattern Matching and pipe forward	211
Pipeline and composition	213
Discriminated Unions and the Record type	214
Active Patterns	217
Asynchronous pattern in F#	**218**
The concept of asynchronous workflow	219
Asynchronous code and examples	220
Functional Reactive Programming	**224**
What is FRP and how is it represented?	225
Introduction to functional reactive programming	226
Collections and functions in a flow	227
FRP and its scenarios	229
Event data flow	229
Push and pull-based domains	232
Examples of scenarios with AsyncSeq	233
Summary	**234**
Chapter 9: Advanced FRP and Best Practices	**235**
Discrete and continuous components	**236**
Discrete components	237
The discrete event example with the discriminated union	239
Continuous components	240
Changing continuous value and event stream	243
Hybrid system	243
Time flow and dynamic change	**244**
Time flow in asynchronous data flow	245
Using F# and collection function for dynamic changing	247
Even more on FRP and F#	**249**
Railway-oriented Programming	250
Making an Observable in FRP	253
Summary	**255**
Index	**257**

Preface

Reactive programming is the programming paradigm for handling continuous changing messages and their notifications. Instead of developing static value changes, we develop data changes. This slight difference leaves the developer facing issues regarding high speed messaging systems that handle such messages in a completely new way. Reactive programming means writing functions that transform messages. This means that something, such as an exception within the reactive world became a message. This book will cover Reactive programming with Reactive extensions for .NET in an increasing complex approach. In the final chapters, the reader will find real-world solutions and learn about F# functional reactive programming.

What this book covers

Chapter 1, *First Steps in Reactive Programming*, covers what Reactive programming is: the idea, the overall design, the available frameworks, and the languages supporting this incredible programming paradigm.

Chapter 2, *Reactive Programming with C#*, will show Reactive programming in action in plain C# coding without the need for any external reference. In this way, any developer may bring reactive programming knowledge to any existing application.

Chapter 3, *Reactive Extension Programming*, explains RX basics, such as the Observable sequence, message consumers (Observer), and the most widely used reactive operators, such as message transforming and message grouping functions.

Chapter 4, *Observable Sequence Programming*, will teach you how to produce, consume, and route messages with subjects and learn the Rx operator catalog. You will also see operators that apply message filtering, aggregation, transformation, generation, and time-based operations.

Chapter 5, *Debugging Reactive Extensions*, will deal with debugging and tracing observable sequences. It focuses on handling exceptions, routing errors, and notifying users about application issues in order to improve application reliability and maintainability.

Chapter 6, *CLR Integration and Scheduling*, covers how to source or send messages with plain CLR objects and how to achieve time scheduling and multithreading easily with Rx programming.

Chapter 7, *Advanced Techniques*, will show Rx in action with real-world solutions and explain how to create new operators or how to use the Rx features in classic .NET development.

Chapter 8, *F# and Functional Reactive Programming*, presents the F# language and key points of functional programming. It describes Functional Reactive Programming (FRP) with a few examples of push-based and pull-based scenarios, the event data flow, and type events in F#.

Chapter 9, *Advanced FRP and Best Practices*, delves deep into advanced FRP concepts through the study of discrete and continuous components and the concepts of time flow and dynamic change. It also discusses Railway-oriented programming and F# observable.

What you need for this book

For this book, you will require an updated version Visual Studio 2013 or 2015.The Reactive Extensions library pack is available from the NuGet package explorer by searching "Rx-main". Examples from the book require other packages as well; in these cases, a reference within the chapter itself will specify the required package's name.

Who this book is for

If you are an experienced C# developer with no pre-existing knowledge of Rx development, this book is for you. The book is useful as a Rx reference manual.

Conventions

In this book, you will find a number of text styles that distinguish between different kinds of information. Here are some examples of these styles and an explanation of their meaning.

Code words in text, database table names, folder names, filenames, file extensions, pathnames, dummy URLs, user input, and Twitter handles are shown as follows: "Later, a counter variable will make the most of the work to find the distance between the two numbers."

A block of code is set as follows:

```
//procedural style
var sourceData = new { TotalAmount = 12345.67, PaidAmount = 12345.67 };
if (sourceData.PaidAmount == sourceData.TotalAmount)
{
    //do something
}
```

The NuGet package names have been changed. The Rx-* and Ix-* packages have been renamed to match their library names, keeping inline with the rest of .NET Core.

- Use `System.Reactive` instead of `Rx-Main`
- Use `System.Interactive` instead of `Ix-Main`
- Use `System.Interactive.Async` instead of `Ix-Async`

New terms and **important words** are shown in bold. Words that you see on the screen, for example, in menus or dialog boxes, appear in the text like this: "As you can see, the diagram depicts three functions held in the Computation Expression that return **Success** or **Failure**."

Warnings or important notes appear in a box like this.

Tips and tricks appear like this.

Reader feedback

Feedback from our readers is always welcome. Let us know what you think about this book—what you liked or disliked. Reader feedback is important for us as it helps us develop titles that you will really get the most out of.

To send us general feedback, simply e-mail `feedback@packtpub.com`, and mention the book's title in the subject of your message.

If there is a topic that you have expertise in and you are interested in either writing or contributing to a book, see our author guide at `www.packtpub.com/authors`.

Customer support

Now that you are the proud owner of a Packt book, we have a number of things to help you to get the most from your purchase.

Downloading the example code

You can download the example code files for this book from your account at `http://www.packtpub.com`. If you purchased this book elsewhere, you can visit `http://www.packtpub.com/support` and register to have the files e-mailed directly to you.

You can download the code files by following these steps:

1. Log in or register to our website using your e-mail address and password.
2. Hover the mouse pointer on the **SUPPORT** tab at the top.
3. Click on **Code Downloads & Errata**.
4. Enter the name of the book in the **Search** box.
5. Select the book for which you're looking to download the code files.
6. Choose from the drop-down menu where you purchased this book from.
7. Click on **Code Download**.

Once the file is downloaded, please make sure that you unzip or extract the folder using the latest version of:

- WinRAR / 7-Zip for Windows
- Zipeg / iZip / UnRarX for Mac
- 7-Zip / PeaZip for Linux

The code bundle for the book is also hosted on GitHub at `https://github.com/PacktPublishing/Reactive-Programming-for-.NET-Developers`. We also have other code bundles from our rich catalog of books and videos available at `https://github.com/PacktPublishing/`. Check them out!

Errata

Although we have taken every care to ensure the accuracy of our content, mistakes do happen. If you find a mistake in one of our books-maybe a mistake in the text or the code-we would be grateful if you could report this to us. By doing so, you can save other readers from frustration and help us improve subsequent versions of this book. If you find any errata, please report them by visiting http://www.packtpub.com/submit-errata, selecting your book, clicking on the **Errata Submission Form** link, and entering the details of your errata. Once your errata are verified, your submission will be accepted and the errata will be uploaded to our website or added to any list of existing errata under the Errata section of that title.

To view the previously submitted errata, go to https://www.packtpub.com/books/content/support and enter the name of the book in the search field. The required information will appear under the **Errata** section.

Piracy

Piracy of copyrighted material on the Internet is an ongoing problem across all media. At Packt, we take the protection of our copyright and licenses very seriously. If you come across any illegal copies of our works in any form on the Internet, please provide us with the location address or website name immediately so that we can pursue a remedy.

Please contact us at copyright@packtpub.com with a link to the suspected pirated material.

We appreciate your help in protecting our authors and our ability to bring you valuable content.

Questions

If you have a problem with any aspect of this book, you can contact us at questions@packtpub.com, and we will do our best to address the problem.

1
First Steps Toward Reactive Programming

Thanks for buying this guide to **Reactive Programming** and **Reactive Extensions** for .NET.

This book will give you an expert overview about the magical world of programming, also known as programming live data or real-time data, instead of programming static data as happens with any other usual programming paradigm.

Do you know Microsoft Excel?

Excel is a software that lets you write raw numbers and functions in a proprietary mathematical form or through a simple scripting programming language (VBA).

The magic happens when you write an Excel function, such as *=A1+A2*, which means that the current cell value will be the sum of the values contained in the *A1* and *A2* cells.

This simple function creates a subscription to the events of cells *A1* and *A2*. This means that any time you update the value of any of these two cells, the function will return a new value. This is the simplest example of functional and reactive programming available.

Now that we have an idea of what reactive is, it is easy to explain that this book will guide developers with any background knowledge about reactive programming toward the understanding of the reactive programming paradigm with a lot of examples of using **Reactive Extensions** (**Rx**) for .NET.

This chapter will give an overview of what **Reactive Programming** (**RP**) is and how it works, starting with programming paradigms and later diving into the RP structure following the schema:

- Programming paradigms
- Dataflow programming
- Functional programming
- Reactive programming

Programming paradigms

Once upon a time, programming languages where extremely different from the ones we have today.

The first-generation programming language was the *machine-code* one. It was made against the hardware itself, and for most, programming in such way meant creating hardware solutions like moving jumpers or switches or adding/removing cables.

The second generation of programming languages was the *assembly* language (such as Assembler). The name was related to the assembling stage of these languages into a machine level one that is able to run in the CPU execution pipelines. This language generation was the first made with text, although it was tightly coupled with hardware architectures.

The third generation of programming languages started the age of English-like languages that were able to run on top of hardware specifications with their own instruction set, no longer coupled with the lower hardware level. It started the reusability era.

These languages were not made in real CPU executable code. Programmers did their job in a *high-level* programming language that, after the compilation stage, translated into a lower-level one that was able to run into the CPU execution pipeline. At the beginning of the high-level programming era, the most diffused languages where IBM ® Fortran and COBOL.

Modern languages, such as .NET, Java, and C/C++, are all of the same generation as their grandparents of the 1950s. Obviously, the current languages have improved features and abilities, because of the long evolution time.

The main differentiation between the previous programming languages and the current ones is the *programming paradigm*—something like a programming approach of structured methodology that changes the way a programmer creates software.

The oldest one is the *imperative programming* paradigm. It is made of a direct sequence of steps, usually numbered from 1 to *N*, that simply executes in a forward-only fashion. In these stages, the ability to jump forward or backward with commands, such as `GoTo`, was definitely a killing feature, while now, with modern programming paradigms, it is absolutely avoided. By programming with such an approach, a simple application made to sum two values was a simple sequence of steps, or instructions, that altogether achieved the desired goal. Here is an example in C#:

```
Console.WriteLine("Step counter: RUNNING");

Console.WriteLine("Write the starting value");
var startingValue = int.Parse(Console.ReadLine());

//value entering starting point
REPEAT:
Console.WriteLine("Write the ending value");
var endingValue = int.Parse(Console.ReadLine());

if (endingValue <= startingValue)
{
    Console.WriteLine("ending value must be greater than starting value");
    goto REPEAT;
}

//this counter represents the distance between startingValue and
endingValue
var counter = 0;

//increments the counter until needed to reach the endingValue
COUNT:
if (endinqValue > ++counter + startinqValue)
    goto COUNT;

Console.WriteLine("You need {0} steps to reach {1} from {2}", counter,
endingValue, startingValue);
Console.WriteLine("END");
```

As you can see in the preceding example, the whole program is only a list of steps where the current actor is at once the computer asking for something on the console and the user writing some response on the console. The program is unable to do multiple things together. Either the computer places a question to the user, or the user enters a digit or something on the keyboard to give the computer a command or some data.

C# is a *general purpose programming language* supporting imperative, procedural, declarative, object-oriented, component-oriented, service-oriented, and functional programming paradigms all together.

There are no interaction constructs (`for`, `for...each`) available in imperative programming, and there is no code factorization into subroutines able to abstract and make reusable single portions of code.

The check logic against the user value is available through a simple `GoTo` statement that is able to move the control's flow pointer (the actual execution row) to a newly desired position. Regarding this check logic, the execution flow simply goes back to some previous line executing and entering a destination value.

Similarly, when it is time to count the distance between the two given values, the logic again uses the `GoTo` statement, changing the current state of the `counter` variable to the updated value. It is the last time the variable will contain the required result.

 It is interesting that throughout the imperative programming paradigm, C# is even faster than when programming in an object-oriented one, because of the higher usage of the stack memory, instead of the heap memory that is slower.
If you are interested in code optimization and high performance programming, you may find it interesting to read my other book *Learning .NET High Performance Programming*.

In imperative programming languages, such as Fortran, Pascal, or COBOL, there was a number for each row to give developers the ability to create interactive constructs, such as recurring jobs or any other interaction logic, by jumping between rows.

Obviously, this choice is not available in modern general-purpose languages, such as C#, which give the same feature with the use of a label (in the preceding example, we used `Repeat` and `Count`) instead of the row number. The result is the same.

To understand imperative programming, we must understand the meaning of the *state*. An application's state is the sum of all the data usually available within the code through fields, properties, and variables. When we started the preceding code, the application state was empty (we will ignore the **Common Language Runtime** (**CLR**) stuff that is in the memory together with our data). During the execution, some variables (`startingValue` and `endingValue`) became available by asking data from the user.

Later, a `counter` variable will make the most of the work to find the distance between the two numbers. What is the heart of the imperative programming paradigm is the *status change* that the code makes against available variables. As visible, the `counter` variable becomes incremented until the wanted value is found.

This status change still happens in other paradigms such as *procedural-programming* or *object-oriented programming*, although these paradigms bring to a higher level abstraction of data structures or a better code reusability.

Dataflow programming

Changing the application state is not something wrong by itself, but there are different programming approaches that may produce better results and together give the developer a more pleasant working experience. A typical use case happens when we deal with *in-move* data (or living data or data stream), where we may find that using interaction logic constructs that change state, such as `if`, `for`, and so on, is a poor performing choice together with a poor design. In-move data is any kind of data stream, such as a video stream, an application insights stream, and so on. Because of its statelessness, it is obvious that a stateless programming approach offers better results than a state-driven one.

We are used to dealing with static data, such as a variable, a database, or anything else such as some binary- or string-based data. All such data is *data-at-rest*, static data, or simply data.

As an example if we execute a `select` statement against a relational database, we will always have a result set containing the exact value contained in the database table at the specific time we executed the query. A second later, the table could experience an `update` statement that could change any row's data without the first client (the one executing the `select` statement) receiving an update on such data changes. To address these kinds of data changes without having to face issues between different relational database clients, there are optimistic and pessimistic concurrency checks (a bit outside the scope of this book). Obviously, the less we need to synchronize code to access a concurrent resource, the better our code will perform.

In imperative programming, *control-flow* is responsible for the good execution of the application. Such flow is usually made of multiple code rows that do something on input/output ports and somehow alter the application's state until the desired result is achieved, whereas in dataflow programming, data flows in and out of the different stages of a flowchart, as it behaves in a workflow.

Obviously, the different types of programming will greatly change the developers' experience and programming capability of the language. It is very difficult (and conceptually a bit wrong) to compute something by executing some interaction logic in data flow programming, because this kind of programming is simply outside the core design of the programming paradigm.

A practical example can be seen in data integrational , **Extract, Transform,** and **Load** (**ETL**) workflows, such as those available in **SQL Server Integration Services** (**SSIS**), as shown in the following screenshot. An ETL workflow has the task of reading (extracting) data from a data source (relational or not) and mapping (transforming) such data by grouping or aggregating it with other data sources or by executing transforming functions. Then, data flows (loads) into a target data store (relational or not) for future simplified access. SSIS is the tool for designing these kinds of workflows within the SQL Server Business Intelligence suite.

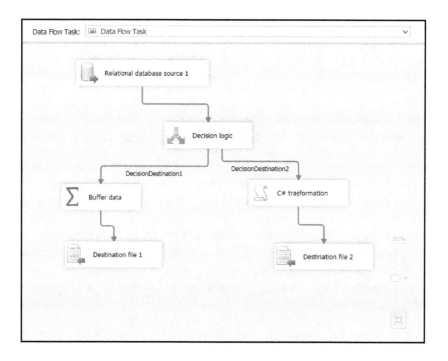

A SSIS dataflow task doing some transformations on data from a relational database

Generally speaking, outside the SQL server-oriented implementation of SSIS, within data flow programming, instead of having a huge code base in a high-level code, we have something like a data workflow. A *digraph* (directed graph)—an ordered version of a usual flowchart. Here is an example:

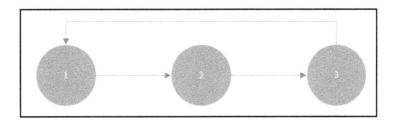

A simple representation of a dataflow digraph made of three recurring stages

Within the Microsoft universe, the only data flow programming compliant language is the *Microsoft Visual Programming Language* available for the Microsoft Robotics Developer Studio environment for robotics programming. Instead, SSIS simply uses data flows to handle data integrations between databases.

Statelessness

The unavailability of the state, a key concept of data flow programming, is the opposite of what happens in all imperative or object-oriented programming-based applications. This behavior drastically changes the programming experience.

A stateless design never stores (temporary or persisted) application or user data with the need of changing it in time for computational needs.

We cannot use temporary variables to store changeable values, such as the total of an invoice. We cannot use an index to jump around a collection or an array, and we cannot iterate it. Obviously, if we need to write a function that needs a variable, we cannot use a variable anymore; in other words, we can't use variables that act as a business logic state persistence.

When we write a function, the data will simply have an origin, a target, and one or multiple transformations in multiple stages.

Thanks to this stateless design of the whole application, it is easy to see that each stage can run on a different thread together and each input or output endpoint can run on another thread and so on. The stateless design is the key that makes the design able to scale out quite perfectly according to *Amdahl's Law*.

As well as performance results, a stateless design brings higher testability rates of the whole application (bear in mind ASP.NET WebForms versus ASP.NET MVC) together with a more modern approach in programming style that avoids the use of interactive loops such as `for`, `for...each`, and relatives.

The data-driven approach

The last evolution of the imperative programming paradigm is object-oriented programming. Such paradigms request we model our business world into a high-level domain model. This means that, in our code, we will find an object representing any living entity of our business model; a invoice or a customer are examples of such objects. Such models drive business logic. They do not need to be persisted in a one-to-one representation from the model to the persistence store (usually, a relational database). This approach is called domain-driven design. The opposite of such an approach is the data-driven design that makes direct actions against data without a real discrimination between data and business.

Because of the intrinsic behavior of dataflow programming, a data-driven design is the natural choice when designing a solution based on such programing paradigms.

But in the modern .NET-based programming style, the use of business-related entities in the various stages of the dataflow execution is available and suggested too.

Data streams

A data stream is the flow of some data in time, usually of a unique format, that is available to one or multiple readers.

Examples are television video streams, YouTube video streams, Twitter or RSS feeds, Azure EventHub, and so on. Those who are used to C# programming will remember the namespace `System.IO` that contains different classes made for stream programming, such as `BinaryReader`/`BinaryWriter` that makes available streaming any CLR low-level type or `StreamReader`/`StreamWriter` that makes available streaming any text supporting various encodings from ASCII to UTF32.

In other words, a data stream is some data in a specific time instance. Time is the key concept for understanding a data stream. It is all about running data or in-move data. Without the time component, data can never flow in a stream.

Depending on the stream, it may support *seeking* operations, such as the ability to go forward and backward along the stream to start flowing data exactly at the desired time. Television video streams do not support such a feature. Microsoft Azure EventHub (a data stream) instead supports the feature in a configured time window of usually some hours.

The Azure EventHub is a paralleled stream service for streaming any data, usually used for **Internet of Things** (**IoT**) devices, telemetry values, or diagnostic purposes as an application insights collection. A similar choice within the Azure offering is the IoT Hub, another streamed service totally oriented to IoT devices that support more specific protocols.

Observer pattern

The `Observer` pattern, is a published subscribe style pattern; it defines the ability to register for data change or event signaling. Although written words may be something new to read about, the observer pattern is something absolutely overused in the event-driven programming paradigm of the Microsoft oriented languages in the last 20 years.

When we handle the `Button` click event, either in Visual Basic (from version 1 to 6) or in modern .NET Windows Forms, WPF applications, or even ASP.NET applications, we are simply using an implementation of the observer pattern.

The pattern defines an event generator, also known as *subject*, that fires the event and one or multiple event listeners or *observers* (in .NET, also known as event handlers) that will do something in reaction to the data state change or event signaling.

When dealing with data flow programming, the observer pattern is the one responsible for the acknowledgment between stages of the new data available. Each stage informs the following stages of new data available with a signal. Stages do not know about the overall design of the digraph. They simple signal the new data availability event; all subsequent stages that are observing the previous one for new data will be then acknowledged. This design makes useless the need of an overall data state, thus the design is stateless. Each stage observes or is being observed. That is all. Such data flowing between stages are data streams.

Functional programming

Functional programming is a programming paradigm that relies on the functional transformation of data between stages, not so different from the dataflow programming we just saw. The main addendum to the data flow paradigm is that, within the functional one, there is a specific functional transformation, while in the data flow paradigm such transformations occur in a specific idiom-based way that can be functional-based, script-based (imperative paradigm), component-based, or anything else.

In functional programming, data is always immutable and functions are responsible for data transformation. Anything in functional style is a data transformation. Although a decisional statement (`if`) cannot exist, a functional transformation from data containing predicate to data containing the Boolean result may occur:

```
//procedural style
var sourceData = new { TotalAmount = 12345.67, PaidAmount = 12345.67 };
if (sourceData.PaidAmount == sourceData.TotalAmount)
{
    //do something
}

//functional style
//a simple enumerable
new[] { new { TotalAmount = 12345.67, PaidAmount = 12345.67 } }
//transformation block
.Select(x => new
{
    x.TotalAmount,
    x.PaidAmount,
    CanContinue = x.TotalAmount == x.PaidAmount,
})
//if
.Where(x => x.CanContinue)
//do something
.ToArray();
```

A widely known design pattern is the data mapper one. This design tries to decouple and translate objects of a layer (for historic purposes, the domain layer) into another one (for historic purposes, the data model one).

Here is a simple procedural (imperative with subroutines) programming style example in C#:

```
class Program
{
    static void Main(string[] args)
```

```
    {
        //retrieve invoices from DB
        var invoicesFromDB = GetInvoicesFromDB();

        //map those invoices to business model objects
        var invoicesForBusiness =
ConvertInvoicesForBusiness(invoicesFromDB);
    }

    /// <summary>
    /// Reads invoices from a (fake) database
    /// </summary>
    /// <returns></returns>
    static InvoiceFromDB[] GetInvoicesFromDB()
    {
        var result = new InvoiceFromDB[3];

        result[0] = new InvoiceFromDB
            {
                CustomerName = "Mr. Black",
                Number = "100/2015/BBC",
                BaseAmount = 24560,
                VATMultiplier = 1.22,
            };

        result[1] = new InvoiceFromDB
            {
                CustomerName = "White Co Ltd",
                Number = "240/2015/BBC",
                BaseAmount = 422480,
                VATMultiplier = 1.22,
            };

        result[2] = new InvoiceFromDB
            {
                CustomerName = "Green Woods inc.",
                Number = "22/2015/BBC",
                BaseAmount = 8500,
                VATMultiplier = 1.22,
            };

        return result;
    }

    /// <summary>
    /// Converts invoices from database to invoices for business needs
    /// </summary>
    static InvoiceBusiness[] ConvertInvoicesForBusiness(InvoiceFromDB[]
```

```
        source)
          {
                var result = new InvoiceBusiness[source.Length];

                for (int i = 0; i < source.Length; i++)
                     result[i] = new InvoiceBusiness
                     {
                          Number = source[i].Number,
                          CustomerName = source[i].CustomerName,
                          BaseAmount = source[i].BaseAmount,
                          VATMultiplier = source[i].VATMultiplier,
                     };

                return result;
          }
    }

    public class InvoiceFromDB
    {
        public string CustomerName { get; set; }
        public string Number { get; set; }
        public double BaseAmount { get; set; }
        public double VATMultiplier { get; set; }
    }

    public class InvoiceBusiness
    {
        public string CustomerName { get; set; }
        public string Number { get; set; }
        public double BaseAmount { get; set; }
        public double VATMultiplier { get; set; }
        public double Total
        {
            get { return BaseAmount * VATMultiplier; }
        }
    }
```

In a functional style, the same program will benefit from the use of the enumerator pattern (for static data such as this one) or triggers that will notify for observed data changes.

Later, the transformation logic will take place within a function.

Here is the same preceding example in a functional style made with LINQ querying in C#:

```
    class Program
    {
        static void Main(string[] args)
        {
```

```
        var businessInvoices =
            //stage 1 - read db data
            GetInvoicesFromDB()
            //stage 2 - make transfomation
            .Select(dbinvoice => new InvoiceBusiness
            {
                Number = dbinvoice.Number,
                BaseAmount = dbinvoice.BaseAmount,
                CustomerName = dbinvoice.CustomerName,
                VATMultiplier = dbinvoice.VATMultiplier,
            })
            //force execution of the whole enumerator
            .ToArray();
    }

    static IEnumerable<InvoiceFromDB> GetInvoicesFromDB()
    {
        yield return new InvoiceFromDB
        {
            CustomerName = "Mr. Black",
            Number = "100/2015/BBC",
            BaseAmount = 24560,
            VATMultiplier = 1.22,
        };

        yield return new InvoiceFromDB
        {
            CustomerName = "White Co Ltd",
            Number = "240/2015/BBC",
            BaseAmount = 422480,
            VATMultiplier = 1.22,
        };

        yield return new InvoiceFromDB
        {
            CustomerName = "Green Woods inc.",
            Number = "22/2015/BBC",
            BaseAmount = 8500,
            VATMultiplier = 1.22,
        };
    }
}

public class InvoiceFromDB
{
    public string CustomerName { get; set; }
    public string Number { get; set; }
    public double BaseAmount { get; set; }
```

```
        public double VATMultiplier { get; set; }
    }

    public class InvoiceBusiness
    {
        public string CustomerName { get; set; }
        public string Number { get; set; }
        public double BaseAmount { get; set; }
        public double VATMultiplier { get; set; }
        public double Total
        {
            get { return BaseAmount * VATMultiplier; }
        }
    }
```

What makes the preceding example different from the previous one is that the `GetInvoicesFromDB` method returns an enumerable collection. Although an array is enumerable too, an array is a finite item collection. In the procedural example, all contained objects must already be in our memory before the method returns values creating a huge data state. Later, in the imperative example, such a state will be changed by the other method `ConvertInvoicesForBusiness` that is responsible for creating business objects containing business stuff (`Total` in the preceding example).

In the functional style example, instead of having an interactive statement that processes data in the memory, we will simply write a new function able to transform the data-oriented object into the business-oriented one. This transformation is declaratively defined with a function. The function simply states how the transformation must happen. Thus, to trigger the concrete computation and the storage (in memory) of the transformed data, we will use the `.ToArray()` LINQ extension method that will evaluate the functional result and store such results into a finite item collection, the array.

 We will delve more deeply into functional programming and functional reactive programming in `Chapter 8`, *F# and Functional Reactive Programming*, and `Chapter 9`, *Advanced FRP and Best Practices*, of this book.

Reactive programming

At this point, the preceding functional programming examples should convince any reader that data-driven programming of in-move data in many programming scenarios may achieve a higher performance than imperative programming could ever do.

Reactive programming is the art of programming the propagation of changes. Think of an Excel function =*A1+B2*. This function will always contain the sum of the two cells; it will never contain a raw (or static) value that represents the sum at a specific time. It will always contain the updated sum of the two cells' values. Anytime the related cells raise a value update event (*A1* and *A2*), the resulting cell will update the sum and show the new value. In C#, a similar behavior is available in a computed property, where the result is available only as a computation instead of a state value:

```
public double TotalAmount { get { return 10d * 10d; } }
```

Obviously, reactive programming is not simply a function or computed property. Specific designs and technologies are available and needed to develop using reactive programming. Let's start understanding such a new paradigm by reading its idea and its main characteristics and the available languages and idioms.

Reactive manifesto

The reactive programming experience starts with the reactive manifesto, the idea, the vision, the goal, and the overall design that should be behind any reactive application.

The manifesto is available here: http://www.reactivemanifesto.org.

The vision is actually simple: modern application needs are incompatible with widely used (and often legacy) designs and architectures. The goals are lovely; they are as follows:

- A *message-based* overall design with improved *lose-coupling* (between application and external modules), improved horizontal scalability, high responsiveness, and *graceful failure handling*.
- A high *scalability* rate means the ability to scale out with a thin overhead in a sessionless design. This traduces in the ability to handle a huge amount of tasks all together by using multiple computational systems.
- Improved *responsive* design because of the event-based design. The whole application will react to any request in a short time, letting the `Observer` module do its job without having the subject wait for completion time.
- Improved *resiliency* design because of the ability to gracefully handle applications and user faults thanks to execution context isolation, software module and data replication, and other features.

From this overview of the manifesto, you learned that reactive applications are all about the asynchronous programming of data and event messages flowing between multiple computational isolated stages.

The programming experience

Reactive programming means programming reactions to asynchronously streamed events. This means programming components that receive and produce messages. In between, we can add a transformation or a filter, or components that only produce or receive messages. Sometimes, in other programming paradigms, such message routing components are called message pump.

A time-based programming is drastically different from static data programming. For example, think of an invoice. Instead of programming its data (the total, the VAT amount, and other values), we will handle how the invoice changes in time.

Let's look at the difference, as follows:

Time stages	Imperative style	Reactive style
T0	A new `Invoice` object is instantiated. Its total is `0.00`.	A new `Invoice` object is instantiated.
T1	A product line is added to the invoice. The invoice's total changes to `450.00`.	A new `InvoiceAdditionItem` object is instantiated.
T2	A product line is added to the invoice. The invoice's total changes to `1450.00`.	A new `InvoiceAdditionItem` object is instantiated.
T3	A product line is added to the invoice. The invoice's total changes to `2450.00`.	A new `InvoiceAdditionItem` object is instantiated.

The main difference is that, in the reactive style, we have a time-based system, that is, we know exactly what the total invoice value at **T3** or **T2** was, even years later.

In database programming, there is the ability to create time-based tables. In reactive programming, we do something similar, but at an improved level because in reactive programming, anything is time-based and asynchronous.

A typical explanation about persist the result or all the actors of a function is that, when we persist each message, we do something more real and more similar to how data originates. While we persist the result as a data state, we persist something easier to read later. This second choice is an easier way of programming and is often less disk consuming within a database server, although it may bring unwanted mistakes and further updates of data-state because of some events or needs.

A simple example is available in any Excel worksheet. If Excel was not reactive, at the *A1* cell value update, the *A2* cell formula pointing to *A1* would not be updated, causing the developer to do more work later and exposing this work to a high error rate. Luckily, Excel is reactive; this means that any time we change any cell value, any formula will update its value.

This means that, in more cases, reactive programming behaves and performs better than state-driven programming, but this is not a universal solution. There are cases when state-driven programming is better than anything (typically, when dealing with other state-driven systems), and there are cases when we need to create a lightweight state to improve performances such as caching function results and so on.

When dealing with reactive programming, there are three kinds of message we can deal with. They are as follows:

- A *value* message containing a new valid value
- An *error* message containing an error that will flow to any message consumer
- A *completed* message that signals that the flow is ending

The daily reactive programming receipt contains a lot of alterations to the flow of the subscribed streams, such as event filtering, event composition from multiple streams, event routing, event buffering (compacting multiple similar events occurring quite at the same time), event mapping (converting an event data to another one), and so on.

Change propagation and cancellation

Whenever a new message containing a value flows throughout a stream, a *change propagation* occurs. It is not a simple binary message containing some values; this message actually informs of a data change. As we are dealing with a value of some types and are programming a time-based system, this flowing data assumes the name *data-in-motion*.

 Data-in-motion is data in real time, such as an application insight stream. Analysis of such data happens on the same data stream, although some stages later. Data-in-motion messages may translate into other messages by morphing or mapping to other messages, but the original message can never change.

Data-in-motion starts flowing by itself in a push style. We do not need asking for a refreshed value (pull style) simply because, in a reactive application, data always flows from the subject (the data producer) to the subscribing observers, notifying always any new value with the change propagation. This means that any observer will always have the last value. Obviously, this design has a heavy constraint: we need to be always online with the data source.

However, in stateful systems, the change propagation may not occur. We simply ask for refreshed data, but in the meantime, we can work with *disconnected* (offline) data.

There are multiple examples of pull-based systems working with data streams. For example, any CNC system gives updates (push way) on data changes in addition to the pull-based way of reading data.

Change propagation introduces another interesting feature: the ability of specifying a timeout value by which any elaboration must occur, otherwise it is cancelled. Similar is the ability to flow a specific cancellation message to request the premature end of executing elaborations against a data changed message.

These features are now available to any stateful system thanks to **Task Parallel Library** (**TPL**) that extends the low level thread API available in the CLR with specific task-oriented features, such as the task cancellation. However, not everything may execute within a `task` class, while in reactive programming, we may always have the ability to cancel a value-changed message elaboration.

Linguistic characteristics

Developing applications by using the reactive programming paradigm means applying to a specified paradigm and nothing else. There is not a specific language to use to comply with reactive programming tenets. Thus, it is possible to create a reactive application by using a specific reactive-oriented language to design the overall application's design and, later, write each computational node (a computational stage on the path of the data stream) in imperative, procedural, or object-oriented programming. This is usually called an *implicit* reactive programming language. While languages that accept only their own constructs or components are *explicit* reactive programming languages.

In the Microsoft universe, an implicit reactive programming style designer is available in the BizTalk Server SDK in the map (transformational graphical-based flowchart) designer. Here, specific transformational components, called `Functoids`, while there is the ability to use `plain` .NET languages or external .NET Assemblies (libraries). Effectively, the BizTalk Server has a lot of reactive programming although different.

A reactive-based programming language may be *static* or *dynamic*, exactly as it happens for nonreactive languages. In this context, a static language is the one that statically links multiple nodes between the others. While in a dynamic reactive programming language, these links become dynamic routes that may change because of a specific logic, giving a message of the direction of a node or another with the ability to change direction per message.

A mandatory feature of any reactive programming language is the ability to manipulate different streams with features, such as the ability to *merge* multiple streams like a `join` statement makes against multiple relational tables or *divide* a single stream into multiple ones.

Another must-have feature is the ability to configure a *Quality of service* priority list of messages within the stream. This is because not all the messages have the same priority. A canonical example is about any real-time control console of hardware systems, where pressure on any key on the keyboard or any button on the board must give an immediate feedback to the user on the screen or with a light or a sound. Conversely, an informative message or notification from the system to the user does not need the same priority, because the use may simply be somewhere other than at the front of the console. This means that some millisecond of delay is valid.

Programming languages and frameworks

There are many reactive programming and compliant form programming languages available to any developer with any background.

For any Microsoft-oriented developer, the obvious choice is learning the Microsoft *Reactive Extensions*—a library for adding all the needed features to .NET and other languages to comply with reactive programming. This is available for .NET as *Rx.NET*, for JavaScript languages as *RxJS*, and for Visual C++ developers such as *RxCpp*.

For JavaScript developers, there are multiple libraries adding reactive features, such as *Reactive.js*, *React* (by Facebook), *Node.js*, *ProAct.js*, and others, available for client development in ASP.NET MVC or WebForms. Links to some of these libraries are listed here:

- Reactive Extensions: `https://msdn.microsoft.com/en-us/data/gg577609.aspx`
- Reactive.js: `http://www.ractivejs.org/`
- React: `https://facebook.github.io/react/`
- Elm: `http://elm-lang.org/`
- Meteor: `https://www.meteor.com/`

Reactive programming approaches

When programming using the reactive programming paradigm in implicit style, we can mix different subparadigms into the computational stages that will handle stream processing. As already mentioned, implicit reactive programming languages give the ability to design an overall (or part of) reactive application and add nonreactive programming scripts or blocks into components, controls, or modules that will execute single stream logic, such as aggregation, filtering, mapping, and so on.

In these computational blocks (that represent data flow stages), we can use functional programming, object-oriented programming, and imperative or declarative programming. For most cases, such as the BizTalk Server mapping, a simple C# script (single or multiple lines) is available as a programmable component for a single stage. In the case of using such features extensively, the paradigm takes the name *imperative reactive programming*.

When we use general-purpose programming languages, such as C#, we will obtain reactive programmability by adding libraries to the core base classes like `Rx.NET`.

The C# now available gives us the ability to use *object-oriented reactive programming*. This means that we can use object-oriented programming in a single reactive stage or inverse the situation by using reactive programming in a single module or class or an object-oriented application. We can use both the alternatives together in the same application too, although this last choice will make the maintainability of the code difficult for the developer.

The more pure *visual reactive programming* style instead gives the developer only visual components to do their job. This is what happens in the SSIS data flow diagram, although not a reactive programming language.

If, in the computational stage, we make use of functional programming or languages, such as F#, the overall paradigm will take the name *functional reactive programming*.

Further reading

Although this book is about reactive programming, the most transforming modules we will write will observe the object-oriented programming paradigm. This is a good thought. Simply consider the following assertion: the best programming style or language is the best only in a few conditions. Accordingly, try your programming style to the task you're facing.

Here are some suggestions:

- *Patterns of Enterprise Application Architecture, Martin Fowler, Pearson Education, Inc*
- *Domain-Driven Design: Tackling Complexity in the Heart of Software, Eric Evans, Pearson Education, Inc*

Summary

In this chapter, we had the opportunity to give an overall description of reactive programming frameworks and languages. Specific key concepts and designs are available for this programming paradigm.

In the next chapter, we will put into practice all such theoretic notions, writing examples in pure C#, and trying to understand all the key concepts and designs explained here.

2
Reactive Programming with C#

In the previous chapter, we gave an overall introduction to reactive programming and related languages and frameworks.

In this chapter, we will see a practical example of reactive programming with pure C# coding.

The following topics will be discussed here:

- `IObserver` interface
- `IObservable` interface
- Subscription life cycle
- Sourcing events
- Filtering events
- Correlating events
- Sourcing from CLR streams
- Sourcing from CLR enumerables

IObserver interface

This core level interface is available within the **Base Class Library** (**BCL**) of .NET 4.0 and is available for the older 3.5 as an add-on.

The use is pretty simple and the goal is to provide a standard way of handling the most basic features of any reactive message consumer.

As already seen in the previous chapter, reactive messages flow by a producer and a consumer and subscribe for some messages. The `IObserver` C# interface is available to construct message receivers that comply with the reactive programming layout by implementing the three main message-oriented events: a *message* received, an *error* received, and a task *completed* message.

The `IObserver` interface has the following sign and description:

```
// Summary:
//     Provides a mechanism for receiving push-based notifications.
//
// Type parameters:
//   T:
//     The object that provides notification information.This type
parameter is
//     contravariant. That is, you can use either the type you
specified or any
//     type that is less derived. For more information about covariance
and contravariance,
//     see Covariance and Contravariance in Generics.
public interface IObserver<in T>
{
    // Summary:
    //     Notifies the observer that the provider has finished sending
push-based notifications.
    void OnCompleted();
    //
    // Summary:
    //     Notifies the observer that the provider has experienced an
error condition.
    //
    // Parameters:
    //   error:
    //     An object that provides additional information about the
error.
    void OnError(Exception error);
    //
    // Summary:
    //     Provides the observer with new data.
    //
    // Parameters:
    //   value:
    //     The current notification information.
    void OnNext(T value);
}
```

Any new message to flow to the receiver implementing such an interface will reach the OnNext method. Any error will reach the OnError method, while the task completed acknowledgement message will reach the OnCompleted method.

The use of an interface means that we cannot use generic premade objects from the BCL. We need to implement any receiver from scratch by using such an interface as a service contract. In Chapter 3, *Reactive Extension Programming*, we will be able to use subjects that will give us the chance not to implement such interfaces anytime, but for now, let's play this way.

Let's see an example, because talking about a code example is always simpler than talking about something theoretical. The following examples show how to read from a console application command from a user in a reactive way:

```
class Program
{
    static void Main(string[] args)
    {
        //creates a new console input consumer
        var consumer = new ConsoleTextConsumer();

        while (true)
        {
            Console.WriteLine("Write some text and press ENTER to send a
            message\r\Press ENTER to exit");
            //read console input
            var input = Console.ReadLine();

            //check for empty messate to exit
            if (string.IsNullOrEmpty(input))
            {
                //job completed
                consumer.OnCompleted();

                Console.WriteLine("Task completed. Any further message will
                generate an error");
            }
            else
            {
                //route the message to the consumer
                consumer.OnNext(input);
            }
        }
    }
}
public class ConsoleTextConsumer : IObserver<string>
{
```

```csharp
    private bool finished = false;
    public void OnCompleted()
    {
        if (finished)
        {
            OnError(new Exception("This consumer already finished it's
lifecycle"));
            return;
        }

        finished = true;
        Console.WriteLine("<- END");
    }

    public void OnError(Exception error)
    {
        Console.WriteLine("<- ERROR");
        Console.WriteLine("<- {0}", error.Message);
    }

    public void OnNext(string value)
    {
        if (finished)
        {
            OnError(new Exception("This consumer finished its lifecycle"));
            return;
        }

        //shows the received message
        Console.WriteLine("-> {0}", value);
        //do something

        //ack the caller
        Console.WriteLine("<- OK");
    }
}
```

The preceding example shows the IObserver interface usage within the
ConsoleTextConsumer class that simply asks a command console (DOS-like) for the user
input text to do something. In this implementation, the class simply writes out the input
text because we simply want to look at the reactive implementation.

The first important concept here is that a message consumer knows nothing about how messages are produced. The consumer simply reacts to one of the three events (not CLR events). Besides this, some kind of logic and cross-event ability is also available within the consumer itself. In the preceding example, we can see that the consumer simply showed any received message again on the console. However, if a *complete* message puts the consumer in a finished state (by signaling the finished flag), any other message that comes on the OnNext method will be automatically routed to the error one. Likewise, any other complete message that reaches the consumer will produce another error once the consumer is already in the finished state.

IObservable interface

The IObservable interface, the opposite of the IObserver interface, has the task of handling message production and the observer subscription. It routes right messages to the OnNext message handler and errors to the OnError message handler. As its life cycle ends, it acknowledges all the observers on the OnComplete message handler.

To create a valid reactive observable interface, we must write something that is not locking against user input or any other external system input data. The observable object acts as an infinite message generator, something like an infinite enumerable of messages; although in such cases, there is no enumeration.

Once a new message is available somehow, observer routes it to all the subscribers.

In the following example, we will try creating a console application to ask the user for an integer number and then route such a number to all the subscribers. Otherwise, if the given input is not a number, an error will be routed to all the subscribers.

This is observer similar to the one already seen in the previous example. Take a look at the following codes:

```
/// <summary>
/// Consumes numeric values that divides without rest by a given number
/// </summary>
public class IntegerConsumer : IObserver<int>
{
    readonly int validDivider;
    //the costructor asks for a divider
    public IntegerConsumer(int validDivider)
    {
        this.validDivider = validDivider;
    }
```

```
    private bool finished = false;
    public void OnCompleted()
    {
        if (finished)
            OnError(new Exception("This consumer already finished it's
lifecycle"));
        else
        {
            finished = true;
            Console.WriteLine("{0}: END", GetHashCode());
        }
    }

    public void OnError(Exception error)
    {
        Console.WriteLine("{0}: {1}", GetHashCode(), error.Message);
    }

    public void OnNext(int value)
    {
        if (finished)
            OnError(new Exception("This consumer finished its lifecycle"));

        //the simple business logic is made by checking divider result
        else if (value % validDivider == 0)
            Console.WriteLine("{0}: {1} divisible by {2}", GetHashCode(),
value, validDivider);
    }
}
```

This `observer` consumes integer numeric messages, but it requires that the number is divisible by another one without producing any rest value. This logic, because of the encapsulation principle, is within the `observer` object. The `observable` interface, instead, only has the logic of the message sending of valid or error messages.

This filtering logic is made within the receiver itself. Although that is not something wrong, in more complex applications, specific filtering features are available in the publish-subscribe communication pipeline. In other words, another object will be available between `observable` (publisher) and `observer` (subscriber) that will act as a message filter.

Back to our numeric example, here we have the `observable` implementation made using an inner `Task` method that does the main job of parsing input text and sending messages. In addition, a cancellation token is available to handle the user `cancellation` request and an eventual `observable` dispose:

```
//Observable able to parse strings from the Console
//and route numeric messages to all subscribers
public class ConsoleIntegerProducer : IObservable<int>, IDisposable
{
    //the subscriber list
    private readonly List<IObserver<int>> subscriberList = new
List<IObserver<int>>();

    //the cancellation token source for starting stopping
    //inner observable working thread
    private readonly CancellationTokenSource cancellationSource;
    //the cancellation flag
    private readonly CancellationToken cancellationToken;
    //the running task that runs the inner running thread
    private readonly Task workerTask;
    public ConsoleIntegerProducer()
    {
        cancellationSource = new CancellationTokenSource();
        cancellationToken = cancellationSource.Token;
        workerTask = Task.Factory.StartNew(OnInnerWorker,
cancellationToken);
    }
    //add another observer to the subscriber list
    public IDisposable Subscribe(IObserver<int> observer)
    {
        if (subscriberList.Contains(observer))
            throw new ArgumentException("The observer is already subscribed
to this observable");

        Console.WriteLine("Subscribing for {0}", observer.GetHashCode());
        subscriberList.Add(observer);

        return null;
    }

    //this code executes the observable infinite loop
    //and routes messages to all observers on the valid
    //message handler
    private void OnInnerWorker()
    {
        while (!cancellationToken.IsCancellationRequested)
        {
```

```csharp
            var input = Console.ReadLine();
            int value;

            foreach (var observer in subscriberList)
                if (string.IsNullOrEmpty(input))
                    break;
                else if (input.Equals("EXIT"))
                {
                    cancellationSource.Cancel();
                    break;
                }
                else if (!int.TryParse(input, out value))
                    observer.OnError(new FormatException("Unable to parse given
                    value"));
                else
                    observer.OnNext(value);
        }
        cancellationToken.ThrowIfCancellationRequested();
    }


    //cancel main task and ack all observers
    //by sending the OnCompleted message
    public void Dispose()
    {
        if (!cancellationSource.IsCancellationRequested)
        {
            cancellationSource.Cancel();
            while (!workerTask.IsCanceled)
                Thread.Sleep(100);
        }

        cancellationSource.Dispose();
        workerTask.Dispose();

        foreach (var observer in subscriberList)
            observer.OnCompleted();
    }

    //wait until the main task completes or went cancelled
    public void Wait()
    {
        while (!(workerTask.IsCompleted || workerTask.IsCanceled))
            Thread.Sleep(100);
    }
}
```

To complete the example, here there is the program `Main`:

```
static void Main(string[] args)
{
    //this is the message observable responsible of producing messages
    using (var observer = new ConsoleIntegerProducer())
    //those are the message observer that consume messages
    using (var consumer1 = observer.Subscribe(new IntegerConsumer(2)))
    using (var consumer2 = observer.Subscribe(new IntegerConsumer(3)))
    using (var consumer3 = observer.Subscribe(new IntegerConsumer(5)))
        observer.Wait();

    Console.WriteLine("END");
    Console.ReadLine();
}
```

The `cancellationToken.ThrowIfCancellationRequested` may raise an exception in your Visual Studio when debugging. Simply go next by pressing *F5*, or test such a code example without the attached debugger by starting the test with *Ctrl + F5* instead of *F5* alone.

The application simply creates an `observable` variable, which is able to parse user data. Then, register three observers specifying to each `observer` variable the required valid divider value.

Then, the `observable` variable will start reading user data from the console and valid or error messages will flow to all the observers. Each `observer` will apply its internal logic of showing the message when it divides for the related divider.

Here is the result of executing the application:

Observables and observers in action

Subscription life cycle

What will happen if we want to stop a single observer from receiving messages from the observable event source? If we change the program Main from the preceding example to the following one, we could experience a wrong observer life cycle design. Here's the code:

```
//this is the message observable responsible of producing messages
using (var observer = new ConsoleIntegerProducer())
//those are the message observer that consume messages
using (var consumer1 = observer.Subscribe(new IntegerConsumer(2)))
using (var consumer2 = observer.Subscribe(new IntegerConsumer(3)))
{
    using (var consumer3 = observer.Subscribe(new IntegerConsumer(5)))
    {
        //internal lifecycle
    }

    observer.Wait();
}

Console.WriteLine("END");
Console.ReadLine();
```

Here is the result in the output console:

The third observer unable to catch value messages

By using the `usingconstruct` method, we should stop the life cycle of the consumer object. However, we do not, because in the previous example, the `Subscribe` method of the `observable` simply returns a `NULL` object.

To create a valid observer, we must handle and design its life cycle management. This means that we must eventually handle the external disposing of the `Subscribe` method's result by signaling the right `observer` that his life cycle reached the end.

We have to create a `Subscription` class to handle an eventual object disposing in the right reactive way by sending the message for the `OnCompleted` event handler.

Here is a simple `Subscription` class implementation:

```
/// <summary>
/// Handle observer subscription lifecycle
/// </summary>
public sealed class Subscription<T> : IDisposable
{
    private readonly IObserver<T> observer;
    public Subscription(IObserver<T> observer)
    {
        this.observer = observer;
    }
```

```
            //the event signalling that the observer has
            //completed its lifecycle
            public event EventHandler<IObserver<T>> OnCompleted;

            public void Dispose()
            {
                if (OnCompleted != null)
                    OnCompleted(this, observer);

                observer.OnCompleted();
            }
        }
```

The usage is within the `observableSubscribe` method. Here's an example:

```
    //add another observer to the subscriber list
    public IDisposable Subscribe(IObserver<int> observer)
    {
        if (observerList.Contains(observer))
            throw new ArgumentException("The observer is already subscribed to
    this observable");

        Console.WriteLine("Subscribing for {0}", observer.GetHashCode());
        observerList.Add(observer);

        //creates a new subscription for the given observer
    var subscription = new Subscription<int>(observer);
    //handle to the subscription lifecycle end event
        subscription.OnCompleted += OnObserverLifecycleEnd;
        return subscription;
    }

    void OnObserverLifecycleEnd(object sender, IObserver<int> e)
    {
        var subscription = sender as Subscription<int>;
        //remove the observer from the internal list within the observable
        observerList.Remove(e);
        //remove the handler from the subscription event
        //once already handled
        subscription.OnCompleted -= OnObserverLifecycleEnd;
    }
```

As shown, the preceding example creates a new `Subscription<T>` object to handle this `observer` life cycle with the `IDisposable.Dispose` method.

Here is the result of such code edits against the full example available in the previous paragraph:

The observer will end their life as we dispose their life cycle tokens

This time, an `observer` ends its life cycle prematurely by disposing the `subscription` object. This is visible by the first `END` message. Later, only two observers remain available at the application ending; when the user asks for `EXIT`, only two such observers end their life cycle by themselves rather than by the `Subscription` disposing.

In real-world applications, observers often subscribe to observables and later unsubscribe by disposing the `Subscription` token. This happens because we do not always want a reactive module to handle all the messages. In this case, this means that we have to handle the `observer` life cycle by ourselves, as we already did in the previous examples, or we need to apply filters to choose which messages flow to which `subscriber`, as shown in the later section *Filtering events*. Kindly consider that although filters make things easier, we will always have to handle the `observer` life cycle.

Sourcing events

Sourcing events is the ability to obtain from a particular source where few useful events are usable in reactive programming.

If you are searching for the EventSourcing pattern, take a look at Chapter 7, *Advanced Techniques*.

As already pointed out in the previous chapter, reactive programming is all about event message handling. Any event is a specific occurrence of some kind of handleable behavior of users or external systems. We can actually program event reactions in the most pleasant and productive way for reaching our software goals.

In the following example, we will see how to react to CLR events. In this specific case, we will handle filesystem events by using events from the System.IO.FileSystemWatcher class that gives us the ability to react to the filesystem's file changes without the need of making useless and resource-consuming polling queries against the file system status.

Here's the observer and observable implementation:

```
public sealed class NewFileSavedMessagePublisher : IObservable<string>,
IDisposable
{
    private readonly FileSystemWatcher watcher;
    public NewFileSavedMessagePublisher(string path)
    {
        //creates a new file system event router
        this.watcher = new FileSystemWatcher(path);
        //register for handling File Created event
        this.watcher.Created += OnFileCreated;
        //enable event routing
        this.watcher.EnableRaisingEvents = true;
    }

    //signal all observers a new file arrived
    private void OnFileCreated(object sender, FileSystemEventArgs e)
    {
        foreach (var observer in subscriberList)
            observer.OnNext(e.FullPath);
    }

    //the subscriber list
    private readonly List<IObserver<string>> subscriberList = new
List<IObserver<string>>();
```

```
    public IDisposable Subscribe(IObserver<string> observer)
    {
        //register the new observer
        subscriberList.Add(observer);

        return null;
    }

    public void Dispose()
    {
        //disable file system event routing
        this.watcher.EnableRaisingEvents = false;
        //deregister from watcher event handler
        this.watcher.Created -= OnFileCreated;
        //dispose the watcher
        this.watcher.Dispose();

        //signal all observers that job is done
        foreach (var observer in subscriberList)
            observer.OnCompleted();
    }
}

/// <summary>
/// A tremendously basic implementation
/// </summary>
public sealed class NewFileSavedMessageSubscriber : IObserver<string>
{
    public void OnCompleted()
    {
        Console.WriteLine("-> END");
    }

    public void OnError(Exception error)
    {
        Console.WriteLine("-> {0}", error.Message);
    }

    public void OnNext(string value)
    {
        Console.WriteLine("-> {0}", value);
    }
}
```

The `observer` interface simply gives us the ability to write text to the console. I think there is nothing to say about it.

On the other hand, the `observable` interface makes the most of the job in this implementation.

The `observable` interface creates the `watcher` object and registers the right event handler to catch the wanted reactive events. It handles the life cycle of itself and the internal `watcher` object. Then, it correctly sends the `OnComplete` message to all the observers.

Here's the program's initialization:

```
static void Main(string[] args)
{
    Console.WriteLine("Watching for new files");
    using (var publisher = new NewFileSavedMessagePublisher(@"[WRITE A PATH
    HERE]"))
    using (var subscriber = publisher.Subscribe(new
NewFileSavedMessageSubscriber()))
    {
        Console.WriteLine("Press RETURN to exit");
        //wait for user RETURN
        Console.ReadLine();
    }
}
```

Any new file that arises in the folder will let route full `FileName` to `observer`. This is the result of a copy and paste of the same file three times:

```
-> [YOUR PATH]\out - Copy.png
-> [YOUR PATH]\out - Copy (2).png
-> [YOUR PATH]\out - Copy (3).png
```

By using a single `observable` interface and a single `observer` interface, the power of reactive programming is not so evident. Let's begin with writing some intermediate object to change the message flow within the pipeline of our message pump made in a reactive way with filters, message correlator, and dividers.

Filtering events

As said in the previous section, it is time to alter message flow.

The `observable` interface has the task of producing messages, while conversely `observer` consumes such messages. To create a message filter, we need to create an object that is both a publisher and a subscriber together.

The implementation must take into consideration the filtering need and the message routing to underlying observers that subscribe to the filter `observable` object instead of the main one.

Here's an implementation of the filter:

```
/// <summary>
/// The filtering observable/observer
/// </summary>
public sealed class StringMessageFilter : IObservable<string>,
IObserver<string>, IDisposable
{
    private readonly string filter;
    public StringMessageFilter(string filter)
    {
        this.filter = filter;
    }

    //the observer collection
    private readonly List<IObserver<string>> observerList = new
List<IObserver<string>>();
    public IDisposable Subscribe(IObserver<string> observer)
    {
        this.observerList.Add(observer);
        return null;
    }

    //a simple implementation
    //that disables message routing once
    //the OnCompleted has been invoked
    private bool hasCompleted = false;
    public void OnCompleted()
    {
        hasCompleted = true;
        foreach (var observer in observerList)
            observer.OnCompleted();
    }

    //routes error messages until not completed
    public void OnError(Exception error)
    {
        if (!hasCompleted)
            foreach (var observer in observerList)
                observer.OnError(error);
    }

    //routes valid messages until not completed
    public void OnNext(string value)
```

```
    {
        Console.WriteLine("Filtering {0}", value);

        if (!hasCompleted &&
value.ToLowerInvariant().Contains(filter.ToLowerInvariant()))
            foreach (var observer in observerList)
                observer.OnNext(value);
    }

    public void Dispose()
    {
        OnCompleted();
    }
}
```

This filter can be used together with the example from the previous section that routes the FileSystemWatcher events of created files. This is the new program initialization:

```
static void Main(string[] args)
{
    Console.WriteLine("Watching for new files");
    using (var publisher = new NewFileSavedMessagePublisher(@"[WRITE A PATH
HERE]"))
        using (var filter = new StringMessageFilter(".txt"))
        {
            //subscribe the filter to publisher messages
            publisher.Subscribe(filter);
            //subscribe the console subscriber to the filter
            //instead that directly to the publisher
            filter.Subscribe(new NewFileSavedMessageSubscriber());

            Console.WriteLine("Press RETURN to exit");
            Console.ReadLine();
        }
}
```

As we can see, this new implementation creates a new filter object that takes a parameter to verify valid filenames to flow to the underlying observers.

The filter subscribes to the main observable object, while the observer subscribes to the filter itself. It is like a chain where each chain link refers to the next one.

This is the output console of the running application:

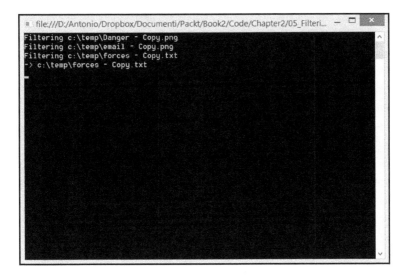

The filtering observer in action

Although I made a copy of two files (a `.png` and a `.txt` file), we can see that only the text file reached the internal `observer` object, while the image file reached the `OnNext` of `filter` because the invalid against the `filter` argument never reached the internal `observer`.

Correlating events

Sometimes, especially when dealing with integration scenarios, there is a need for correlating multiple events that don't always came together. This is the case of a header file that came together with multiple body files.

In reactive programming, correlating events means correlating multiple `observable` messages into a single message that is the result of two or more original messages. Such messages must be somehow correlated to a value (an `ID`, `serial`, or metadata) that defines that such initial messages belong to the same correlation set.

Useful features in real-world correlators are the ability to specify a timeout (that may be infinite too) in the correlation waiting logic and the ability to specify a correlation message count (infinite too).

Here's a `correlator` implementation made for the previous example based on the `FileSystemWatcher` class:

```
public sealed class FileNameMessageCorrelator : IObservable<string>,
IObserver<string>, IDisposable
{
    private readonly Func<string, string> correlationKeyExtractor;
    public FileNameMessageCorrelator(Func<string, string>
correlationKeyExtractor)
    {
        this.correlationKeyExtractor = correlationKeyExtractor;
    }

    //the observer collection
    private readonly List<IObserver<string>> observerList = new
List<IObserver<string>>();
    public IDisposable Subscribe(IObserver<string> observer)
    {
        this.observerList.Add(observer);
        return null;
    }

    private bool hasCompleted = false;
    public void OnCompleted()
    {
        hasCompleted = true;
        foreach (var observer in observerList)
            observer.OnCompleted();
    }

    //routes error messages until not completed
    public void OnError(Exception error)
    {
        if (!hasCompleted)
            foreach (var observer in observerList)
                observer.OnError(error);
    }
```

Let's pause. Up to this row, we simply created the reactive structure of the `FileNameMessageCorrelator` class by implementing the two main interfaces. Here is the core implementation that correlates messages:

```
//the container of correlations able to contain
```

```
//multiple strings per each key
private readonly NameValueCollection correlations = new
NameValueCollection();

//routes valid messages until not completed
public void OnNext(string value)
{
    if (hasCompleted) return;

    //check if subscriber has completed
    Console.WriteLine("Parsing message: {0}", value);

    //try extracting the correlation ID
    var correlationID = correlationKeyExtractor(value);

    //check if the correlation is available
    if (correlationID == null) return;

    //append the new file name to the correlation state
    correlations.Add(correlationID, value);

    //in this example we will consider always
    //correlations of two items
    if (correlations.GetValues(correlationID).Count() == 2)
    {
        //once the correlation is complete
        //read the two files and push the
        //two contents altogether to the
        //observers

        var fileData = correlations.GetValues(correlationID)
            //route messages to the ReadAllText method
            .Select(File.ReadAllText)
            //materialize the query
            .ToArray();

        var newValue = string.Join("|", fileData);

        foreach (var observer in observerList)
            observer.OnNext(newValue);

        correlations.Remove(correlationID);
    }
}
```

This `correlator` class accepts a `correlation` function as a constructor parameter. This function is later used to evaluate `correlationID` when a new `filename` variable flows within the `OnNext` method.

Once the function returns valid `correlationID`, such IDs will be used as key for `NameValueCollection`, a specialized string collection to store multiple values per key. When there are two values for the same key, `correlation` is ready to flow out to the underlying observers by reading file data and joining such data into a single string message.

Here's the application's initialization:

```
static void Main(string[] args)
{
    using (var publisher = new NewFileSavedMessagePublisher(@"[WRITE A PATH
HERE]"))
    //creates a new correlator by specifying the correlation key
    //extraction function made with a Regular expression that
    //extract a file ID similar to FILEID0001
    using (var correlator = new
FileNameMessageCorrelator(ExtractCorrelationKey))
    {
        //subscribe the correlator to publisher messages
        publisher.Subscribe(correlator);

        //subscribe the console subscriber to the correlator
        //instead that directly to the publisher
        correlator.Subscribe(new NewFileSavedMessageSubscriber());

        //wait for user RETURN
        Console.ReadLine();
    }
}

private static string ExtractCorrelationKey(string arg)
{
    var match = Regex.Match(arg, "(FILEID\\d{4})");
    if (match.Success)
        return match.Captures[0].Value;
    else
        return null;
}
```

The initialization is almost the same as the filtering example seen in the previous section. The biggest difference is that the `correlator` object, instead of a string `filter` variable, accepts a function that analyses the incoming filename and produces the eventually available `correlationID` variable.

I prepared two files with the same ID in the `filename` variable. Here's the console output of the running example:

Two files correlated by their name

As can be seen, `correlator` fulfilled its job by joining the two file's data into a single message regardless of the order in which the two files were stored in the filesystem.

These examples regarding the filtering and correlation of messages should show you that we can do anything with received messages: we can put a message in standby until a correlated message comes, we can join multiple messages into one, we can produce multiple times the same message, and so on.

This programming style opens the programmer's mind to a lot of new application designs and possibilities.

Sourcing from CLR streams

Any class that extends `System.IO.Stream` is some kind of cursor-based flow of data. The same happens when we want to see a video stream, a sort of locally not persisted data that flows only in the network with the ability to go forward and backward, stop, pause, resume, play, and so on. The same behavior is available while streaming any kind of data, thus, the `Stream` class is the base class that exposes such behavior for any need.

There are specialized classes that extend `Stream`, helping work with the streams of text data (`StreamWriter` and `StreamReader`), binary serialized data (`BinaryReader` and `BinaryWriter`), memory-based temporary byte containers (`MemoryStream`), network-based streams (`NetworkStream`), and many others.

Regarding reactive programming, we are dealing with the ability to source events from any stream regardless of its type (network, file, memory, and so on).

Real-world applications that use reactive programming based on streams are cheats, remote binary listeners (socket programming), and any other unpredictable event-oriented application. On the other hand, it is useless to read a huge file in a reactive way, because there is simply nothing reactive in such cases.

It is time to look at an example. Here's a complete example of a reactive application made for listening to a TPC port and routing string messages (CR + LF divides multiple messages) to all the available observers. The program `Main` and the usual `ConsoleObserver` methods are omitted for better readability:

```csharp
    public sealed class TcpListenerStringObservable : IObservable<string>,
IDisposable
    {
        private readonly TcpListener listener;
        public TcpListenerStringObservable(int port, int backlogSize = 64)
        {
            //creates a new tcp listener on given port
            //with given backlog size
            listener = new TcpListener(IPAddress.Any, port);
            listener.Start(backlogSize);

            //start listening asynchronously
listener.AcceptTcpClientAsync().ContinueWith(OnTcpClientConnected);
        }

        private void OnTcpClientConnected(Task<TcpClient> clientTask)
        {
            //if the task has not encountered errors
            if (clientTask.IsCompleted)
```

```csharp
                    //we will handle a single client connection per time
                    //to handle multiple connections, simply put following
                    //code into a Task
                    using (var tcpClient = clientTask.Result)
                    using (var stream = tcpClient.GetStream())
                    using (var reader = new StreamReader(stream))
                        while (tcpClient.Connected)
                        {
                            //read the message
                            var line = reader.ReadLine();

                            //stop listening if nothing available
                            if (string.IsNullOrEmpty(line))
                                break;
                            else
                            {
                                //construct observer message adding client's
remote
                                endpoint address and port
                                var msg = string.Format("{0}: {1}",
                                 tcpClient.Client.RemoteEndPoint, line);

                                //route messages
                                foreach (var observer in observerList)
                                    observer.OnNext(msg);
                            }
                        }


        //starts another client listener
listener.AcceptTcpClientAsync().ContinueWith(OnTcpClientConnected);
        }

        private readonly List<IObserver<string>> observerList = new
        List<IObserver<string>>();
        public IDisposable Subscribe(IObserver<string> observer)
        {
            observerList.Add(observer);

            //subscription lifecycle missing
            //for readability purpose
            return null;
        }

        public void Dispose()
        {
            //stop listener
            listener.Stop();
        }
```

```
    }
```

The preceding example shows how to create a reactive TCP listener that acts as an `observable` of string messages.

The `observable` method uses an internal `TcpListener` class that provides mid-level network services across an underlying `Socket` object. The example asks the listener to start listening and starts waiting for a client into another thread with the use of a `Task` object. When a remote client becomes available, its communication with the internals of `observable` is guaranteed by the `OnTcpClientConneted` method that verifies the normal execution of `Task`. Then, it catches `TcpClient` from `Task`, reads the network stream, and appends `StreamReader` to such a network stream to start a reading feature.

Once the message reading feature is complete, another `Task` starts repeating the procedure. Although, this design handles a backlog of pending connections, it makes available only a single client per time. To change such designs to handle multiple connections altogether, simply encapsulate the `OnTcpClientConnected` logic. Here's an example:

```
    private void OnTcpClientConnected(Task<TcpClient> clientTask)
    {
        //if the task has not encountered errors
        if (clientTask.IsCompleted)
            Task.Factory.StartNew(() =>
                {
                    using (var tcpClient = clientTask.Result)
                    using (var stream = tcpClient.GetStream())
                    using (var reader = new StreamReader(stream))
                        while (tcpClient.Connected)
                        {
                            //read the message
                            var line = reader.ReadLine();

                            //stop listening if nothing available
                            if (string.IsNullOrEmpty(line))
                                break;
                            else
                            {
                                //construct observer message adding client's
remote
                                  endpoint address and port
                                var msg = string.Format("{0}: {1}",
                                tcpClient.Client.RemoteEndPoint, line);

                                //route messages
                                foreach (var observer in observerList)
                                    observer.OnNext(msg);
```

```
                                    }
                                }
                            }, TaskCreationOptions.PreferFairness);

                    //starts another client listener
                    listener.AcceptTcpClientAsync().ContinueWith(OnTcpClientConnected);
        }
```

This is the output of the reactive application when it receives two different connections by using `telnet` as a client (`C:\>telnet localhost 8081`). The program `Main` and the usual `ConsoleObserver` methods are omitted for better readability:

The observable routing events from the telnet client

As you can see, each client starts connecting to the listener by using a different remote port. This gives us the ability to differentiate multiple remote connections although they connect altogether.

Sourcing from CLR enumerables

Sourcing from a finite collection is quite useless with regard to reactive programming. However, specific enumerable collections are perfect for reactive uses. These collections are the changeable collections that support collection change notifications by implementing the `INotifyCollectionChanged(System.Collections.Specialized)` interface like the `ObservableCollection(System.Collections.ObjectModel)` class and any infinite collection that supports the enumerator pattern with the use of the `yield` keyword.

Changeable collections

The `ObservableCollection<T>` class gives us the ability to understand, in an event-based way, any change that occurs against the collection content. Kindly consider that changes regarding collection child properties are outside of the collection scope. This means that we are notified only for collection changes like the one produced from the `Add` or `Remove` methods. Changes within a single item do not produce an alteration of the collection size, thus, they are not notified at all.

Here's a generic (non reactive) example:

```
static void Main(string[] args)
{
    //the observable collection
    var collection = new ObservableCollection<string>();
    //register a handler to catch collection changes
    collection.CollectionChanged += OnCollectionChanged;

    collection.Add("ciao");
    collection.Add("hahahah");

    collection.Insert(0, "new first line");
    collection.RemoveAt(0);

    Console.WriteLine("Press RETURN to EXIT");
    Console.ReadLine();
}

private static void OnCollectionChanged(object sender,
NotifyCollectionChangedEventArgs e)
{
    var collection = sender as ObservableCollection<string>;

    if (e.NewStartingIndex >= 0) //adding new items
        Console.WriteLine("-> {0} {1}", e.Action,
collection[e.NewStartingIndex]);
    else //removing items
        Console.WriteLine("-> {0} at {1}", e.Action, e.OldStartingIndex);
}
```

As shown, `collection` notifies all the adding operations, giving the ability to catch the new message. The `Insert` method signals an `Add` operation; although with the `Insert` method, we can specify the index and the value will be available within `collection`. Obviously, the parameter containing the index value (`e.NewStartingIndex`) contains the new index according to the right operation. However, the `Remove` operation, although notifying the removed element index, cannot give us the ability to read the original message before the removal, because the event triggers after the remove operation has already occurred.

In a real-world reactive application, the most interesting operation against `ObservableCollection` is the `Add` operation. Here's an example (console observer omitted for better readability):

```
class Program
{
    static void Main(string[] args)
    {
        //the observable collection
        var collection = new ObservableCollection<string>();

        using (var observable = new
NotifiableCollectionObservable(collection))
        using (var observer = observable.Subscribe(new
ConsoleStringObserver()))
        {
            collection.Add("ciao");
            collection.Add("hahahah");

            collection.Insert(0, "new first line");
            collection.RemoveAt(0);

            Console.WriteLine("Press RETURN to EXIT");
            Console.ReadLine();
        }
    }
}

public sealed class NotifiableCollectionObservable : IObservable<string>,
IDisposable
{
    private readonly ObservableCollection<string> collection;
    public NotifiableCollectionObservable(ObservableCollection<string>
collection)
    {
        this.collection = collection;
        this.collection.CollectionChanged += collection_CollectionChanged;
    }
```

```
    private readonly List<IObserver<string>> observerList = new
List<IObserver<string>>();
    public IDisposable Subscribe(IObserver<string> observer)
    {
        observerList.Add(observer);

        //subscription lifecycle missing
        //for readability purpose
        return null;
    }

    public void Dispose()
    {
        this.collection.CollectionChanged -= collection_CollectionChanged;

        foreach (var observer in observerList)
            observer.OnCompleted();
    }
}
}
```

The result is the same as the previous example of ObservableCollection without the reactive objects. The only difference is that observable only routes messages when the Action values add.

The ObservableCollection signaling its content changes

Infinite collections

Our last example is regarding sourcing events from an infinite `collection` method.

In C#, it is possible to implement the enumerator pattern by signaling each object to enumerate per time, thanks to the `yield` keyword. Here's an example:

```
static void Main(string[] args)
{
    foreach (var value in EnumerateValuesFromSomewhere())
        Console.WriteLine(value);
}

static IEnumerable<string> EnumerateValuesFromSomewhere()
{
    var random = new Random(DateTime.Now.GetHashCode());
    while (true) //forever
    {
        //returns a random integer number as string
        yield return random.Next().ToString();
        //some throttling time
        Thread.Sleep(100);
    }
}
```

This implementation is powerful because it doesn't materialize all the values into the memory. It simply signals that a new object is available to the enumerator that the `foreach` structure internally uses itself. The result is forever writing numbers onto the output console.

Somehow, this behavior is useful for reactive use, because it doesn't create a useless state like a temporary array, list, or generic collection. It simply signals new items available to the enumerable.

Here's an example:

```
    public sealed class EnumerableObservable : IObservable<string>,
IDisposable
    {
        private readonly IEnumerable<string> enumerable;
        public EnumerableObservable(IEnumerable<string> enumerable)
        {
            this.enumerable = enumerable;
            this.cancellationSource = new CancellationTokenSource();
            this.cancellationToken = cancellationSource.Token;
            this.workerTask = Task.Factory.StartNew(() =>
                {
```

```
                foreach (var value in this.enumerable)
                {
                    //if task cancellation triggers, raise the proper
exception
                    //to stop task execution
                    cancellationToken.ThrowIfCancellationRequested();

                    foreach (var observer in observerList)
                        observer.OnNext(value);
                }
            }, this.cancellationToken);
        }

        //the cancellation token source for starting stopping
        //inner observable working thread
        private readonly CancellationTokenSource cancellationSource;
        //the cancellation flag
        private readonly CancellationToken cancellationToken;
        //the running task that runs the inner running thread
        private readonly Task workerTask;
        //the observer list
        private readonly List<IObserver<string>> observerList = new
List<IObserver<string>>();
        public IDisposable Subscribe(IObserver<string> observer)
        {
            observerList.Add(observer);

            //subscription lifecycle missing
            //for readability purpose
            return null;
        }

        public void Dispose()
        {
            //trigger task cancellation
            //and wait for acknoledge
            if (!cancellationSource.IsCancellationRequested)
            {
                cancellationSource.Cancel();
                while (!workerTask.IsCanceled)
                    Thread.Sleep(100);
            }

            cancellationSource.Dispose();
            workerTask.Dispose();

            foreach (var observer in observerList)
                observer.OnCompleted();
```

```
        }
    }
```

This is the code of the program startup with the infinite enumerable generation:

```
class Program
{
    static void Main(string[] args)
    {
        //we create a variable containing the enumerable
        //this does not trigger item retrieval
        //so the enumerator does not begin flowing datas
        var enumerable = EnumerateValuesFromSomewhere();

        using (var observable = new EnumerableObservable(enumerable))
        using (var observer = observable.Subscribe(new
ConsoleStringObserver()))
        {
            //wait for 2 seconds than exit
            Thread.Sleep(2000);
        }

        Console.WriteLine("Press RETURN to EXIT");
        Console.ReadLine();
    }

    static IEnumerable<string> EnumerateValuesFromSomewhere()
    {
        var random = new Random(DateTime.Now.GetHashCode());
        while (true) //forever
        {
            //returns a random integer number as string
            yield return random.Next().ToString();
            //some throttling time
            Thread.Sleep(100);
        }
    }
}
```

As against the last examples, here we have the use of the `Task` class. The `observable` uses the enumerable within the asynchronous `Task` method to give the programmer the ability to stop the execution of the whole operation by simply exiting the *using* scope or by manually invoking the `Dispose` method.

This example shows a tremendously powerful feature: the ability to yield values without having to source them from a concrete (finite) array or collection by simply implementing the enumerator pattern. Although few are used, the `yield` operator gives the ability to create complex applications simply by pushing messages between methods. The more methods we create that cross send messages to each other, the more complex business logics the application can handle.

Consider the ability to catch all such messages with observables, and you have a little idea about how powerful reactive programming can be for a developer.

Summary

In this chapter, we had the opportunity to test the main features that any reactive application must implement: message sending, error sending, and completing acknowledgement. We focused on plain C# programming to give the first overview of how reactive classic designs can be applied to all main application needs, such as sourcing from streams, from user input, from changeable and infinite collections.

In the following chapters, we will divert Reactive Extensions for .NET features that will give us the ability to test more complex solutions to comply with more complex reactive needs.

3
Reactive Extension Programming

This chapter will lead readers through the first steps in **Reactive Extension (Rx)** programming. We will give an overview of the Rx architecture with information on how to configure our application to use the framework and how to use its main components.

We will cover the following arguments:

- Setting up `Rx.NET`
- Marble diagrams
- Subjects
- Transforming operators
- Combining operators
- Filtering operators
- Mathematical operators
- Logic operators

The NuGet package names have been changed. The Rx-* and Ix-* packages have been renamed to match their library names, keeping inline with the rest of .NET Core.

- Use `System.Reactive` instead of `Rx-Main`
- Use `System.Interactive` instead of `Ix-Main`

- Use `System.Interactive.Async` instead of `Ix-Async`

Setting up Rx.NET

To configure our .NET-based application to use the Rx.NET classes, we can simply ask **NuGet** to download the Rx-Main (**Reactive Extensions - Main Library**) package.

This action will register all .NET assemblies in our application, including other NuGet packages, such as Rx-Core, Rx-Interfaces, Rx-PlatformServices, and Rx-Linq, all from Microsoft Corp.

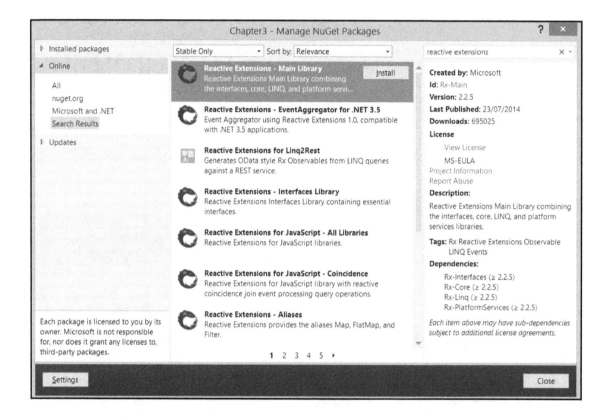

NuGet Rx-Main package

Other packages are available using NuGet. This book will cover only the mainline of such package distributions.

At the time of writing this book, Rx was available in version 2.2.5 that was released in July 2014. Although in May 2015 a version 2.3.0 beta was available throughout NuGet, a stable 2.3.x release is still not available.

A stable version 2.x was available in August 2012, supporting .NET 4.0, 4.5, 4.5 for Store Apps, Windows Phone 7.5, and Silverlight 5.

Marble diagrams

A marble diagram exposes graphically a sequence of `observable` items in a time fashion.

This simple diagram is the standard de facto of exposing observable sequences when composed with observable operators, such as `merge`, `delay`, `scan`, and so on.

The most practical example is available on `http://rxmarbles.com`.

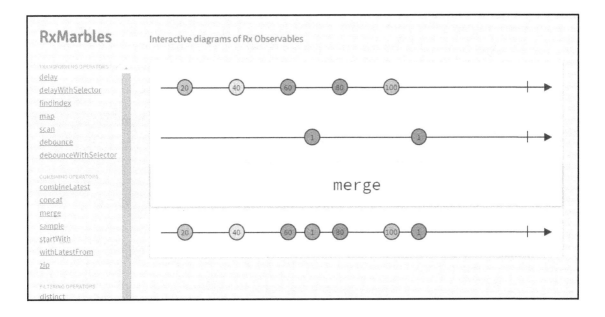

A marble diagram showing a merge operation

In the preceding screenshot, we can see two time-based sequences of observable numeric values in the first two lines. The balls are the values. The little vertical lines are the `OnCompleted` messages that define when a sequence ends its life cycle.

The third line shows the merged observable sequence containing all the values from the first two sequences.

The website offers a great selection of examples regarding the most used reactive operators by using marble diagrams. This is useful to understand the operator job before diving into coding.

Subjects

A `subject` class is an observable sequence that is an observer too. A subject may produce and consume values; in other words, it is a value publisher and a value subscriber.

In real-world reactive applications, there are various (some times hundreds) subjects interacting with each other.

In the previous section, when we saw the `merge` operation in the marble diagram, we pressed two sequences into another one to give us the ability to subscribe an `Observer` to the new merged sequence. This merged sequence is a subject because it receives values from the nonmerged sequences and then produces values to the related observer.

This is only an example of the infinite subjects available in any application.

A `subject` class gives us the ability to create sequences or observers without having to always create a specific class and implement the relative interface, as seen in the previous examples with pure C# coding. Here is an example:

```
//a new sequence
var s = new Subject<string>();
//subscribe such new observer OnNext implementation
s.Subscribe(Console.WriteLine);
//some push value
s.OnNext("value1");
s.OnNext("value2");
Console.ReadLine();
```

The ability to create sequences with minimal effort is one of the killing features of a `subject`.

As shown in the previous example, we do not need to implement any interface or create any custom class to achieve the desired result. The only required task is providing the `OnNext` method implementation by executing the `Subscribe` method. This method asks for `Action<T>`. We can pass such a parameter by writing a lambda or by passing the method itself (as seen in the example).

The `Subject` class itself implements the `OnCompleted` method and the `OnError` method by routing the proper message to all the subscribers and then disposing all the subscriber tokens.

When using Rx, we have lot of extension methods available to access the huge amount of operations available against `subjects`. Later, in this chapter, we will give an overview of the most widely used ones.

`Subject` is only the head of the dragon. A lot of other classes extends `Subject` by adding other features.

ReplaySubject

`ReplaySubject<T>` gives a time buffer feature.

Normally, when we use `Subject` by pushing values into the subject, only already subscribed `observers` will receive the new value from the first subject, as seen in the example:

```
var simpleSubject = new Subject<string>();
simpleSubject.OnNext("value1");
simpleSubject.OnNext("value2");
simpleSubject.Subscribe(Console.WriteLine);
simpleSubject.OnNext("value3");
simpleSubject.OnNext("value4");
```

Instead, by using `ReplaySubject`, the subject will route all the pushed messages to its subscribers like a normal subject does, adding the ability to store all such messages, making them available to later subscribers.

In this case, words are a bit more confusing than code:

```
var replaySubject = new ReplaySubject<string>();
replaySubject.OnNext("value1");
replaySubject.OnNext("value2");
replaySubject.Subscribe(Console.WriteLine);
replaySubject.OnNext("value3");
replaySubject.OnNext("value4");
```

The difference between those two identical examples is that, in the `simpleSubject` example at the beginning of the *Subjects* section, only `value3` and `value4` will be outputted to the console. In the example of the *ReplaySubject* section, all the values will reach the console output.

`ReplaySubject` will buffer all the received messages in its memory and will later produce all such messages to the new subscriber.

Obviously, because the memory is finite, we have the ability to specify in the constructor a numeric buffer amount or a time-based amount with `TimeSpan`:

```
var a = new ReplaySubject<string>(10);
var b = new ReplaySubject<string>(TimeSpan.FromSeconds(10));
```

BehaviorSubject

This alternative extension of the `Subject` class is similar to `ReplaySubject` with the difference that `BehaviorSubject` always stores the latest available value (or the initial value if we're at the beginning of its life). This means that a default value must be provided through its constructor. Here is an example:

```
var behaviorSubject = new BehaviorSubject<DateTime>(new DateTime(2001, 1,
1));
Thread.Sleep(1000);
//the default value will flow to the new subscriber
behaviorSubject.Subscribe(x => Console.WriteLine(x));
Thread.Sleep(1000);
//a new value will flow to the subscriber
behaviorSubject.OnNext(DateTime.Now);
Thread.Sleep(1000);
//this new subscriber will receive the last available message
//regardless is was not subscribing at the time the message arise
behaviorSubject.Subscribe(x => Console.WriteLine(x));
Thread.Sleep(1000);
```

In any case, if `observer` subscribes to `subject`, it receives the last available value. However, when a subscriber already subscribes `subject` when a new value is available, this value will normally flow to the subscriber.

This behavior is very specific in reactive programming because it allows us to ensure that a value will always flow to any subscriber regardless of the availability of new values.

In the real world, this subject is used in cases where we want to have the opportunity to subscribe, take some updated value, unsubscribe, and then be able to subscribe again in the future, thus repeating the behavior. This is a bit unreactive, but there are cases when this is useful.

Consider the case when you interface to a **Programmable Logic Controller** (**PLC**) to read analogic data. You may want the ability to stop collecting data and the ability to connect our subscribers again to the PLC reactive interface by receiving immediately the last value of all the wanted variables/analogic ports without having to wait until each PLC variable produces a new value to flow to our subscribers.

AsyncSubject

AsyncSubject is another single message subject. Although similar to BehaviorSubject, it routes only the last message it receives, waiting for the OnComplete message before routing its single OnNext message:

```
var asyncSubject = new AsyncSubject<string>();
asyncSubject.OnNext("value1"); //this will be missed
asyncSubject.Subscribe(Console.WriteLine);
asyncSubject.OnNext("value2"); //this will be missed
asyncSubject.OnNext("value3"); //this will be routed once OnCompleted
raised
Console.ReadLine();
asyncSubject.OnCompleted();
```

AsyncSubject is very useful for cases when we need to work in a message-based way with the need of a message flow logic. The most used case is in combination to other sequences that produce a rolling average or a rolling total from a sequence of values. This subject gives us the ability to catch only the end result from the rolling one.

Custom subjects

If out-of-the box subjects cannot satisfy our needs, we can create our custom subject class by implementing the ISubject interface. This interface offers the ability to create subjects with the same type argument in receiving and sending messages, like in all the subject classes seen in the previous examples. An interesting feature is the ability to create subjects with different in/out type arguments. Here's an example:

```
public sealed class MapperSubject<Tin, Tout> : ISubject<Tin, Tout>
{
    readonly Func<Tin, Tout> mapper;
    public MapperSubject(Func<Tin, Tout> mapper)
    {
        this.mapper = mapper;
    }
```

```csharp
public void OnCompleted()
{
    foreach (var o in observers.ToArray())
    {
        o.OnCompleted();
        observers.Remove(o);
    }
}

public void OnError(Exception error)
{
    foreach (var o in observers.ToArray())
    {
        o.OnError(error);
        observers.Remove(o);
    }
}

public void OnNext(Tin value)
{
    Tout newValue = default(Tout);
    try
    {
        //mapping statement
        newValue = mapper(value);
    }
    catch (Exception ex)
    {
        //if mapping crashed
        OnError(ex);
        return;
    }

    //if mapping succeded
    foreach (var o in observers)
        o.OnNext(newValue);
}

//all registered observers
private readonly List<IObserver<Tout>> observers = new
List<IObserver<Tout>>();
public IDisposable Subscribe(IObserver<Tout> observer)
{
    observers.Add(observer);
    return new ObserverHandler<Tout>(observer, OnObserverLifecycleEnd);
}

private void OnObserverLifecycleEnd(IObserver<Tout> o)
```

```
    {
        o.OnCompleted();
        observers.Remove(o);
    }

    //this class simply informs the subject that a dispose
    //has been invoked against the observer causing its removal
    //from the observer collection of the subject
    private class ObserverHandler<T> : IDisposable
    {
        private IObserver<T> observer;
        Action<IObserver<T>> onObserverLifecycleEnd;
        public ObserverHandler(IObserver<T> observer, Action<IObserver<T>>
        onObserverLifecycleEnd)
        {
            this.observer = observer;
            this.onObserverLifecycleEnd = onObserverLifecycleEnd;
        }

        public void Dispose()
        {
            onObserverLifecycleEnd(observer);
        }
    }
}
```

Here's the usage:

```
var mapper = new MapperSubject<string, double>(x => double.Parse(x));
mapper.Subscribe(x => Console.WriteLine("{0:N4}", x));
mapper.OnNext("4.123");
mapper.OnNext("5.456");
mapper.OnNext("7.90'?");
mapper.OnNext("9.432");
```

This example shows how to create a mapping subject that translates messages into another type before routing all the data to the waiting observers.

The `subject` class uses an `ObserverHandler` class that handles the `observer` life cycle by signaling the subject an eventual `observerDispose` invoke by removing it from the `observer` list.

Subject from IObservable/IObserver

An interesting feature available as the factory method from the `Subject` class is the ability to create a new `Subject` class using the given `IObservable` and `IObserver` couple. This gives us the ability to create mixed subjects from the external `observable/observer` objects or by reusing the `IObservable` or the `IObserver` part of other subject objects into a new `subject` class.

 Kindly bear in mind that the `IObserver` implementation of `subject` is simply the message routing to its underlying observers. Here is an example:

```
var receiverSubject = new Subject<string>();
//the final observer implementation
receiverSubject.Subscribe(x => Console.WriteLine("s1=>{0}", x));

//the source of all messages
var senderSubject = new Subject<string>();
//no observers here

//the router made with the Observer part of
//the receiverSubject and the Observable part
//of the senderSubject
var routerSubject = Subject.Create(receiverSubject, senderSubject);
//another observer for testing purposes
routerSubject.Subscribe(x => Console.WriteLine("s3=>{0}", x));

senderSubject.OnNext("value1");
senderSubject.OnNext("value2");
```

This example shows us how to use the `Subject.Create` factory method.

When creating a new subject by using `Subject.Create`, the first parameter is `IObserver` that will receive messages, and the second parameter is the `IObservable` that will produce messages.

Although this example uses two subjects for creating `routerSubject` (`receiverSubject` and `senderSubject`), any `IObservable` and any `IObserver` are valid in their place.

 All the operators are usually available as extension methods by including the `System.Reactive.Linq` namespace in all the `IObservables` classes.

Transforming operators

Transforming operators transform a message into another type or transform the sequence message order or flow.

Delay

A `delay` operation adds some time delay to each message flowing within a sequence.

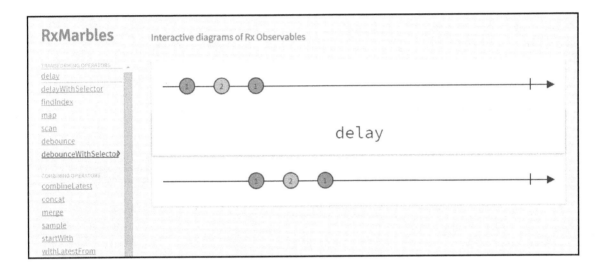

A marble diagram showing a delay operation

Here's an example:

```
var s3 = new Subject<string>();
var delay = s3.Delay(TimeSpan.FromSeconds(10));
delay.Subscribe(Console.WriteLine);

s3.OnNext("value1");
s3.OnNext("value2");
```

Map

The map operator creates a new sequence that will flow messages from the sourcing sequence translated into another type. The translation may change the intrinsic value (as a mathematic operation similar to the example shown in the following screenshot) or may be a type transformation:

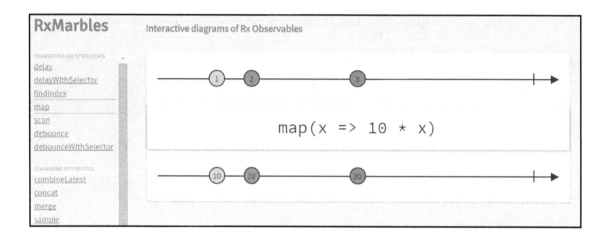

A marble diagram showing a map operation

Here's an example:

```
var s4 = new Subject<string>();
//a numeric sequence
var map = s4.Select(x => double.Parse(x));
map.Subscribe(x => Console.WriteLine("{0:N4}", x));
s4.OnNext("10.40");
s4.OnNext("12.55");
```

Scan

A scan operation works by applying a transformation to each message within a sequence with the ability to interact with the last transformed value. The following example shows how to create a running total, as the one available within Microsoft Excel, to have a real-time invoice total amount.

During the first execution, the transformation `Func` is not executed.

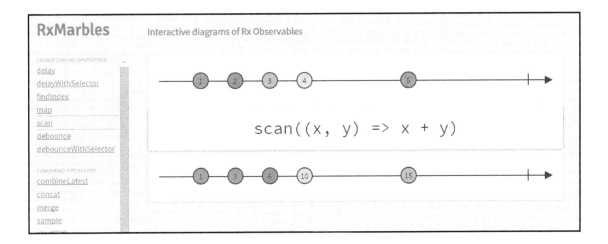

A marble diagram showing a scan operation

Here's an example:

```
var invoiceSummarySubject = new Subject<double>();
var invoiceSummaryScanSubject = invoiceSummarySubject.Scan((last, x) => x +
last);
//register an observer for printing total amount
invoiceSummaryScanSubject.Subscribe(new Action<double>(x =>
Console.WriteLine("Total amount: {0:C}", x)));
//register some invoice item total
invoiceSummarySubject.OnNext(1250,50); //add a notebook
invoiceSummarySubject.OnNext(-50.0); //discount
invoiceSummarySubject.OnNext(44.98); //a notebook bag
```

> `Scan` produces a sequence containing a running total; alternative if the
> ending total is your only interest, you can use the `Aggregate` extension
> method.

Debounce

A `Debounce` operator avoids messages from flowing in at a higher rate by setting a time-based throttling between messages. This means that messages cannot flow at a rate higher than the set one. In Rx, the operator name is Throttle, because it slows down the message flow when too many messages flow altogether in a short period.

Real world uses are the need to slow down useless high rate notifications that have to reach a UX, where anything other than 30 fps is only a resource waste, or when we make an analog-to-digital parsing that we don't want to exceed a parsing rate per second.

When we use the `Throttle` extension method, we must specify the minimum time from the last message so that the new sequence will wait to ensure the last message has flown out.

The `Debounce` operator adds a time delay and regulates the flow of messages when the source observable is still producing a lot of messages:

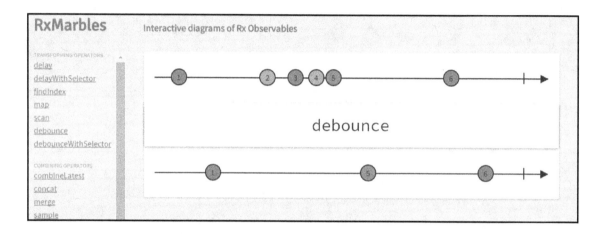

A marble diagram showing a debounce operation

Here's an example:

```
var s5 = new Subject<DateTime>();
var throttle = s5.Throttle(TimeSpan.FromMilliseconds(500));
throttle.Subscribe(x => Console.WriteLine("{0:T}", x));

//produce 100 messages
for (int i = 0; i < 100; i++)
    s5.OnNext(DateTime.Now);
```

Amb

The Amb operator will produce a new sequence that will flow messages from the fastest to produce the first message between the sourcing sequences. This means that the first sequence that flows a message into the Amb operator's sequence will became the only sourcing sequence of the Amb operator regardless of whether this sequence later completes prematurely while other initial sourcing sequences are still alive. This kind of operator is great when we need the *Speculative Execution* logic with reactive sequences. With this logic design, we can start or simply wait until multiple functions doing the same task with different parameters (think of a web search with the user's raw search criteria, or similar words from an anagram dictionary) execute, usually taking the result only from the fastest to results.

It is a routing sequence that accepts multiple source sequences (of the same message type), as other routing sequences, the Amb simply routes messages without applying any transformation. It simply chooses a single sourcing sequence between all those available by selecting the fastest one to produce any message:

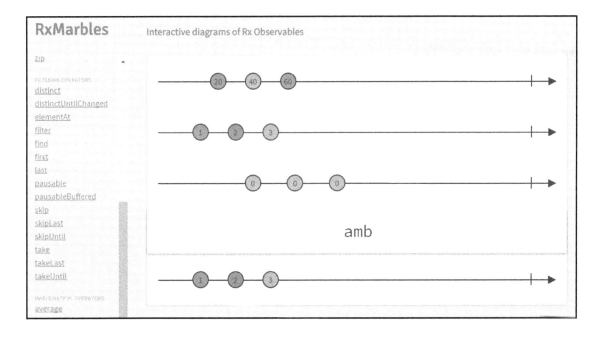

A marble diagram showing an amb operation

Here's an example:

```
var s20 = new Subject<string>();
var s21 = new Subject<string>();
var amb = s20.Amb(s21);
amb.Subscribe(Console.WriteLine);

//the first message will let amb operator
//choose the definite source sequence

s21.OnNext("value1");
//messages from the other sequences are ignored
s20.OnNext("value2");
```

Combining operators

Combining operators combine multiple sequences into a new sequence, eventually with a specific design to reduce message flow.

Combine latest

The `CombineLatest` operator produces a new sequence that combines multiple sourcing sequences by joining such messages to produce a new composite message. Kindly consider that anytime each of the source enumerable flows a new message, regardless of being the first or the second sequence, a new composite message will flow throughout the combined latest sequence.

The new sequence will start flowing messages when all the sourcing sequences produce their first message.

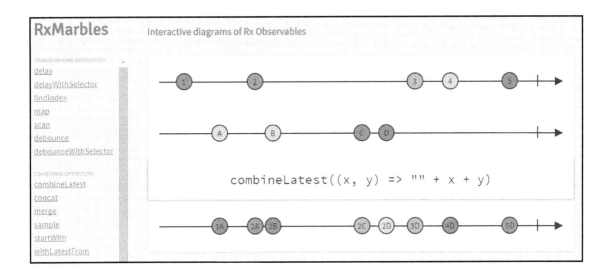

A marble diagram showing a combine latest operation

Here's an example:

```
var s6 = new Subject<string>();
var s7 = new Subject<int>();
var clatest = s6.CombineLatest(s7, (x, y) => new { text = x, value = y, });
clatest.Subscribe(x => Console.WriteLine("{0}: {1}", x.text, x.value));

//some message
s6.OnNext("Mr. Brown");
s7.OnNext(10);
s7.OnNext(20);
s6.OnNext("Mr. Green");
s6.OnNext("Mr. White");
s7.OnNext(30);
```

Concat

The Concat operator creates a new sequence that contains the concatenation of multiple sourcing sequences, as they are registered as sourcing sequence.

In other words, as shown in the following screenshot, the `Concat` sequence will start flowing messages from the first sourcing sequence and will then start flowing messages from the second sourcing sequence and so on. An important aspect is that this operator will start flowing messages from a new sequence only after the previous sequence completes (by flowing the `OnComplete` message) correctly. In other words, this operator sequentially flows messages from multiple sequences. For the parallel version, take a look at the `Merge` operator in the following section.

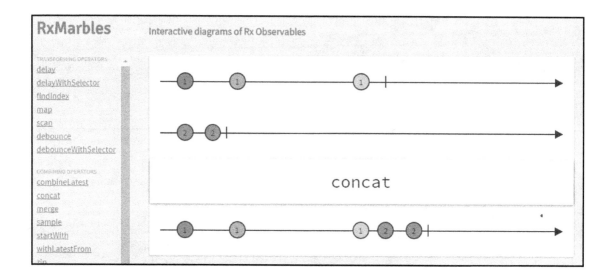

A marble diagram showing a Concat operation

Here's an example:

```
var s8 = new Subject<string>();
var s9 = new Subject<string>();
var concat = s8.Concat(s9);
concat.Subscribe(Console.WriteLine);

//some message
s8.OnNext("value1");
s8.OnNext("value2");
s9.OnNext("value3"); //missed
s9.OnNext("value4"); //missed
s8.OnNext("value5");
//close first sequence
s8.OnCompleted();
//only now messages from second sequence will start flowing
s9.OnNext("value6");
```

Merge

The Merge operation flattens messages of the same type between multiple sequences into a single output sequence. In other words, it combines values from a multiple sequence in a parallel way.

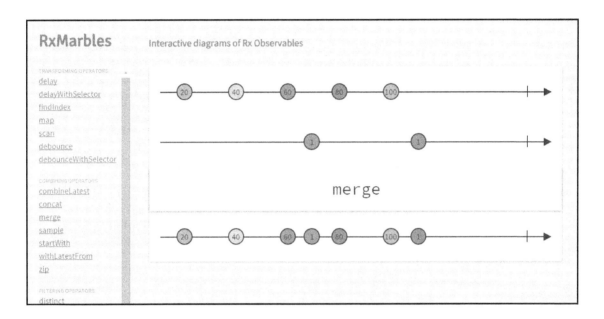

A marble diagram showing a merge operation

Here's an example.

```
var s1 = new Subject<string>();
var s2 = new Subject<string>();
var merge = s1.Merge(s2);
merge.Subscribe(Console.WriteLine);

s1.OnNext("value1"); //first subject
s2.OnNext("value2"); //second subject
```

Sample

A `Sample` sequence lets the values flow from another sequence only when a value flows from another sequence that works like a metronome when playing music. The second sequence simply defines the time when a message can flow. The first sequence, however is the source of all the messages that will flow within the sampling. This is something like a polling-based design.

Consider the case when we read data from a PLC analogic port. The PLC usually works in a reactive way by itself (PLC's SDK may support multiple data paradigm outputs); this means that it flows out new analogic port values only when these change the value changes. Rather, if we need sampling data at a fixed time, as happens in digital audio, we may use the Sample operator by reading raw data from the PLC sourcing sequence, and a clock message from another sequence. With this design, we will be able to sample at a fixed time from a source that flows values as they're available with few efforts in a full reactive design.

In Rx, the `Sample` extension method has two overloads. One overload accepts a `DateTime` parameter useful to sample at a fixed time. Another overload accepts another sequence to sample when sampling messages flow. Although an overload accepting a fixed time parameter is available with the `Scan` operator, the canonical one is the overload with two sequence parameter overloads.

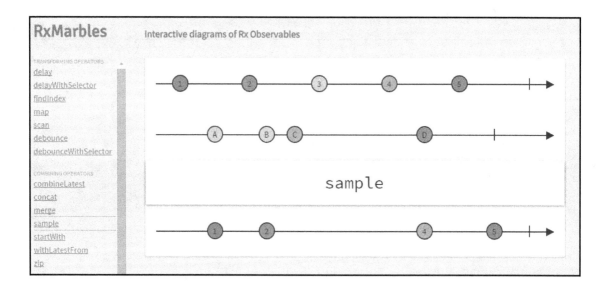

A marble diagram showing a sample operation

Here's an example:

```
var samplingValueSequence = new Subject<int>();
var samplingTimeSequence = new Subject<object>();
var samplingSequence = samplingValueSequence.Sample(samplingTimeSequence);
//register an observer
samplingSequence.Subscribe(new Action<int>(x => Console.WriteLine(x)));

//some value
samplingValueSequence.OnNext(10); //ignored
samplingValueSequence.OnNext(20);
//raise a message into the sampling time sequence
samplingTimeSequence.OnNext(null); //last value will be outputted now
samplingValueSequence.OnNext(30); //ignored
samplingValueSequence.OnNext(40);
//raise a message into the sampling time sequence
samplingTimeSequence.OnNext(null); //last value will be outputted now
```

StartWith

The `StartWith` operator is similar to the `Concat` operator because they concatenate values of sequences with the difference that `StartWith` inserts a specific value at the beginning of its sourcing sequence. The other difference is that `StartWith` does not work on multiple sequences. It simply uses a defined group of values, such as an array or any `IEnumerable`.

`StartWith` is very useful when combined with the `Scan` operator because it gives the `Scan` operator a value to start the running total (or any other running operation).

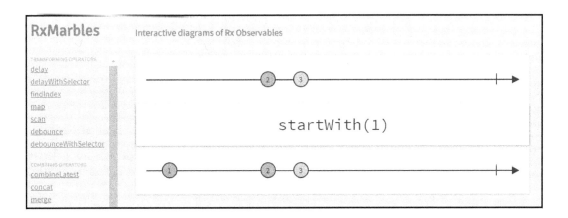

A marble diagram showing a startwith operation

Here's an example:

```
var s10 = new Subject<string>();
var swith = s10.StartWith("value0");
swith.Subscribe(Console.WriteLine);
s10.OnNext("value1");
s10.OnNext("value2");
```

Zip

The `Zip` operator is similar to the combine latest operator, producing values from two other sequences only when each source sequence has a new value. The difference is that the combine latest operator produces messages wherever any source sequence produces a new message, eventually reusing the same value from the other sequence. Instead, the `Zip` operator synchronizes the two sequences using the message index number as a correlation ID to flow messages always together, eventually waiting for the two sequences to have the new couple of messages to produce the new one.

As the combine latest operator, the `Zip` operator translates the two source messages into a new message by executing a transformation operation.

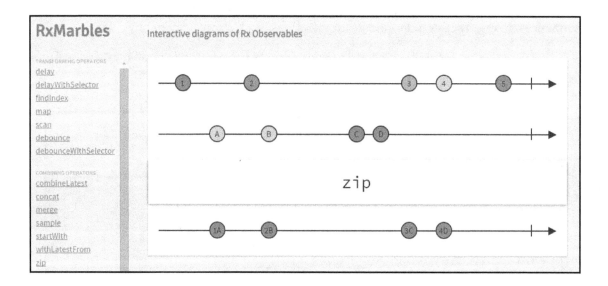

A marble diagram showing a zip operation

Here's an example:

```
var s11 = new Subject<string>();
var s12 = new Subject<double>();
var zip = s11.Zip(s12, (x, y) => new { text = x, value = y });
zip.Subscribe(x => Console.WriteLine("{0}: {1}", x.text, x.value));
//same example of combine latest
s11.OnNext("Mr. Brown");
s12.OnNext(10);
s12.OnNext(20);
s11.OnNext("Mr. Green");
s11.OnNext("Mr. White");
s12.OnNext(30);
//this time the output is synchronized
```

Filtering operators

Filtering operators act as the `where` operators of any `LINQ` query. They reduce, take, or peek a value (or multiple values) from a sequence when messages comply with a given filtering function.

Filter

The easiest filtering operator, filter, simply applies a filtering condition that allows or prevents messages from flowing throughout the newly created sequence. In Rx, the filter operator in made by using the `Where` extension method like in any other `LINQ` query.

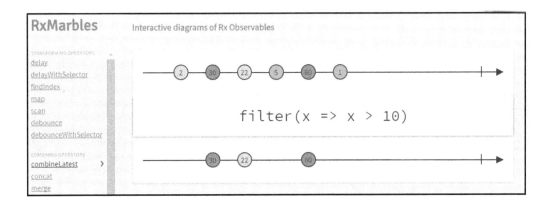

A marble diagram showing a filter operation

Here's an example:

```
var s12 = new Subject<string>();
var filtered = s12.Where(x => x.Contains("e"));
filtered.Subscribe(Console.WriteLine);
s12.OnNext("Mr. Brown");
s12.OnNext("Mr. White");
```

Distinct

The distinct operator, similar to what happens in any SQL statement, creates a new sequence that prevents duplicated values from flowing out from the source sequence.

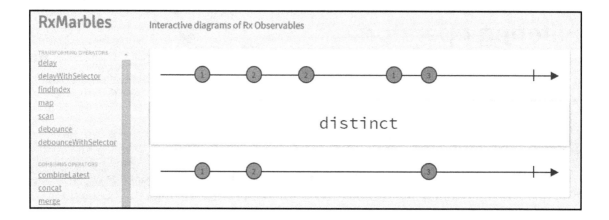

A marble diagram showing a distinct operation

Here's an example:

```
var s13 = new Subject<string>();
var distinct = s13.Distinct();
distinct.Subscribe(Console.WriteLine);
s13.OnNext("value1");
s13.OnNext("value2");
s13.OnNext("value1");
s13.OnNext("value2");
```

DistinctUntilChanged

Different from the simple distinct operator, the `DistinctUntilChanged` operator avoids duplicated values flowing into a new sequence only when those duplicated values are contiguous.

This is a powerful operator for any raw value sampling, such as when dealing with analog or digital sensors from IoT applications, preventing high rate sampling from creating multiple duplicated values because the sampling rate is higher than the value change rate.

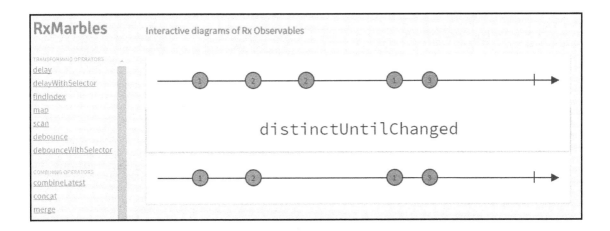

A marble diagram showing a DistinctUntilChanged operation

Here's an example:

```
var s24 = new Subject<string>();
var distinct = s24.DistinctUntilChanged();
distinct.Subscribe(Console.WriteLine);
s24.OnNext("value1"); //ok
s24.OnNext("value2"); //ok
s24.OnNext("value2"); //ignored
s24.OnNext("value3"); //ok
s24.OnNext("value4"); //ok
s24.OnNext("value1"); //ok
s24.OnNext("value2"); //ok
s24.OnNext("value2"); //ignored
s24.OnNext("value3"); //ok
s24.OnNext("value4"); //ok
```

Bear in mind that the operator avoids duplicated values when these flow sequentially, otherwise duplicates may exist. Thus, in the preceding example, we saw that we can flow out messages from 1 to 4 two times. Only the two duplicates are ignored.

ElementAt

The ElementAt operator makes available accessing a new sequence that will flow a single message when its index in the source sequence equals the requested index.

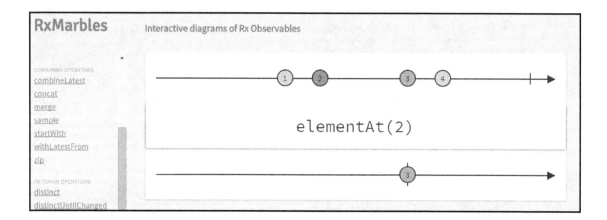

A marble diagram showing a ElementAt operation

Here's an example:

```
var s13 = new Subject<string>();
var indexed = s13.ElementAt(2);

indexed.Subscribe(Console.WriteLine);
s13.OnNext("value1"); //ignored
s13.OnNext("value2"); //ignored
s13.OnNext("value3"); //OK
s13.OnNext("value4"); //ignored
```

Skip

The `Skip` operator creates a new sequence that will skip some messages from the source sequence before it starts flowing messages.

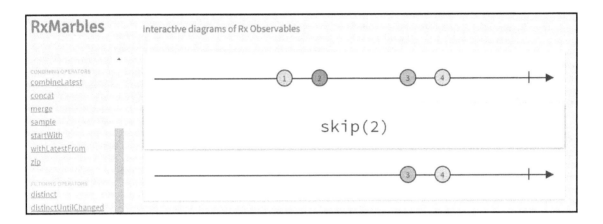

A marble diagram showing a skip operation

Here's an example:

```
var s14 = new Subject<string>();
var skip = s14.Skip(2);
skip.Subscribe(Console.WriteLine);
s14.OnNext("value1"); //ignored
s14.OnNext("value2"); //ignored
s14.OnNext("value3"); //ok
s14.OnNext("value4"); //ok
```

Take

The `Take` operator, as the opposite of the skip operator, creates a new sequence that will flow only an initial amount of messages from the source sequence.

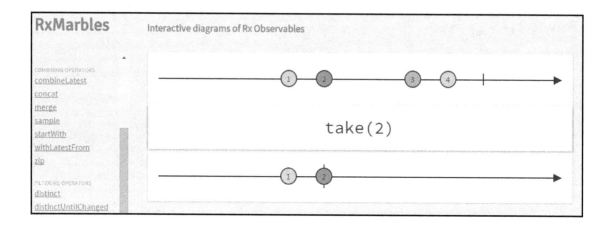

A marble diagram showing a take operation

Here's an example:

```
var s15 = new Subject<string>();
var take = s15.Take(2);
take.Subscribe(Console.WriteLine);
s15.OnNext("value1"); //ok
s15.OnNext("value2"); //ok
s15.OnNext("value3"); //ignored
s15.OnNext("value4"); //ignored
```

Mathematical operators

Mathematical operators are all the operators that deal with mathematics aggregations. All such operators work on aggregated values.

Min/Max/Avg/Sum/Count

All these operators create a new sequence that will flow a single message containing the minimum, maximum, averaged, sum, or count value ever entered in the operator from the source sequence. The new sequence will flow out its message only when the source sequence is complete.

Here is an example:

```
var s16 = new Subject<double>();
var min = s16.Min(); //register for finding the min
var max = s16.Max(); //register for finding the max
var avg = s16.Average(); //register for finding the average
var sum = s16.Sum(); //register for finding the count
var count = s16.Count(); //register for finding the sum

min.Subscribe(x => Console.WriteLine("min: {0}", x));
max.Subscribe(x => Console.WriteLine("max: {0}", x));
avg.Subscribe(x => Console.WriteLine("avg: {0}", x));
sum.Subscribe(x => Console.WriteLine("sum: {0}", x));
count.Subscribe(x => Console.WriteLine("count: {0}", x));

//some value
var r = new Random(DateTime.Now.GetHashCode());
for (int i = 0; i < 10; i++)
    s16.OnNext(r.NextDouble() * 100d);

//now aggregation operators will flow their message
s16.OnCompleted();
```

Logic operators

Logic operators deal with Boolean results, giving the programmer the ability to take decisions on sequence values in a reactive way by producing other sequences. They are the respective of LINQAny, All, and similar operators.

Every/Some/Includes

All these operators produce a new sequence containing a single message that will contain a result of a Boolean question.

The `Every` operator is the reactive version of the LINQ All operator, returning if all the elements of a sequence comply with a specified statement.

The `Some` operator is the reactive version of the LINQ `Any` operator, returning if any element in a sequence complies with a specified statement.

The `Includes` operator is the reactive version of the LINQ `Contains` operator, returning if any element in the sequence is the one specified.

Boolean operators, similar to mathematical ones, need the source sequence complete before flowing their response messages.

Here's an example:

```
var s17 = new Subject<double>();
var every = s17.All(x => x > 0);
var some = s17.Any(x => x % 2 == 0);
var includes = s17.Contains(4d);

every.Subscribe(x => Console.WriteLine("every: {0}", x));
some.Subscribe(x => Console.WriteLine("some: {0}", x));
includes.Subscribe(x => Console.WriteLine("includes: {0}", x));

//some value
var r = new Random(DateTime.Now.GetHashCode());
for (int i = 0; i < 10; i++)
    s17.OnNext(r.NextDouble() * 100d);

//now operators will flow their message
s17.OnCompleted();
```

SequenceEqual

The `SequenceEqual` operator, similar to mathematical and Boolean operators, creates a new sequence that will flow a single message containing the result if multiple source sequences have the same message values respecting the original order, eventually ignoring time-based differences. This means that the two sequences are not synchronized in their message flow timings. The only interest is in the message order and values.

The new sequence will flow its result message only when all the source sequences are complete.

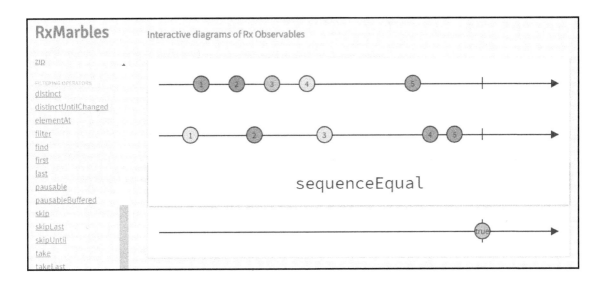

A marble diagram showing a SequenceEqual operation

Here's an example:

```
var s18 = new Subject<int>();
var s19 = new Subject<int>();
var equals = s18.SequenceEqual(s19);
equals.Subscribe(x => Console.WriteLine("sequenceEqual: {0}", x));
s18.OnNext(10),
s18.OnNext(20);
s19.OnNext(10);
s19.OnNext(20);
s18.OnNext(30);
s19.OnNext(30);

//completes to flow out the sequenceEqual result message
s18.OnCompleted();
s19.OnCompleted();
```

References

Interesting reading on observer patterns can be found at the following link:

`http://reactivex.io/.`

An operator list and detailed explanation is provided at the following link:

`http://reactivex.io/documentation/operators.html.`

Summary

In this chapter, we took a first look at Reactive Extensions for .NET-based languages.

We took some steps toward programming with subjects and with the huge operator library available as Extension Methods.

In the next chapter, we will continue our Rx programming tour by looking at creational factories and other sequence manipulation operators.

4
Observable Sequence Programming

This chapter will give the reader a specific idea of sequence creation and manipulation. We will see the Reactive Extension framework's abilities to interact with sequences with the huge operator's availability through a lot of extension methods available to any observable sequence.

During this chapter, we will focus on the following arguments:

- Sequence creation basics
- Time-based sequence creation
- Sequence manipulation and filtering
- Sequence partitioning
- Advanced operators

Sequence creation basics

In the previous chapter, we saw how to create sequences other than simply implementing the IObservable interface by creating our custom observables using the Subject class that gives us an initial implementation which is useful in a lot of cases, thus reducing the bootstrap time when programming in a reactive way.

We can create a new `observable` subject simply with the `new` keyword of the C# programming language. The same happens in regard to customized observable sequences (by implementing the `IObservable` interface). Other than this, we can create generic observable sequences with the factory methods available within the `observable` helper class that give us the ability to create sequences from the scratch without having to create custom classes, or by other values or other CLR objects, such as events and so on. These sequences are only observable sequences; they are not subjects and they are not observers.

A lot of the following factory methods will simply translate state-based (variables) data into flowing data by returning the same value wrapped into a sequence. Although this may seem like a change of minimal importance, the truth is that by changing the layout of data, we are also changing the kind of application design.

Empty/Never

The simplest sequence is the empty sequence. This kind of sequence may be useful to start/end some kind of operations or may be useful to comply with some operator method signs.

Each of the two operators are available as factory methods from the `Observable` helper. Each of these two operators (`Empty` and `Never`) produces a virtually empty sequence. The difference is that the `Empty` factory method produces a sequence without values that inform of its emptiness by flowing a completed message. On the other hand, the `Never` method produces a sequence that will either never end (infinite sequence) or never send any message:

```
//an empty sequence ended with a completed message
IObservable<string> s2ended = Observable.Empty<string>();
//an infinite sequence
IObservable<string> s2infinite = Observable.Never<string>();
```

Return

When we need a sequence from an already available value, to bring such a value into the reactive world, we can simply use the `Return` factory method. This factory gives us the ability to go from the state-based application design to the reactive one:

```
//a sequence from a value
IObservable<double> s3 = Observable.Return(40d);
```

Throw

Identical to the `Return` factory, `Throw` lets the error message flow to the underlying observers. It produces a new sequence with a single error message that originates from `Exception`:

```
//a faulty sequence
IObservable<DateTime> s4 = Observable.Throw<DateTime>(new
Exception("Now"));
```

Create

The `Create` factory method is the most complex of the group. It does not simply change the type of the resulting object. It actually is a factory method that returns a factory for creating arbitrary sequences, such as message sources, to interact with observers.

We are not creating a self-messaging sequence. Instead, we will actually write a code that will produce messages per each observer ever attached to such a sequence. This is extremely different to any other sequence we have already seen (and even others in the next chapters), because all the sequences produce the same message that routes to all the observers, while the sequence born with the `Create` factory method produces different messages based on any logic.

The `Create` operator gives us the ability to specify a `Func<IObserver<T>, IDisposable>` delegate that will contain the message sourcing logic. This delegated implementation will definitely produce messages (that is, by materializing a database query) that each subscriber will consume, only when the subscription occurs, in a lazy fashion. Bear in mind that each subscription will cause the execution of the delegate that will start flowing messages. The ability to have different implementations per subscriber makes this operator unique. Thus, only with the `Create` operator, we have the ability to interact with the observer itself from within the sequence operator chain itself.

Before trying to understand such sequences in detail, let's take a look at an example:

```
var s5 = Observable.Create<DateTime>(observer =>
    {
        Console.WriteLine("Registering subscriber {0} of type {1}",
        observer.GetHashCode(), observer);
        //here you can handle by hand your observer interaction logic
        Task.Factory.StartNew(() =>
            {
                //some (time based) message
                for(int i=0;i<10;i++)
```

```
            {
                observer.OnNext(DateTime.Now);
                Thread.Sleep(1000);
            }
            //end of observer life
            observer.OnCompleted();
        });
        return () => Console.WriteLine("OnCompleted {0} of type {1}",
        observer.GetHashCode(), observer);
    });

    //subscribe an anonymous observer
    s5.Subscribe(d =>
        {
            Console.WriteLine("OnNext : {0}", d);
        });
```

The preceding example creates a sequence that accepts `Action` that contains the executing code that represents the observable sequence logic for a given observer. Based on such a logic, different observers may even receive different messages.

In the example, we created `Task` that will produce messages containing current `DateTime`. At the end, a completed message reached the observer, killing it.

Instead of returning a simple `Action` method representing the handler of the completed message that will reach the observer, we can produce a `Disposable` object that is actually an end-of-life token. Once disposed, such tokens will kill the observer subscription even prematurely. The result is identical to the solution with the `Action` already seen in the preceding code.

It is interesting see the ability to use the `Disposable` helper module that gives us the opportunity to have empty disposable objects or disposable objects that execute some specific code once the disposing happens by specifying `Action`. The previous example routes the written `Action` method into the `Disposable.Create` helper method, thus producing the same result of the following code with the difference being that, in the following example, we can stop prematurely the observer's life cycle:

```
    var s5 = Observable.Create<DateTime>(observer =>
        {
            Console.WriteLine("Registering subscriber {0} of type {1}",
            observer.GetHashCode(), observer);
            //here you can handle by hand your observer interaction logic
            Task.Factory.StartNew(() =>
                {
                    //some (time based) message
                    for (int i = 0; i < 10; i++)
```

```
            {
                observer.OnNext(DateTime.Now);
                Thread.Sleep(1000);
            }
            //end of observer life
            observer.OnCompleted();
        });
    return Disposable.Create(() => Console.WriteLine("Disposing..."));
});

//subscribe an anonymous observer
var disposableObserver = s5.Subscribe(d =>
    {
        Console.WriteLine("OnNext : {0}", d);
    });

//wait some time and press RETURN
//to dispose the observer
Console.ReadLine();

disposableObserver.Dispose();

Console.ReadLine();
```

Range

The `Range` factory method creates a sequence that will produce messages from a specific value range using the `Int32` message type. This is something like creating a range of values by executing the `Enumerable.Range()` method that is later flowed in an observable sequence. Here's an example:

```
//a ranged sequence
var range = Observable.Range(0, 1000);
//an observer will get values
//anytime it will subscribe
range.Subscribe(value =>
    {
        Console.WriteLine("range -> {0}", value);
    });
```

The `Range` operator creates something like a sourcing message pattern. This means that each subscribing observer will benefit by the same result. In other words, if we specify a range of `1000` items, each subscriber will receive `1000` messages. This also means that if there are no existing subscribers, nothing will happen and no message will flow to the consuming resources.

Generate

The Generate factory method is some kind of aberration within the reactive world. We should deal with functions; instead, it is a For statement made reactive.

In other words, we have an index value (i=0), an evaluation statement (i<10), an index iteration addition function, and a body function, exactly the same as any For statement. Here's an example:

```
//a reactive For statement
//similar to for(int i=0;i<10;i++)
var generated = Observable.Generate<int, DateTime>(0, i => i < 10, i => i +
1, i => new DateTime(2016, 1, 1).AddDays(i));

generated.Subscribe(value =>
    {
        Console.WriteLine("generated -> {0}", value);
    });
```

Although it is strange to see an iterative statement in the reactive world, sometimes, it may be useful.

Time-based sequence creation

In the previous sections, we had the opportunity to create simple sequences from known values or by executing some specific code.

Although these opportunities give us the chance to create useful message sequences, in the real world, reactive programming deals with some kind of time-based messages.

Interval

The easiest form of time-based interaction is the polling design. This design, typical of nonreactive programming, happens anytime we ask for a value or a state at a fixed time interval. Similarly, within the reactive programming, we may produce messages at a fixed time interval running in a push design to use the value itself or to trigger other logics available in the following sequence chain.

The `Interval` operator produces a similar design by specifying the wanted time interval, receiving a counter of the current tick as the `Int64` value.

Here's an example:

```
static void Main(string[] args)
{
    //this sequence produces a message per second
    var sequence = Observable.Interval(TimeSpan.FromSeconds(1));
    sequence.Subscribe(ObserverOnNext);

    Console.ReadLine();
}

private static void ObserverOnNext(long obj)
{
    Console.WriteLine("{0} -> {1}", obj, DateTime.Now);
}
```

The greatest benefit here is the asynchronous implementation of the sequence that came from the `Observable.Interval` helper method at actually no cost for the developer.

Instead of creating threads or tasks, we simply asked for a sequence to produce messages at a timely basis and that is what we have.

The sequence always produces the `Int64` values starting from zero. This is a message counter. Useful for some hardcoded, antireactive solution/design, the suggestion is to ignore such values.

Timer

The `Timer` factory method adds another feature to the `Interval` one. Like `Interval`, `Timer` may give us the ability to produce messages at a fixed time interval, but the real use of the `Timer` method is the ability to defer the execution at a given time or mix two features together. Here's an example:

```
//a timer used for defer the message sending
var defer = Observable.Timer(TimeSpan.FromSeconds(5));
defer.Subscribe(value =>
    {
        Console.WriteLine("defer -> {0}", value);
    });

//a polling timer that will produce
//messages at fixed time interval
```

```
var loop = Observable.Timer(TimeSpan.FromSeconds(5),
TimeSpan.FromSeconds(0.5));
loop.Subscribe(value =>
{
    Console.WriteLine("loop -> {0}", value);
});

Console.ReadLine();
```

Similar to the `Interval` factory method, the `Timer` produces a sequence to work in an asynchronous way without having the developer doing the hard job of creating threads or tasks.

Timeout

The `Timeout` factory method creates a new sequence to throw `TimeoutException` if the system time exceeds a specific time (absolute timeout) or if a message flows by a time that exceeds a given time by the previous message (relative timeout).

This powerful sequence can help in addressing a lot of network-related needs or multiple message correlations based on specific synchronization times.

Here's a complete example of the two working modes:

```
class Program
{
    static void Main(string[] args)
    {
        //this sequence must complete by 5 seconds from now
        var absoluteTimeoutSequence =
Observable.Interval(TimeSpan.FromSeconds(1))
            .Select(id => DateTime.UtcNow)
            .Timeout(DateTimeOffset.Now.AddSeconds(5));

        absoluteTimeoutSequence.Subscribe(new ConsoleObserver());

        Console.WriteLine("Press RETURN to start the following example");
        Console.ReadLine();

        //this sequence's messages must flow
        //by 2 seconds
        var relativeTimeoutSequence =
Observable.Create<DateTime>(newObserver =>
            {
                Console.WriteLine("Registering observer...");
                Console.WriteLine("Starting message flow...");
```

```
                        //handle the new subscriber message flow
                        Task.Factory.StartNew(() =>
                        {
                            //the message flow will slow down until timeout
                            int i = 100;
                            while (true)
                            {
                                newObserver.OnNext(DateTime.UtcNow);
                                //the delay will increase each iteration
                                Thread.Sleep(i += 100);
                            }
                        }, TaskCreationOptions.PreferFairness);

                        return new Action(() =>
                        {
                            Console.WriteLine("Completed");
                        });
                    })
                    .Timeout(TimeSpan.FromSeconds(2));

            relativeTimeoutSequence.Subscribe(new ConsoleObserver());

            Console.ReadLine();
        }
    }

    public class ConsoleObserver : IObserver<DateTime>
    {
        public void OnCompleted()
        {
            Console.WriteLine("Observer completed!");
        }

        public void OnError(Exception error)
        {
            Console.WriteLine("Observer error: {0}", error);
        }

        public void OnNext(DateTime value)
        {
            Console.WriteLine("{0}", value);
        }
    }
```

TimeInterval/Timestamp

The `TimeInterval` factory method is a very useful factory method that creates a sequence to record the time interval that exists between messages flowing from a sourcing sequence. It is absolutely useful for diagnostic purposes.

Similarly useful is the `Timestamp` factory method that creates a sequence that flows out messages with a timestamp (`DateTimeOffset`) which is useful for tracing/logging message flows.

Here's a complete example of a fixed time interval sourcing sequence:

```
class Program
{
    static void Main(string[] args)
    {
        //a sourcing sequence
        var sourcingSequence =
         Observable.Interval(TimeSpan.FromSeconds(1)).Select(id =>
         DateTime.UtcNow);
         sourcingSequence.Subscribe(value =>
            {
                Console.WriteLine("{0}", value);
            });

        //a sequence recording the time interval of the sourcing sequence
        var diagnosticSequence = sourcingSequence.TimeInterval();
        diagnosticSequence.Subscribe(interval =>
            {
                Debug.WriteLine(string.Format("Message flowing in
{0:N0}ms",
                    interval.Interval.TotalMilliseconds));
            });

        var diagnosticSequence2 = sourcingSequence.Timestamp();
        diagnosticSequence2.Subscribe(new MessageTimeStampLogger());

        Console.ReadLine();
    }
}

public class MessageTimeStampLogger : IObserver<Timestamped<DateTime>>
{
    public void OnCompleted()
    {
        Console.WriteLine("Observer completed!");
    }
```

```
    public void OnError(Exception error)
    {
        Console.WriteLine("Observer error: {0}", error);
    }

    public void OnNext(Timestamped<DateTime> value)
    {
        Debug.WriteLine(string.Format("{0} -> Now flowing: {1}",
value.Timestamp, value.Value));
    }
}
```

Sequence manipulation and filtering

Manipulation and filtering of sequence messages helps in the development of complex messaging designs. The most immediate and widely used operator is Where, which creates a routing sequence of messages already filtered based on its filtering predicate. We have already seen some of the manipulating or filtering factory methods in the previous chapter, such as the Take, Skip, Distinct, and DistinctUntilChanged methods.

Where

The Where factory method creates a new sequence that flows messages from another sequence only when a specific Where predicate succeeds. Here's an example:

```
//fixed-time interval sequence
var fixedTimeBasedSequence = Observable.Interval(TimeSpan.FromSeconds(1));

//convert the message
//into time value
var dateTimeSequence = fixedTimeBasedSequence
    .Select(v=> DateTime.UtcNow );

//filtered sequence of times with even second value
var filteredSequence = dateTimeSequence.Where(dt => dt.Second % 2 == 0);

//outputs the value
filteredSequence.Subscribe(dt =>
    {
        Console.WriteLine("{0:d} {0:T}", dt);
    });

Console.ReadLine();
```

Join

The `Observable.Join` factory method (available as the `Extension` method) creates a single sequence of messages from multiple sequences. To synchronize messages from the sourcing sequences, we must give such messages time to synchronize to others. This time the window makes it evident as to how much reactive programming is time-based. This is different from state-driven paradigms in which an eventual `Join` clause would use a specific value to synchronize to another value, as what happens within the SQL language.

Before I try to explain further, let's take a look at an example:

```
//two sourcing sequences of time-based values
var sourceSequence1 =
Observable.Interval(TimeSpan.FromSeconds(2)).Select(nr => DateTime.UtcNow);
var sourceSequence2 =
Observable.Interval(TimeSpan.FromSeconds(3)).Select(nr => DateTime.UtcNow);

//a joined sequence of messages
var joinedSequence = sourceSequence1.Join(sourceSequence2,
    v => Observable.Return(v).Delay(TimeSpan.FromMilliseconds(100)),
    v => Observable.Return(v).Delay(TimeSpan.FromMilliseconds(100)),
    (v1, v2) => new { fromSequence1 = v1, fromSequence2 = v2 });

joinedSequence.Subscribe(x =>
    {
        Console.WriteLine("{0} / {1}", x.fromSequence1, x.fromSequence2);
    });
```

The preceding example shows the usage of the `Join` clause. There are two sourcing sequences of values, one emitting messages 2 seconds each and another emitting messages 3 seconds each. To make things easier, the two sequences produce the `DateTime` values.

The `Join` method needs the sourcing sequences, two time window function generators and a function that creates the new object from the two sourcing ones.

The most interesting things here are the two time window generator functions. These functions create other sequences of messages with little delay in the message flow. This delay is in the time window that the joined sequence uses to match messages from the two sourcing sequences.

In the preceding example, we take values from two sourcing sequences. To match values based on the time (messages must arise from the sourcing sequences in the same moment), we need to create something like a time buffer to let messages from the two sequences match the other. To make this happen, we will create (with two identical lambda functions) two new sequences with a time delay from the value of the sourcing sequence. These sequences produce a message that is like a time to leave for the sourcing message itself. In other words, it is a matching timeout of the sourcing messages. When the two sourcing sequences flow messages that overlap the timeout of the message from the other source, the two messages match the Join operator filter and flow out with the resulting sequence.

If

The `If` factory method of the `Observable` helper module returns a sequence that chooses which sourcing sequence to return to each subscriber based on a conditional function. This is similar to the usual `If` statement of C# with a difference that such reactive versions will execute the conditional function to evaluate which sourcing sequence to return each time a new subscriber asks for registering. Here's a complete example:

```
//two sourcing sequences of time values

var sourcingSequence1 = Observable.Interval(TimeSpan.FromSeconds(2))
    .Select(id => DateTime.UtcNow);

var sourcingSequence2 = Observable.Interval(TimeSpan.FromSeconds(3))
    .Select(id => DateTime.UtcNow);


//a selection function to choose
//which sourcing sequence to use
var mustUseTheFirstSequenceSelector = new Func<bool>(() =>
    {
        var isFirst = DateTime.UtcNow.Second % 2 == 0;
        Console.WriteLine("IsFirst: {0}", isFirst);
        return isFirst;
    });

//a conditional sequence of values from
// the first or the second sourcing sequence
var conditionalSequence = Observable.If(mustUseTheFirstSequenceSelector,
sourcingSequence1, sourcingSequence2);

for (int i = 0; i < 3; i++)
{
    Console.WriteLine("Subscribing new observer...");
```

```
        conditionalSequence.Subscribe(x =>
            {
                Console.WriteLine("{0}", x);
            });
        Thread.Sleep(1000);
    }

Console.ReadLine();
```

TakeUntil/TakeWhile/SkipUntil/SkipWhile

These factory methods are available as the `Extension` methods to any observable sequence and manipulate the message's availability as follows:

- The `TakeUntil` operator sources values until a timeout occurs
- The `TakeWhile` operator sources values while a condition remains true
- The `SkipUntil` operator will avoid flowing messages until a timeout occurs
- The `SkipWhile` operator will avoid flowing messages while a condition remains true

Here's a group example:

```
//a sourcing sequence
var sourcingSequence =
Observable.Interval(TimeSpan.FromSeconds(1)).Select(id => DateTime.UtcNow);

//will flow messages for next 5 seconds
var takeUntil =
sourcingSequence.TakeUntil(DateTimeOffset.Now.AddSeconds(5));
takeUntil.Subscribe(value =>
    {
        Console.WriteLine("Until5Seconds: {0}", value);
    });

var begin=DateTime.UtcNow;
//will flow messages while in the
//same minute of the begin
var takeWhile = sourcingSequence.TakeWhile(x => begin.Minute == x.Minute);
takeWhile.Subscribe(value =>
    {
        Console.WriteLine("WhileSameMinute: {0}", value);
    });

//skip messages for 5 seconds
var skipUntil =
```

```
sourcingSequence.SkipUntil(DateTimeOffset.Now.AddSeconds(5));
skipUntil.Subscribe(value =>
    {
        Console.WriteLine("SkipFor5Seconds: {0}", value);
    });

//skip messages of the same minute
var skipWhile = sourcingSequence.SkipWhile(x => begin.Minute == x.Minute);
skipWhile.Subscribe(value =>
    {
        Console.WriteLine("SkipSameMinute: {0}", value);
    });
Console.ReadLine();
```

TakeLast/SkipLast

These two factory methods give us the ability to create sequences that deal with the last messages of a sourcing sequence. The difference between these two implementations is that, with the TakeLast, we will obtain a new sequence that will produce only a small numeric amount of messages (given a specific count or time window) just before the sourcing sequence completes its life. On the other hand, SkipLast will flow all the messages, except the last amount of messages (given a specific count or time window).

Here's a group example:

```
Console.WriteLine("Starting: {0}", DateTime.Now);
//a sourcing sequence for a time-window of 5 seconds
var sourcingSequence =
Observable.Interval(TimeSpan.FromSeconds(1)).Select(id => DateTime.UtcNow)
    .TakeUntil(DateTimeOffset.Now.AddSeconds(5));

//skip last messages within a time-window of 3 seconds
var skipLast = sourcingSequence.SkipLast(TimeSpan.FromSeconds(3));
skipLast.Subscribe(value =>
    {
        Console.WriteLine("SkipLast: {0}", value);
    });

//take last messages within a time-window of 3 seconds
var takeLast = sourcingSequence.TakeLast(TimeSpan.FromSeconds(3));
takeLast.Subscribe(value =>
{
    Console.WriteLine("TakeLast: {0}", value);
});

Console.ReadLine();
```

Sequence partitioning

Partitioning is the ability to split data into multiple strips.

When dealing with reactive sequences, partitioning means splitting a sourcing sequence into multiple subsequences. The goal may be to maintain message flow consistency when dealing with multiple parallel sequences. In this case, although we may prefer working with data from all the sourcing sequences in a single sequence chain for simplicity and maintainability, at a time, we will need to split the messages from their original flow by grouping them by one (or more) properties.

In reactive programming, we never partition for performance needs (such as parallelizing processing) because this is achieved by default using the reactive framework itself if we use the proper overall design (refer to `Chapter 6, CLR Integration and Scheduling`, for a more in-depth the argument).

GroupBy

The king of the partitioning functions is the `GroupBy` one. This is the same within Rx, thus we have the `GroupBy` extension method that will produce a grouping observable sequence (`IGroupedObservable<T>`) of small sequences to deal with a single group item per time.

These sequences will flow out the grouping sequence in a lazy way. Once a new message, requiring a new subsequence, flows out the sourcing sequence, the grouping sequence will flow out a new grouping sequence. This is why we need a two-level subscribing method, because at the first level, we register the new subsequence, and at the second one we register the message observer as usual for nongrouped sequences.

Here's an example:

```
//a sourcing sequence
var sourcingSequence =
Observable.Interval(TimeSpan.FromSeconds(1)).Select(id => DateTime.UtcNow);

//sequence partitioning by seconds
var partitions = sourcingSequence.GroupBy(x => Math.Floor(x.Second / 10d));

//register the partition per group key
partitions.Subscribe(partition =>
    {
        Console.WriteLine("Registering observer for: {0}", partition.Key);

        //register the observer per partition
```

```
        partition.Subscribe(value =>
            {
                Console.WriteLine("partition {0}: {1}", partition.Key,
value);
            });
        });
```

```
Console.ReadLine();
```

Nested subscriptions, although useful for demonstration purposes, are something we should avoid in the real world because they may cause difficulties in maintainability and debugging, and (most importantly) because they reduce our control on the overall flow because of the nested delegates we need to write to handle nested sequences. Although we will see other nested sequences here, the suggestion when dealing with real-world coding is to write something like the following example of the `GroupBy` operator. The only difference is that, to avoid nesting, we need to flatten the multiple stripes into a single sequence of new messages containing the original value and the group key. Although we're still logically grouping, we don't actually need multiple real subsequences:

```
//register the partition per group key
//without nested sequences partitions
//transform inner groups into new objects
//containing the key and the value altogether
.SelectMany(group => group.Select(x => new { key =
group.Key, value = x }))
.Subscribe(msg => Console.WriteLine("partition {0}: {1}",
msg.key, msg.value));
```

Aggregate

The `Aggregate` factory method creates a new sequence that will interact with each source message, returning a single output message that will produce any operation we want. In the following example, there is an accumulator function that simply adds each message value to the next:

```
//a sourcing sequence of random doubles
var sourcingSequence = Observable.Create<double>(observer =>
    {
        var r = new Random(DateTime.Now.GetHashCode());

        for (int i = 0; i < 5; i++)
        {
```

```
            observer.OnNext((r.NextDouble() - 0.5d) * 10d);
            Thread.Sleep(1000);
        }

        observer.OnCompleted();

        return () =>
        {
            Console.WriteLine("Completed");
        };
    });

//aggregate values to compute a single ending value
var aggregationSequence = sourcingSequence.Aggregate(0d, (rolling, value)
=>
{
    Console.WriteLine("Aggregating: {0} + {1}", rolling, value);
    return rolling + value;
});
aggregationSequence.Subscribe(value => Console.WriteLine("Aggregated value:
{0}", value));

Console.ReadLine();
```

In the `Aggregate` factory method, the first parameter is the starting accumulation function value. Then, we simply need to write the accumulation function in the preceding example, which will show the input value on the console for better understanding of the operation.

MaxBy/MinBy

When dealing with aggregations, there are premade sequences. The `MaxBy` and `MinBy` factory methods create sequences that group by the sourcing value for the given key and then return only messages where the key is equal to the min or max value found in the sourcing sequence.

Each of these sequences will produce a single message that contains multiple sourcing messages. The sequence will produce no messages until the sourcing sequence fires its completed message. Here's a group example:

```
//a sourcing sequence of 2 messages per second
var sourcingSequence = Observable.Interval(TimeSpan.FromSeconds(0.5))
    //a transformation into DateTime
    //skipping milliseconds/nanoseconds
    .Select(id => new DateTime(DateTime.UtcNow.Year, DateTime.UtcNow.Month,
DateTime.UtcNow.Day, DateTime.UtcNow.Hour, DateTime.UtcNow.Minute,
```

```
DateTime.UtcNow.Second))
    //we take messages only for 5 seconds
    .TakeUntil(DateTimeOffset.Now.AddSeconds(5));

//the maxby sequence
var maxBySequence = sourcingSequence.MaxBy(d => d.Ticks);
maxBySequence.Subscribe(ordered =>
{
    foreach (var value in ordered)
        Console.WriteLine("MaxBy: {0}", value);
});

//the minby sequence
var minBySequence = sourcingSequence.MinBy(d => d.Ticks);
minBySequence.Subscribe(ordered =>
{
    foreach (var value in ordered)
        Console.WriteLine("MinBy: {0}", value);
});

Console.ReadLine();
```

Usually, primitive types already implement the `IComparable` interface. To make our types comparable, we may implement the same interface. To compare types that don't implement the `IComparable` interface by themselves, we can create an external comparer by implementing the `IComparer<T>` interface. Once we have the comparer, another overload of the `MaxBy`/`MinBy` operator will accept the value selector and the comparer as the second parameter to let us use the operator with our custom comparer.

Advanced operators

Sometimes, we need functions to create message repetitions or to manipulate or reuse a subscription with multiple observers. This is the time when advanced operators come into play.

IgnoreElements

The `IgnoreElements` factory method creates a new sequence that will ignore any value message. Instead, errors and completion messages will normally flow out from the sourcing sequence.

This method is particularly useful to create multiple acknowledgements or simply to append some completion code to a sourcing sequence. Here's an example:

```
//the sourcing sequence of errors or completed messages
var sourcingSequence = Observable.Throw<object>(new Exception("Test"));

//a sequence able to handle only errors or completed messages
var ignoredElements = sourcingSequence.IgnoreElements();
ignoredElements.Subscribe(new ConsoleObserver());
```

The `ConsoleObserver` class is the same as that of the previous examples. See the *Interval* or *Create* sections in this chapter.

Repeat

The `Repeat` factory method creates a sequence that will flow out sourcing sequence messages multiple (or infinite) times. Here's an example:

```
//a sourcing sequence of 5 elements
var sourcingSequence = Observable.Range(1, 5);

//the repeating sequence
var repeatFor2Times = sourcingSequence.Repeat(2);
repeatFor2Times.Subscribe(value => Console.WriteLine("Value: {0}", value));
```

Although the `Repeat` factory method is pretty simple to use, it is perfect to show the reader a possible unintended behavior. Anytime we subscribe a sequence, most of the premade factory methods restart their implementation. When dealing with simple integers, it is difficult to notice such behavior, but when dealing with the `DateTime` values, this is immediate. Here's an example:

```
//a sourcing sequence of 5 elements
var sourcingSequence = Observable.Range(1, 5)
    //slow down
    .Select(i => { Thread.Sleep(1000); return i; })
    //take the actual time
    .Select(i => DateTime.Now);

//the repeating sequence
```

```
var repeatFor2Times = sourcingSequence.Repeat(2);
repeatFor2Times.Subscribe(value => Console.WriteLine("Value: {0}", value));
```

In this example, we cannot use the `Interval` factory method, because this one lacks the completion message that is required for the `Repeat` method.

By using a `DateTime` value, you will immediately see that the `Repeat` sequence will subscribe two times the sourcing sequence that came from a `Range` factory method. This means that the integer values are valued two times in the `Select` transformation providing new `DateTime` values, instead of repeating the original ones. If this is an unintended behavior, we can use the `Publish` factory method just before.

Publish/Connect

The `Publish` method produces a single subscription sequence available to any other following subscriber. As it has already been said before, any subscription may cause the sourcing sequence to produce different values. Here's an example based on a random value:

```
var r = new Random(DateTime.Now.GetHashCode());
//a randomic value sequence
var sourcingSequence = Observable.Range(1, 5)
    //slow down
    .Select(i => { Thread.Sleep(500); return i; })
    //take the actual time
    .Select(i => r.Next());

//multiple subscriptions causing different
//values being printed onto the console
sourcingSequence.Subscribe(value => Console.WriteLine("Observer#1: {0}",
value));
sourcingSequence.Subscribe(value => Console.WriteLine("Observer#2: {0}",
value));
sourcingSequence.Subscribe(value => Console.WriteLine("Observer#3: {0}",
value));
```

The preceding example will print to the console as follows:

```
Observer#1: 1387437772
Observer#1: 1673597686
Observer#1: 407780858
Observer#1: 630401573
Observer#1: 336086919
Observer#2: 1071679403
Observer#2: 302043112
Observer#2: 1359704606
```

```
Observer#2:  413086291
Observer#2:  1357199039
Observer#3:  1918565397
Observer#3:  1660389991
Observer#3:  1852413164
Observer#3:  1520275706
Observer#3:  1750871851
```

As we can see, each subscription will start with a new ranged source sequence. Instead, the `Publish` method will create a single subscription sequence that will be available to multiple subscribers, routing the messages to all the observers. To start publishing messages, we need to turn on (and eventually off) the flowing by invoking the `Connect` method of the publishing sequence. Once we complete our task, we will dispose such connection flags. Here's another example:

```
//the sourcing sequence
var publishedSequence = Observable.Interval(TimeSpan.FromSeconds(0.5))
    .Select(i => DateTime.Now)
    .Publish();

//attach subscribers before connecting the publisher
publishedSequence.Subscribe(value => Console.WriteLine("Observer#1: {0}",
value));
publishedSequence.Subscribe(value => Console.WriteLine("Observer#2: {0}",
value));
publishedSequence.Subscribe(value => Console.WriteLine("Observer#3: {0}",
value));

while (true)
{
    Console.WriteLine("Press RETURN to connect the published sequence");
    Console.ReadLine();
    using (var connected = publishedSequence.Connect())
    {
        Console.WriteLine("Press RETURN to quit the connection");
        Console.ReadLine();
    }
    //now we disconnected from the published sequence
}
```

Now, we have the same value flowing to all the subscribers, thus such subscribers receive their value, value by value, instead of having each subscriber wait for the previous subscriber to read the whole sequence as it happened in the previous example.

RefCount

Similar to the Publish/Connect operator pattern, RefCount returns a sequence of the published messages to its subscribers by subscribing only once to the sourcing sequence.

The difference is that RefCount automatically connects and disconnects from the published sequence while there is at least one subscriber. Once the last subscriber unsubscribes, the RefCount operator will automatically disconnect from the sourcing sequence. This is a powerful operator because it avoids the implementation of the Publish/Connect pattern by ourselves, and because this implementation avoids the occurrence of a race condition between the Publish and the Subscribe operators that in some cases may happen.

Here's an example:

```
//the sourcing sequence
var publishedSequence = Observable.Interval(TimeSpan.FromSeconds(0.5))
    .Select(i => DateTime.Now)
    .Publish()
    .RefCount();

while (true)
{
    Console.WriteLine("Press return to subscribe");
    Console.ReadLine();
    using (var subscription = publishedSequence.Subscribe(value =>
    Console.WriteLine("Observer: {0}", value)))
    {
        Console.WriteLine("Press return to unsubscribe");
        Console.ReadLine();
    }
    //now we disconnected from the published sequence
}
```

Another significant difference between the Publish/Connect pattern and the RefCount operator is that RefCount subscribers will start receiving messages as soon as they subscribe, while the Publish/Connect subscribers must wait for the Connect method to start receiving messages.

However, having a sequence without subscribers often is a performance improvement because the sequence consumes fewer resources.

PublishLast

If you want to simply publish the last value instead of the whole sequence, the choice is to use the `PublishLast` factory method:

```
//the sourcing sequence
var publishedSequence = Observable.Interval(TimeSpan.FromSeconds(0.5))
    .Select(i => DateTime.Now)
    .Take(5)
    .PublishLast();

publishedSequence.Subscribe(value => Console.WriteLine("Last: {0}",
value));
publishedSequence.Connect();
```

Keep in mind that the difference between such implementations and a classical `Last` one is that, with `PublishLast`, we make a single subscription to the sourcing sequence.

Replay

The `Replay` factory method creates a single subscription sequence that will buffer messages of the sourcing sequence for the given buffer size. The replayed sequence will be identical to the sourcing sequence for message values and timings. This means that buffered messages will not flow altogether to the first subscriber. Instead, they will flow out as if they were just produced from the sourcing sequence. Here's an example:

```
//the sourcing sequence will fire
//for 5 seconds
var publishedSequence = Observable.Interval(TimeSpan.FromSeconds(1))
    .Select(i => DateTime.Now)
    .Take(5)
    .Replay(10);

//we wait for 2 seconds
Thread.Sleep(2000);

//now we connect the subscriber that will
//recover all messages thanks to the replay behaviour
publishedSequence.Subscribe(value => Console.WriteLine("Value: {0}",
value));
publishedSequence.Connect();

Console.ReadLine();
```

In the preceding example, we are taking only 5 messages from the sourcing sequence by setting a replay buffer of 10 items, which is obviously to contain the whole sourcing sequence. In real-world applications, this buffer acts as a cache, allowing lazy subscribers to catch all the messages they want to reduce losses.

Multicast

The `Multicast` factory method is the father of all the previously seen methods that produces a single subscription against the sourcing sequence. All the other methods are built on the `Multicast` one, returning `Subject` or another to produce the right implementation.

This explains the internals of all the seen single subscription methods. They use `Subject` to read and produce messages from the sourcing sequence to the target subscribers.

We can use such factory methods to create our own implementations. Here's an example:

```
//the sourcing sequence
var sourcingSequence = Observable.Interval(TimeSpan.FromSeconds(1))
    .Select(i => DateTime.Now);

//the subject that will route messages
var multicastingSubject = new Subject<DateTime>();
//the publisher sequence
var multicastSequence = sourcingSequence.Multicast(multicastingSubject);

//subscribers
multicastSequence.Subscribe(value => Console.WriteLine("Observer#1: {0}",
value)));
multicastSequence.Subscribe(value => Console.WriteLine("Observer#2: {0}",
value));

//connect the publisher sequence
multicastSequence.Connect();

Console.ReadLine();
```

This example shows an implementation similar to the classic `Publish` factory method. The difference here is that this implementation gives the developer the chance of using a personally extended version of the subject, creating new publishing sequence implementations.

Summary

In this chapter, we had the opportunity to deal with sequence creation and manipulation. The knowledge of a wide amount of factory methods gives the reactive programming developer the ability to write reactive functions that can deal with all the real-world demands. Together, this knowledge is mandatory before reading the next chapters that will bring the reader into deeper Rx and reactive programming understanding.

5
Debugging Reactive Extensions

Debugging Reactive Extensions (Rx) for .NET means something more than simply using the visual studio debugger. This chapter focuses on how to trace the executing operations against all the sequences that behave within our application and how to use diagnostic-oriented sequences that strongly improve developer debugging times. Here's a short list of arguments we're going to cover in this chapter:

- Tracing sequences
- Inspecting sequences
- Exception handling
- Playing with sequences

Tracing sequences

The most widely used diagnostic solution is application tracing; in a few words, it is the art of logging the application execution flow with emphasis on the event type and its description.

This is the same in reactive programming, thus, we have the ability to use specific sequences that mark messages with additional metadata or log out messages to analyze (or dump for further usages) the sequence flow in addition to the usual tracing tools available within the .NET world.

More than a simple reactive way of tracing, we can design specific diagnostic sequence flows with related filtering or manipulation, and the ability to use any other reactive operator to help us isolate interesting diagnostic information.

Materialize

The `Materialize` extension method produces a new sequence for diagnostic purposes that flows messages containing additional metadata information about the messages flowing in the sourcing sequence.

The great advantage of materializing a sequence is the ability to know the message's type (`OnNext`, `OnComplete`, or `OnError`), inspecting its sourcing data or exceptions without having to fit within the original sequence chain. This is actually, a powerful feature. However, this has a cost in resource needs. This is why we cannot materialize every sequence just to have access to related metadata until we definitely need it.

In other words, `Materialize` is something similar to what `Reflection` is for normal types, giving us the ability to write a code to read the object's property by simply looping across all those available because we don't need to write code in a static way. In fact, with reflection, there is huge additional resource cost, and with reflection, we definitely need it often.

You have just another use case to look at before you dive into code: think about the ability to handle any reactive message at a single point by simply analyzing the message metadata and routing to the required concrete handler. Keep the resource usage in mind before you think that this is a great feature at all; although in some cases, this may be definitely a great feature.

The usage is definitely simple. Here's an example:

```
//a simple sequence of DateTime
var sequence1 = new Subject<DateTime>();

//a console observer
sequence1.Subscribe(x => Console.WriteLine("{0}", x));

//a tracing sequence
//of materialized notifications
IObservable<Notification<DateTime>> tracingSequence =
sequence1.Materialize();
tracingSequence.Subscribe(notification =>
{
    //this represents the operation
    Console.WriteLine("Operation: {0}", notification.Kind);

    //has a value
    if (notification.HasValue)
        Console.WriteLine("Value: {0}", notification.Value);
```

```
    //has an exception
    else if (notification.Exception != null)
        Console.WriteLine("Exception: {0}", notification.Exception);
});

//flows a new value
sequence1.OnNext(DateTime.Now);

//flows the oncomplete message
sequence1.OnCompleted();

Console.ReadLine();
```

The preceding example shows the basic usage of the `Materialize` operator. This gives us a new sequence of the `Notification<T>` messages, where `T` is the original message type. These messages will contain full information/metadata about the flowing message. The `Notification<T>` method contains everything we need to trace out our messages or dump message data by reading its `Kind`, `Value`, or `Exception` properties as visible in the preceding example.

Regarding performance, the suggestion is to avoid the massive usage of materialized sequences because these are very expensive considering the overall resource usage.

 By using the `Sample` or the `Throttle` operator together with the `Materialize` operator, we can trace messages at a slower rate. This may be an interesting compromise when we want to trace without destroying the overall performance of our application. Their description is available in the *Transforming operators* or *Combining operators* sections of `Chapter 3`, *Reactive Extension Programming*.

Dematerialize

Once we have a materialized sequence of the `Notification<T>` messages, if we need to produce a value sequence, we can use the `Dematerialize` extension method.

Obviously, recreating the original value sequence from a materialized sequence is odd, but it is sometimes necessary. Here's an example:

```
//a dematerialized sequence
var valueSequence = tracingSequence.Dematerialize();
//a console observer
valueSequence.Subscribe(x => Console.WriteLine("D: {0}", x));
```

Regarding performance, the usage of the `Materialize/Dematerialize` sequences produces some visible overheads. Other than when debugging, the suggestion is to avoid the usage of similar sequences.

A similar feature is available when debugging with Visual Studio under the name `IntelliTrace`. With this feature, Visual Studio logs all that is happening in our executing code with the ability to replay specific code portions or verify already handled exceptions that don't bubble up in the debugger. The same feature is obviously available when programming with Rx, but `Materialize/Dematerialize` gives a coarse-grained ability to reproduce the message flow of a production environment without the cost of having a debugger online, as `IntelliTrace` needs.

TimeInterval

Although we have already seen this sequence in `Chapter 4`, *Observable Sequence Programming*, kindly consider that its usage in debugging is visibly useful. Here's a short example.

Let's assume that we're writing an application that reads data from an IO port as a serial or TCP port. We want the messages to always come on time. In other words, we cannot accept delays of more than a specific duration because we're writing a real-time application.

 Bear in mind that a real-time application must have a deterministic execution time in addition to fast/immediate reactions to events/input.

We can use the `TimeInterval` operator to skip messages that are outside our timing policy and produce a log of these messages for further analysis or simply as a waste sequence.

Here's an example:

```
var r = new Random(DateTime.Now.GetHashCode());

//an infinite message source
var source = Observable.Interval(TimeSpan.FromSeconds(1))
    .Select(i =>
    {
        //let's add some random delay
        Thread.Sleep(r.Next(100, 1000));

        return DateTime.Now;
    });
```

```
//the timing tracing sequence
var timingsTracingSequence = source.TimeInterval();

//valid messages
var validMessagesSequence = timingsTracingSequence.Where(x =>
x.Interval.TotalMilliseconds <= 1200);
//var exceeding messages
var exceedingMessagesSequence = timingsTracingSequence.Where(x =>
x.Interval.TotalMilliseconds > 1200);

//some console output
validMessagesSequence.Subscribe(x => Console.WriteLine(x.Value));
exceedingMessagesSequence.Subscribe(x => Console.WriteLine("Exceeding
timing limits for: {0} ({1:N0}ms)", x.Value,
x.Interval.TotalMilliseconds));

Console.ReadLine();
```

Do

The Do extension method is very similar to the Materialize one with a single great difference. The Materialize method produces a new sequence of Notification<T> that will add message-related metadata information to each sourcing message, while the Do method will return the same sourcing sequence, registering and passing each message of each type to the proper C# handler (Action or Action<Exception>).

In other words, the Do method gives us the ability to specify an external message handler in a way similar to CLR event handling with the usage of delegates (Action, Action<Exception>).

Although this option may seem more comfortable to any experienced state-driven programmer, here, in any reactive programming project, it may bring more issues than it resolves. This is because of the different programming approach that is very useful for diagnostics needs and contemporarily very dangerous in production time execution because it may lead the developer into an undesired Action at a distance anti-pattern.

Here's a complete example:

```
static void Main(string[] args)
{
    var source = Observable.Interval(TimeSpan.FromSeconds(1))
        .Select(x => DateTime.Now)
        .Take(5)
        .Select(x =>
        {
            if (x.Second % 10 == 0)
                throw new ArgumentException();

            return x;
        })
        .Do(OnNext, OnError, OnCompleted)
        .Catch(Observable.Empty<DateTime>());

    //starts the source
    source.Subscribe();

    Console.ReadLine();
}

private static void OnError(Exception ex)
{
    Console.WriteLine("-> {0}", ex.Message);
}

private static void OnCompleted()
{
    Console.WriteLine("-> END");
}

private static void OnNext(DateTime obj)
{
    Console.WriteLine("-> {0}", obj);
}
```

The example is very simple: we have a sourcing sequence of no more than 5 messages. In addition, we will raise an error when the timestamp's seconds are divisible by 10.

The Do method expects up to three handlers for the three message types.

Kindly consider, anything that executes within the handlers, actually executes within the sequence change pipeline in a synchronous way.

A side effect happens anytime we produce an action at a distance by editing some state or by executing some logic outside our function. In a reactive world, our function is our sequence chain. We can do anything we want within our chain, but when we interact outside the chain within a single chain node or message transformation/filtering node, we are causing a side effect.

Inspecting sequences

After tracing what flows within a sequence, the second most useful diagnostic feature is to verify the sequence content against a predicted content or a static content (usually for testing purposes with mocking objects) simply because we need to check the message homogeneity. Luckily, there are different operators that help us achieve this.

Contains

This is maybe the easiest case to deal with when we need to check if/when a sequence contains a given value.

In reactive, we always deal with sequences; this is true also when we want to aspect a Boolean value, as in this case, if we were programming in a nonreactive way. The `Contains` extension method produces a new sequence that will fire a single message with a value informing us if we found what we're searching for immediately after the sourcing sequence is complete. This is easily visible by instrumenting Rx materializing our `Contains` sequence. Here's an example:

```
var r = new Random(DateTime.Now.GetHashCode());

//an infinite message source of integer numbers
//running at 10hz
var source = Observable.Interval(TimeSpan.FromMilliseconds(100))
    .Select(x => r.Next(1, 20));

var contains = source.Contains(10)
    //we want message metadata
    .Materialize();

//some console output
source.Subscribe(x => Console.WriteLine(x));
contains.Subscribe(x => Console.WriteLine("FOUND: {0}", x));

Console.ReadLine();
```

Any

Almost identical to the Contains extensions method, Any produces a sequence that flows messages about its search results. The difference is the overload; it needs a Func<T,bool>. Instead, the Contains method needs a raw value.

Here is a short example:

```
var any = source.Any(x => x == 10)
    //we want message metadata
    .Materialize();
any.Subscribe(x => Console.WriteLine("FOUND ANY: {0}", x));
```

All

Similar to the Any method, the All extension method produces a sequence flowing the result of our search. The difference is that the All method fires only when all the sourcing messages succeed in passing the predicate expression, waiting for the completion of the sourcing sequence before sourcing its result message. Instead, if any message fails the validating expression, the All sequence immediately flows out the failure result.

Here's an example:

```
var r = new Random(DateTime.Now.GetHashCode());

var stopperSequence = new Subject<bool>();

//an infinite message source of integer numbers
//running at 10hz
var source = Observable.Interval(TimeSpan.FromMilliseconds(100))
    .Select(x => r.Next(1, 20))
    //take only until we press RETURN
    .TakeUntil(stopperSequence);

source.Subscribe(x => Console.WriteLine(x));

var all = source.All(x => x < 18)
    //we want message metadata
    .Materialize();

all.Subscribe(x => Console.WriteLine("FOUND ALL: {0}", x));

//wait until user press RETURN
Console.ReadLine();
//notify the stop message
```

```
stopperSequence.OnNext(true);
//wait again to see the result
Console.ReadLine();
```

The preceding example is similar to the `Any` method and the `Contains` method. But this one needs a more detailed explanation.

First of all, we're using another sequence (`stopperSequence`) to signal the other sequence (`source`) when to stop flowing messages.

This is accomplished by using the `TakeUntil` method on the `source` sequence that returns a new sequence to flow messages until a message flows from the parameter sequence (`stopperSequence`).

Take a look at the result; it takes only a few seconds. When we press the Enter key, the `All` sequence intercepts the `OnCompleted` message and executes its logic returning result as to whether all the messages are complying with the lambda expression.

In other words, to ensure the `True` result, the `All` sequence waits for the sourcing sequence's `OnCompleted` message, while any failing message immediately produces a `False` result.

SequenceEqual

The `SequenceEqual` extension method produces a sequence almost identical to the one from the `All` method. The difference is that the `All` method checks whether all the messages of a single sourcing sequence comply with a specified predicate, while `SequenceEqual` produces a sequence that returns if two sourcing sequences are identical in their content.

Similar to the `All` sequence, `SequenceEqual` immediately outputs a failing result while waiting for the completion of all sourcing sequences leads to a succeeding result.

Here's an example:

```
//two random generators
//without the random initial seed
var r1 = new Random();
var r2 = new Random();

//two infinite message source of integer numbers running at 1hz
var source1 = Observable.Interval(TimeSpan.FromMilliseconds(1000))
    .Select(x => r1.Next(1, 20));
```

```
var source2 = Observable.Interval(TimeSpan.FromMilliseconds(1000))
    .Select(x => r2.Next(1, 20));

var identical = source1.SequenceEqual(source2)
    .Materialize();

source1.Subscribe(x => Console.WriteLine("1: {0}", x));
source2.Subscribe(x => Console.WriteLine("2: {0}", x));
identical.Subscribe(x => Console.WriteLine("Equals: {0}", x));

Console.ReadLine();
```

Exception handling

Handling exceptions in reactive programming with Rx is something odd. We're used to handling exceptions by writing code that executes when some other code hangs. More precisely, we write multiple execution flows that execute when the application runs properly or badly. The real meaning of exception handling means handling an exception in the usual way of doing something. Exception handling is not error handling.

Although, this being a philosophical definition, we're used to using exception handling to handle unpredictable behaviors.

In Rx, exception handling is identical with the difference that here we don't deal with code rows that execute one by one; we actually deal with the sequences of messages that must continue flowing regardless of whether an exception may invalidate one or multiple messages. In smarter words, the show must go on. Obviously, a single exception must prevent the whole sequence from running anymore.

In other (simpler) words, when we want to handle an exception message, we will define the new sequence that will flow messages in place of the initial source sequence.

Catch

Catch is the main extension method that gives us the ability to handle exceptions in Rx sequences. It simply starts flowing messages from a second source sequence when the first hangs. Kindly consider that in state-driven programming, catching an exception means executing some other code from the one in the Try clause, while in reactive programming, catching an exception means flowing from another sequence. We can choose to source from a fruitful sequence or an empty one to cause the sequence's premature ending.

Here's a complete example:

```
var r = new Random(DateTime.Now.GetHashCode());

//an infinite message source of integer numbers running at 10hz
var source1 = Observable.Interval(TimeSpan.FromMilliseconds(100))
    .Select(x => r.Next(1, 20))
    //raise an exception on high values
    .Select(x =>
    {
        if (x >= 19)
            throw new ArgumentException("Value too high");
        else
            return x;
    })
    //a single shared subscription available to all following subscribers
    .Publish();

//enable the connectable sequence
source1.Connect();

//an infinite message source of integer numbers running at 1hz
var source2 = Observable.Interval(TimeSpan.FromMilliseconds(1000))
    .Select(x => r.Next(20, 40));

//a new sequence that continues with source2 when source1 raise an error
var output = source1.Catch(source2)
    //we want message metadata for out testing purpose
    .Materialize();

//output all values
output.Subscribe(x => Console.WriteLine(x));
//output when source1 raise the error
source1.Materialize()
    .Where(x => x.Kind == NotificationKind.OnError)
    .Subscribe(x => Console.WriteLine("Error: {0}", x.Exception));

Console.ReadLine();
```

The preceding example shows the usage of the `Catch` extension method; we use it to source from `source2` when `source1` faults. Because of testing needs, we have to use the `Publish/Connect` pattern to share a single subscription with the `source1` sequence from the `Catch` operator and from the `Materialize` one we use to see when the exception occurs.

An interesting aspect is the availability of another overload that allows the `Catch` method to accept a specific exception type to handle:

```
//specific exception handling
var output2 = source1.Catch<int, ArgumentException>(exType => source2);
```

As mentioned if we want a premature sequence end, we can simply specify an empty continuing sequence as the parameter for the `Catch` operator:

```
//handle excetion and stop flowing messages
var output3 = source1.Catch(Observable.Empty<int>());
```

Real-world experience says that we have to carefully use this method because it may bring your application into unintentional exception hiding logics. This may make your application difficult to debug or in an inconsistent state, as happens in the case where we hide the exception without logging the event.

OnErrorResumeNext

Similar to the `Catch` method, there is the `OnErrorResumeNext` method. Although many experienced developers may remember this name that was a specific error handling logic in the old `VisualBasic` languages (prior to .NET), the old one from VB was instead identical to the reactive `Catch` implementation. The `OnErrorResumeNext` method produces a sequence concatenation regardless of whether the first sequence experiences some errors or not. The only exception handling here is that if the first sequence hangs, the second sequence immediately starts flowing messages. However, the `Catch` method does not concatenate sourcing sequences. It simply starts flowing messages from another sequence if the first hangs.

Finally

The `Finally` method gives us the ability to execute some code when a sequence completes regardless of whether it completes with an `OnComplete` message or with an `OnError` message. Here's a complete example:

```
var source = Observable.Interval(TimeSpan.FromSeconds(1))
    //stops after 5 seconds
    .TakeUntil(Observable.Return(0).Delay(TimeSpan.FromSeconds(5)));

source.Subscribe(x => Console.WriteLine(x));

//log the completion of the source
```

```
source.Finally(() => Console.WriteLine("END"))
    //force the Finally sequence to
    //start working by registering
    //an empty subscriber
    .Subscribe();

Console.ReadLine();
```

In the preceding example, we can see the `Finally` method in action. The example is extremely useful because it shows a more reactive-styled programming.

First, we will create a sourcing sequence that must flow messages only for 5 seconds. To specify the timeout, we will use another sequence as the parameter that will fire its only message to stop the main sourcing sequence from flowing. Then, by using the `Finally` operator, we will specify `Action` that will fire when the sourcing sequence completes.

An interesting aspect of this example is that to force the `Finally` sequence to start its job we need to attach a subscriber. To accomplish this, we can simply use the `Subscribe` method without passing any concrete subscriber. This happens because the result sequence from the `Finally` operator runs in a lazy fashion, waiting for a subscription to exist before doing its job.

A sequence that starts producing messages only when a subscription exists is a `Cold` sequence. These are lazy execution sequences. On the other hand, a sequence that produces messages regardless of whether a subscriber exists or not is a `Hot` sequence. Although the practical difference when using the two sequence types from other sequences or operators is slightly visible, because all the sequences produce messages once subscribed, the difference when no subscription exists is evident. Another great difference is that, often, the `Cold` sequences produce the same message flow for all their subscribers regardless of how many times we subscribe to the sourcing sequence, while `Hot` observers usually have their own message flow that will continue flowing regardless of whether a subscription exists or not. This means that a message repetition may never occur, but in case we need it, it is possible with external operators.

Retry

Another widely used approach when experiencing unwanted behaviors from external systems or unpredictable functions is the ability to repeat our logic until we get our desired result.

This choice has its pros, such as the ability to avoid unintentional network errors or system low availability. However, the choice has its cons, such as the ability to reduce system response time, increase overall resource usage, and (the terrifying one) the possibility to duplicate data or create inconsistent data stores if we don't properly manage all repeating logics.

The most critical time in a retry logic is when an attempt fails, in other words, when we eventually need to rollback the partially saved data, the partially executed logics, or the partially sent commands (to external systems).

This doesn't mean that the retry logic is wrong in itself. It simply focuses a lot on its usage because it may bring the invisible issues. Here's a complete example (it is better to execute this example without the debugger by pressing *Ctrl + F5*):

```
//a finite sequence of 5 values
var source = Observable.Interval(TimeSpan.FromSeconds(1))
    .Take(5)
    .Select(x => DateTime.Now)
    .Select(x =>
    {
        //lets raise some error
        if (x.Second % 10 == 0)
            throw new ArgumentException("Wrong milliseconds value");
        else
            return x;
    })
    //restart he sourcing sequence on error (max 2 times)
    .Retry(2)
    //materialize to read message metadata
    .Materialize();

source.Subscribe(x -> Console.WriteLine(x));
Console.ReadLine();
```

The preceding example shows a usage of the `Reply` sequence available through the `Reply` extension method.

The execution shows that we have to produce 5 messages. If any message has a timestamp with seconds divisible by 10 an exception raises. When an exception reaches the `Retry` sequence, this simply closes the subscription and starts another subscription, restarting the counter of 5 messages.

At the end of the sequence construction, although we materialize the `Reply` sequence, we will never see the error message. We will simply receive the concatenation of all the messages before and after the error. Obviously, this may bring an unintentional hidden exception that may make it tricky to find unwanted behaviors.

The solution lies in the usage of the `Materialize` operator together with a filter that will let us trace only unwanted exceptions when we're running our application in the production stage. This choice will give us the ability to know when an exception occurred with a light additional resource usage. Differently, once we're trying to investigate an exception we already know, we may edit the filter to trace multiple information other than exceptions to help us find the root cause of the investigating exception.

Summary

In this chapter, we had the opportunity of looking at reactive programming in action with real-world needs: diagnostics and exception handling.

Debugging a reactive application in production is something very different from debugging a typical state-driven application because we deal with sequence chains that are usually very long and articulated. The same applies in the case of exception handling; whereas in reactive, the approach changes totally.

In the next chapter, we will go deeper into Rx programming with advanced features and techniques, such as time scheduling and CLR integration.

6
CLR Integration and Scheduling

This chapter will cover two very important aspects of reactive programming: the ability to configure how time changes within the sequences and their workers (observers/observables) and the ability to interact with all the other elements of the classic CLR, such as events, threads, tasks, and so on. Here's a short index:

- Sourcing from CLR events
- Threading integration
- Asynchronous sourcing
- Time scheduling
- Advanced time scheduling

Sourcing from CLR events

An event is the occurrence of something we can handle somehow with our code. More precisely, in .NET, an event is a kind of `Delegate` object, an object that represents one or multiple actions to run. The `Delegate` object is the .NET implementation of the `Observer` pattern with the addition of other features, such as asynchronous execution.

By convention, any event in .NET uses the `Delegate` implementation specific to `System.EventHandler` or any other childhood according to the inheritance `tenet`. This implementation accepts handlers (subscribers) that must accept two parameters, such as the following example:

```
static void EventHandler1(object o, EventArgs e)
{
    Console.WriteLine("Handling for object {0}", o);
}
```

In place of using the generic `EventArgs` type as an event parameter as specified by the `EventHandler` delegate, when using the related generic version `EventHandler<T>`, we can use any other type as an argument parameter.

By using reactive programming, we can handle events or produce events to interact with classic .NET desktop/mobile applications or server-side workflow/web applications in a simplified way, producing or sourcing events from an observable sequence. In the following section, we will divert all the main operators that help us in this absolutely useful task

FromEventPattern

By using the `FromEventPattern` extension method of the `Observable` class, we can produce a sequence of the `EventPattern` messages containing the firing event parameters as the sender and the argument. Here's a complete example for console applications:

```
public static event EventHandler userIsTiredEvent;
static void Main(string[] args)
{
    //raise the event in 5 seconds
    Task.Factory.StartNew(() =>
    {
        Thread.Sleep(5000);

        //check event is handled
        if (userIsTiredEvent != null)
            userIsTiredEvent("Program.Main", new EventArgs());
    });

    //classic event handler registration
    userIsTiredEvent += EventHandler1;

    //reactive registration
    var eventSequence = Observable.FromEventPattern(typeof(Program),
    "userIsTiredEvent");

    //some output
    eventSequence.Materialize().Subscribe(x => Console.WriteLine("From Rx:
{0}",
    x));

    Console.ReadLine();
}

static void EventHandler1(object o, EventArgs e)
```

```
{
    Console.WriteLine("Handling for object {0}", o);
}
```

The `FromEventPattern` operator wraps events into `EventPattern<T>` that will flow as usual in an observable sequence. In the preceding example, we wrapped the `EventPattern` message into the `Notification` message (with the `Materialize` operator) to receive details about the message's type, as you learned to do in Chapter 5, Debugging Reactive Extensions.

With our code, we created two subscribers to `userIsTiredEvent`; one outputs the result directly to the console as it is usually done by any event handler, while the second subscriber is totally created and handled by the implementation of the `FromEventPattern` method.

In the nonreactive world, we're used to seeing one or more handlers per event because event delegates support multiple subscribers (bear in mind that it's an implementation of the `Observable` pattern). However, we rarely see a single handler handling multiple events. On the other hand, in the Rx world, it's absolutely usual to share handlers with a pipeline of sequences that may use the `EventPattern` parameters to make needed decisions.

Here's a complete example for a **Windows Presentation Foundation (WPF)** desktop application. The following code examples focus only on single application portions to explain event bridging to Rx. The full example is available with the other examples.

The UI XAML codes are as follows:

```
<Grid>
    <DockPanel>
        <UniformGrid Rows="1" DockPanel.Dock="Top">
            <Button Content="- 10" Command="{Binding ChangeValueCommand}"
CommandParameter="-10" />
            <Button Content="- 1" Command="{Binding ChangeValueCommand}"
CommandParameter="-1" />
            <Button Content="+ 1" Command="{Binding ChangeValueCommand}"
CommandParameter="+1" />
            <Button Content="+ 10" Command="{Binding ChangeValueCommand}"
CommandParameter="+10" />
        </UniformGrid>

        <Grid>
            <Viewbox>
                <TextBlock Text="{Binding Result}" />
            </Viewbox>
```

```
        </Grid>
    </DockPanel>
</Grid>
```

This XAML will produce a view similar to the following screenshot:

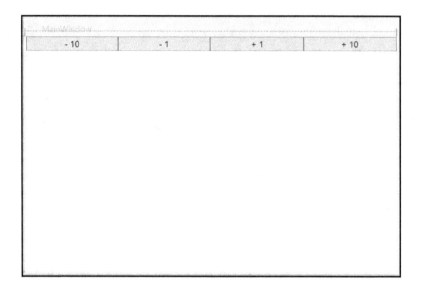

A command based simple UI in WPF

The WPF application has a specific command: `CommandBinding` pattern for implementing events that support natively the **Model View ViewModel** (**MVVM**) pattern. Different from the classic .NET event pattern, the command-binding pattern supports the *N–N* association between command raisers and handlers. Differently, in the .NET event pattern, only the event owner can raise the event, while multiple subscribers may exist.

In the following code, we will register a single command (the event definition) with multiple button subscribers (the event raisers) and a single command-binding (the event handler):

```
public MainWindow()
{
    InitializeComponent();
    DataContext = this;

    //command definition
    ChangeValueCommand = new RoutedCommand(Guid.NewGuid().ToString(),
    typeof(MainWindow));
```

```
    //command binding registration
    CommandBindings.Add(new CommandBinding(ChangeValueCommand,
    OnChangeValueCommand));
}

public event PropertyChangedEventHandler PropertyChanged;

//classic WPF implementation
private void OnChangeValueCommand(object sender, ExecutedRoutedEventArgs e)
{
    Result += Convert.ToInt32(e.Parameter);
    //notify value update
    Notify("Result");
}
```

The preceding example is pretty simple. We passed a numeric value as a command parameter from the view (the XAML) and we added/subtracted such a value parameter to/from the `Result` property that is visible as a label in the middle of the view.

The preceding code uses the MVVM pattern. To keep it short, we flattened the `ViewModel` and the `View` classes into a single class. Because this book focuses on reactive programming, if something is not clear here, kindly read more about MVVM by referring to a more specific book or the Internet as follows:

`https://msdn.microsoft.com/en-us/library/hh848246.aspx`.

The same example is available by handling the command wrapped into an event with the `EventCommand` class and then wrapped into an `EventPattern` message for reactive usage. Here's the code:

```
public MainWindow()
{
    InitializeComponent();
    DataContext = this;

    //command definition
    var command = new EventCommand();
    ChangeValueCommand = command;

    //sequence initialization

    //register to the event from the command
    Observable.FromEventPattern(command, "ExecuteRaised")
    //subscribe to messages from the sequence
    .Subscribe(eventDetail =>
    {
```

```
        //EventArgs contains the Parameter of the command
        Result += Convert.ToInt32(eventDetail.EventArgs);
        //notify the value update
        Notify("Result");
    });
}
```

Here's the `EventCommand` class:

```
//a simplified CommandToEvent command
public class EventCommand : ICommand
{
    public event EventHandler<object> ExecuteRaised;
    public event EventHandler CanExecuteChanged;

    public bool CanExecute(object parameter)
    {
        return true;
    }

    public void Execute(object parameter)
    {
        if (ExecuteRaised != null)
            ExecuteRaised(this, parameter);
    }
}
```

The first difference that exists between the previous example and the one with `ConsoleApplication` in the preceding example is that, here, we injected into `FromEventPattern` a specific object (`instance`) that raises its event, while in the `ConsoleApplication` example, we specified a `Type` parameter because that event is static.

Other than this difference, the example is identical (in its design), because the WPF command-binding pattern is somehow already changing the event design into the Rx direction. What if we use a classic window/web form design? Here's an example:

```
//sequence initialization

//register to buttons
var button1Sequence = Observable.FromEventPattern(button1, "Click")
//create the message to specify right numeric value
.Select(x => -10);

var button2Sequence = Observable.FromEventPattern(button2, "Click")
//create the message to specify right numeric value
.Select(x => -1);
```

```
var button3Sequence = Observable.FromEventPattern(button3, "Click")
//create the message to specify right numeric value
.Select(x => +1);

var button4Sequence = Observable.FromEventPattern(button4, "Click")
//create the message to specify right numeric value
.Select(x => +10);

//create a single merged sequence
button1Sequence.Merge(button2Sequence).Merge(button3Sequence).Merge(button4
Sequence)
//flatten values into a single
.Scan((previous, actual) => previous + actual)
//subscribe to handle value change
.Subscribe(x =>
{
    //notify the value update
    textBox1.Text = x.ToString();
});
```

The preceding example is within the constructor of a form. We have 4 buttons and TextBox for displaying the result. The example is identical to the WPF one, but here, we have a completely different Rx sequence. In Windows Forms, each button raises its Click event; this means that we need to create 4 sequences from the event pattern and merge these sequences into a single sequence. Once we have flattened the changing values, we need to find the result by using the Scan operator that gives us a rolling result. At the end of the sequence, a simple subscription sets the result to the textbox1.Text property.

FromEvent

The FromEvent method, similar to FromEventPattern, returns a sequence of the messages that represent event occurrences. The difference is that FromEvent gives us the ability to interact more deeply with the internals of the FromEvent sequence generation.

Instead of asking for a CLR event, as was the case with FromEventPattern, the FromEvent method asks for two actions. The first (registration) action gives us the internal Action<T> method that FromEvent uses to generate messages. The second (unregister) action give us again the same inner action to inform us to stop using that inner action to produce messages.

Here's a short example:

```
//the action from the FromEvent
Action<string> fromEventAction = null;

//setup the FromEvent sequence
Observable.FromEvent<string>(
    //register the inner action
    innerAction => { fromEventAction = innerAction; },
    //unregister the inner action
    innerAction => { fromEventAction = null; }
    )
    .Subscribe(x => Console.WriteLine("-> {0}", x));

while (true)
{
    //invoke the inner action
    fromEventAction(DateTime.Now.ToString());
    Thread.Sleep(1000);
}
```

This is one of the most powerful implementations within Rx between all the message generator operators available throughout the `Observable` class, because here, we have the ability to produce an arbitrary amount of messages simply with the delegate method available with `Action<T>`, a generic delegate.

Another way of using the `FromEvent` method is by using its inner actions to handle an external event. In a few words, we will receive a couple of delegates to ensure the registration/deregistration of our sequence. Then, we will append these delegates (as an event handler) to the external event we want to intercept to create messages. The message flow will start by intercepting the event.

Here's an example:

```
public static event Action MyStaticEvent;
static void Main(string[] args)
{
    //event sequence
    var sequence = Observable.FromEvent(
        //register the inner action as handler of the static event
        x => MyStaticEvent += x,
        //unregister the inner action from the static event
        x => MyStaticEvent -= x);

    //observer
    sequence.Subscribe(unit => Console.WriteLine(unit));
```

```
    //manually raise the event
    MyStaticEvent();

    Console.ReadLine();
}
```

This usage of the `FromEvent` method is a bit useless because we could use the `FromEventPattern` instead. The difference is always that, with the `FromEvent` method we can register to the event (or to multiple events) by ourselves and later unregister in the same way.

ToEvent

The opposite of handling events as messages in the `observable` sequence is exposing a reactive message as events. This is a useful way of interacting with the existing (usually desktop) applications, because this choice makes available intercepting `OnNext`, `OnCompleted`, and `OnError` messages as events.

Here's a short example:

```
//an infinite sequence
var sequence = Observable.Interval(TimeSpan.FromSeconds(1)).Select(x =>
DateTime.Now);

//the event wrapper
var eventWrapper = sequence.ToEvent();

//register the event handler
eventWrapper.OnNext += x => Console.WriteLine("{0}", x);

Console.ReadLine();
```

Threading integration

With Rx, we have the ability to let our messages flow in specific threads to achieve high concurrency computation or we can define to use the main thread to comply with the UI controls requirements. This kind of thread integration is discussed in the *Scheduling* section.

Differently, in this section, we will cover the ability to flow the result of an asynchronous operation within a sequence.

Sourcing from a Task

A `Task` process is an asynchronous operation wrapped into an object that gives us the ability to create task hierarchy, task cancellation, and so on.

Often, in our applications, we use tasks to handle CPU-bound or IO-bound operations. When we're dealing with reactive applications, the best way to acknowledge a task completion is by routing `ack` as a message within a sequence. This is available throughout the `ToObservable` extension method of the `Task` class. Here's an example:

```
//as simple task
var task = Task.Factory.StartNew(() =>
{
    Thread.Sleep(1000);
    return DateTime.Now;
});

//a sequence to ack the task's result
//need using System.Reactive.Threading.Tasks
var ackSequence = task.ToObservable();

//some output
ackSequence.Subscribe(x => Console.WriteLine(x));

Console.ReadLine();
```

Task cancellation

We can use task cancellation within the sequence creation to have the opportunity to cancel internal subscription executions with the usual task cancellation design. Here's a complete example:

```
//a cancellable sequence
var fromDatabase = Observable.Create<DateTime>(o =>
{
    //a cancellation token source for timeout
    var tks = new CancellationTokenSource(TimeSpan.FromSeconds(5));
    var token = tks.Token;

    //the cancellable task within the sequence
    return Task.Factory.StartNew(() =>
    {
        //run until cancel requested
        while (!token.IsCancellationRequested)
            using (var cn = new SqlConnection(@"data
```

```
source=(local);integrated security=true;"))
            using (var cm = new SqlCommand("select getdate()", cn))
            {
                Thread.Sleep(1000);
                cn.Open();
                //read time from DB
                o.OnNext((DateTime)cm.ExecuteScalar());
            }

        //signal oncompleted
        o.OnCompleted();

        //returns a disposable subscription completed object
        //with an OnCompleted callback
        return Disposable.Create(() => Console.WriteLine("Killing
        subscription"));
    }, token);
});

fromDatabase.Subscribe(x => Console.WriteLine(x));
```

The preceding example shows how to cancel the internal per subscription message generation function. Essentially, it's a classic task cancellation example. The only difference is that this executes within a `Create` operator that specifies the message generation workflow that runs per subscriber. In this example, we specified a 5 seconds timeout that signals `CancellationToken` to end the internal execution of `Task`, exits its execution loop, and correctly completes its job.

Scheduling

Programming observable sequences is a powerful way to achieve a highly modularized programming experience. Although this offers high flexibility, an observable sequence is single-threaded by default and is similar to a lot of other CLR objects. This means that although a sequence can push messages to multiple subscribers, this operation happens in the same thread where the messages originate and then the messages reach all the subscribers, sequentially following their subscription order.

This means that using an observable sequence instead of any other .NET object does not convert automatically our code into a multithreaded one.

Luckily, to address this automatic multithreading need in the Rx world, there are `Schedulers`. These are objects that choose when a message can flow and which thread must handle a message.

It is important to understand the huge difference that exists between using a CLR `delegate/event` and Rx scheduling. When using scheduling in Rx, we would always have an asynchronous implementation in an in-memory queue of messages that act as a message pump supporting **Quality of Service (QoS)** for routing messages at different speeds. These messages flow and are observed in a thread or another based on the scheduler's choice. This is actually the most critical task of a scheduler.

In short, a scheduler is in charge of choosing the `message/thread` association. Let's take a look at this familiar code:

```
var loopBasedSequence = Observable.Create<DateTime>(x =>
{
    while (true)
    {
        Console.WriteLine("{0} -> Yielding new value...",
        Thread.CurrentThread.ManagedThreadId);
        x.OnNext(DateTime.Now);
        Thread.Sleep(1000);
    }
    return Disposable.Empty;
});

loopBasedSequence.Subscribe(x => Console.WriteLine("-> {0}", x));
```

The preceding example shows us a very simple implementation of an infinite sequence. Based on a simple infinite loop, this example produces messages that originate always from the same thread. This is obvious because we are looping within a `While` loop; the same behavior is available in nonreactive coding.

Let's take a look at another example that shows a timer-based sequence:

```
var timerBasedSequence = Observable.Interval(TimeSpan.FromSeconds(1))
.Select(x =>
{
    Console.WriteLine("{0} -> Yielding new value...",
    Thread.CurrentThread.ManagedThreadId);
    return DateTime.Now;
});

timerBasedSequence.Subscribe(x => Console.WriteLine("-> {0}", x));
```

This example shows another infinite sequence that is slightly different from the previous one. This sequence is timer-based, such as when we use `System.Threading.Timer` in classic CLR programming or any similar object. A `Timer` method produces a signal at a fixed time interval. This signal originates from a thread in `ThreadPool`. We cannot choose the thread by ourselves. The same happens in the reactive version of `Timer` available through the `Interval` method.

Other than these built-in behaviors, we have the ability to set up a specific thread for our sequence by specifying the scheduler to be used. Here's an example:

```
var loopBasedSequence = Observable.Create<DateTime>(x =>
{
    while (true)
    {
        Console.WriteLine("{0} -> Yielding new value...",
Thread.CurrentThread.ManagedThreadId);
        x.OnNext(DateTime.Now);
        Thread.Sleep(1000);
    }
    return Disposable.Empty;
});

loopBasedSequence.SubscribeOn(Scheduler.Default).Subscribe(x =>
Console.WriteLine("{0} -> {1}", Thread.CurrentThread.ManagedThreadId, x));
loopBasedSequence.SubscribeOn(Scheduler.Default).Subscribe(x =>
Console.WriteLine("{0} -> {1}", Thread.CurrentThread.ManagedThreadId, x));
loopBasedSequence.SubscribeOn(Scheduler.Default).Subscribe(x =>
Console.WriteLine("{0} -> {1}", Thread.CurrentThread.ManagedThreadId, x));
```

The preceding example shows another implementation of the loop-based infinite sequence. This time, before the subscription, we specified to use a specific `Scheduler` class with the `SubscribeOn` extension method (discussed in detail later in this chapter). In the previous example, only the subscriber creates a subscription on the creation thread (the main thread) that prevented the application to exit from that infinite loop. Differently, in this new example, `Scheduler` assigned a thread to each observer subscription. This means that we have altogether three different threads running their infinite logic.

To use the `Scheduler` helper class, we need to import the `System.Reactive.Concurrency` namespace.

Default schedulers

We have the ability to select the desired scheduler between those available in the `Scheduler` helper class as static properties. Each prebuild scheduler is optimized for a specific kind of usage as background tasks, UI programming, and so on. Here's a short explanation of the available schedulers.

The `Scheduler.Default` (former `Scheduler.ThreadPool`) scheduler is the default concurrent scheduler that lets us interact with multithreaded execution in a simple way. It uses threads from `ThreadPool`. Bear in mind that `ThreadPool` has a finite number of threads and that its threads fulfil the needs of other CLR objects as tasks from `TaskFactory`. Obviously, we can set up the minimum and maximum number of threads with the `ThreadPool.SetMinThreads` and `ThreadPool.SetMaxThreads` static methods.

On the other hand, `Scheduler.Immediate` is definitely the default scheduler that runs when we don't ask for a scheduler. This is the blocking one that executes any subscription life cycle in the main thread.

The `Scheduler.CurrentThread` method is very similar to the `Immediate` one, but the `Immediate` one executes without queuing messages. This means that the `CurrentThread` one schedules messages to execute sequentially on the same creation thread, preventing these messages from creating a race/deadlock condition.

The `Scheduler.Dispatcher` method lets the observers execute on the UI thread for WPF or Silverlight applications.

 To use the `Dispatcher` scheduler, import the NuGet package `Rx-WPF` or `Rx-Silverlight`.

The `NewThreadScheduler.Default` method (former `Scheduler.NewThread`) executes each observer on a new foreground thread (`System.Threading.Thread`) to avoid consuming a thread from `ThreadPool` as it happens with the `Default` scheduler. This means that we can virtually execute the maximum number of threads (~65K) the OS can handle, but this also means that this choice can dramatically reduce the application's (and OS) reliability because there is no throttling on thread amount, causing huge resource usages and the possibility to reach the starvation state that will impact the OS, too.

The `Scheduler.TaskPool` method executes the observer within `Task` from the default task factory. There are two main benefits in using this scheduler: threads in the thread pool (`TaskFactory`, by default, uses threads from `ThreadPool`) are pregenerated; this means that we don't have to wait for their creation (if there are enough threads ready in the pool). This is useful for reducing the delay in the message's response. Another benefit is that the pool contains a finite number of threads, acting as a throttling that doesn't allow an unpredictable number of threads to run together.

Each Rx operator comes with its default scheduler. This means that timer-based schedulers (for instance, Interval) run on the `ThreadPool` scheduler, while sequences that produce few messages will usually run on the `Immediate` scheduler. This design choice is made by preferring the less concurrent scheduler, while, when we select a specific scheduler or when we select the `Default` scheduler, we're asking Rx to configure its message pump to route messages to multiple threads to improve the messages' concurrency.

SubscribeOn/ObserveOn

In the previous example, we had the opportunity of seeing the `SubscribeOn` method in action. This method allows us to specify a scheduler to queue messages on different threads.

The same result is available with the `ObserveOn` method with the difference that the `SubscribeOn` method registers the scheduler on the whole the subscriber and, eventually, the observer code that produces messages related to the same observer. Differently, the `ObserveOn` method registers to the given scheduler only the output message by letting all the messages source from the same thread.

It's time to understand in detail how these methods work. The following example shows a sequence made with the `Create` operator. This operator lets us specify a custom code to produce messages per registration. Later, we will register two subscribers with `SubscribeOn` and then with the `ObserveOn` method specifying the `Default` (`ThreadPool`) scheduler. This will route execution on the thread pool. The two different operators will produce different results because the `SubscribeOn` method will put the whole `Create` operator on the pool's thread, while the `ObserveOn` will only put the resulting messages on the pool's thread. Here's the code:

```
var sequence = Observable.Create<DateTime>(x =>
{
    //let take some time before registering the new observer
```

```
    for(int i=0;i<10;i++)
    {
        Console.WriteLine("Registering observer on thread {0}...",
Thread.CurrentThread.ManagedThreadId);
        Thread.Sleep(100);
    }

    //produce 10 messages
    for(int i=0;i<10;i++)
    {
        x.OnNext(DateTime.Now);
        Thread.Sleep(100);
    }

    //exit
    return Disposable.Empty;
});

//register two subscribers
sequence.SubscribeOn(Scheduler.Default).Subscribe(x =>
Console.WriteLine("{0} -> {1}", Thread.CurrentThread.ManagedThreadId, x));
sequence.SubscribeOn(Scheduler.Default).Subscribe(x =>
Console.WriteLine("{0} -> {1}", Thread.CurrentThread.ManagedThreadId, x));

Console.ReadLine();
```

The example code is identical whether we use the `SubscribeOn` or the `ObserveOn` method. Let's evaluate the behavior of the two methods.

When using the `ObserveOn` method, the two observers will register sequentially. The second observer will register only when the first stops receiving messages. Then, each observer will receive its messages. Talking about the threading design, each observer will register on the same thread (the main one). Then, each observer will receive its messages on another thread of the pool. This means that the observer creational code that runs within the `Create` method will always run in the main thread per each observer. In other words, each subscription will execute on thread *A* (the main one); the first observer will handle messages on thread *B*, and the second observer will handle messages on thread *C*.

When using the `SubscribeOn` method, each observer will get correlated to a specific thread from the subscription to the completion. This means that the first observer will subscribe and receive messages on thread *A* (not the main one), while the second observer will subscribe and receive messages on thread *B* (not the main one).

The immediate result of these two implementations is that, with SubscribeOn, the two subscriptions will run in parallel by avoiding the second observer waiting for the first one to complete its job before registering. Obviously, this method produces the most concurrent result and is preferable in any case if we want to increase parallelism in our coding. However, this method cannot directly interact with UI controls as WPF or Windows Forms controls because all these controls require that the request (in the example, the code within the Create method) comes from the UI thread. In such cases, the ObserveOn method is definitely our choice.

Injecting schedulers

Other than injecting schedulers within the sequence chain by using the SubscribeOn or the ObserveOn method, we can pass a specific scheduler in almost any Rx operator's extension method, changing the default scheduler of the operator itself. Here's an example:

```
Console.WriteLine("Main thread: {0}",
Thread.CurrentThread.ManagedThreadId);

//numeric sequence
var sequence = Observable.Range(1, 10, Scheduler.Default);

//observers
sequence.Subscribe(x => Console.WriteLine("{0} -> {1}",
Thread.CurrentThread.ManagedThreadId, x));
sequence.Subscribe(x => Console.WriteLine("{0} -> {1}",
Thread.CurrentThread.ManagedThreadId, x));
```

In the preceding example, we will see an implementation almost identical to the ObserveOn one because the two observers will run sequentially, receiving the same values from the sourcing sequence. This happens because the Range method produces a Cold sequence.

The Cold sequences are sequences that start their messaging workflow each time an observer subscribes. But, each Hot observer has its own messaging workflow regardless of whether one or multiple subscriptions exist.

Custom scheduling

A Scheduler class, as the name implies, other than something that deals with threads, is something that schedules some action at a given time. We can use Schedulers to schedule jobs of any kind at any absolute or relative or repetitive time. In the real-world reactive programming, we can use scheduled jobs to push messages into sequences or because of their ability to virtualize the time (later explained in the *Virtual time* section).

Here's an example of Immediate scheduling:

```
static void Main(string[] args)
{
    using (var job1 = Scheduler.Default.Schedule(OnJob1Executed))
        //job timeout
        Thread.Sleep(2000);

    Console.WriteLine("END");
    Console.ReadLine();
}

static void OnJob1Executed()
{
    for (int i = 0; i < 10; i++)
    {
        Console.Write(".");
        Thread.Sleep(100);
    }

    Console.WriteLine();
    Console.WriteLine("JOB END");
}
```

The preceding example shows how to schedule a simple job immediately. Consider a real-world usage where we schedule immediate jobs by receiving inputs from a user or by handling an event. Although we could simply execute the same job immediately without Scheduler, by using Scheduler, we may, in future, replay the scheduled job sequence by saving this sequence somewhere. This gives us a great diagnostic tool. More details on it are available in the *Virtual time* section.

Another interesting thing to focus on by looking at this example is the job timeout that we can invoke by simply disposing the job token (in the code, this is the job1 variable).

The token represents the scheduled job, not its implementation. This means that it is cancelling job, preventing it from being executed, but not from breaking an eventual execution if this has already been triggered by Scheduler.

Future scheduling

Future scheduling is the ability to schedule at a given (future) absolute time, or relative time, or periodic time. The usage is pretty identical to the generic scheduling with the addition of a scheduling time value.

An important aspect is that, here, the timeout we give to the job token may actually prevent the scheduled job from firing.

Here are a few examples:

```
//starts a job in absolute time
using (var job2 =
Scheduler.Default.Schedule(DateTimeOffset.Now.AddSeconds(1), ()
.0=> Console.WriteLine("OK")))
    //job timeout
    Thread.Sleep(2000);

//starts a job in relative time
using (var job3 = Scheduler.Default.Schedule(TimeSpan.FromSeconds(10), ()
=> Console.WriteLine("OK")))
    //job timeout
    //this job will never fire because its schedule is greater than how
time timeout will grant
    Thread.Sleep(2000);

//starts a job periodically
using (var job4 =
Scheduler.Default.SchedulePeriodic(TimeSpan.FromSeconds(1), () =>
Console.WriteLine("OK")))
    //timeout at 5 seconds
    Thread.Sleep(5000);

Console.WriteLine("END");
Console.ReadLine();
```

The periodic example (the third) will fire our scheduled job until we don't kill it by disposing the token (job2).

The ability to create custom future scheduling with multiple different Schedulers gives us tremendous chances of designing our solution the best we can.

Virtual time

When we create complex scheduling, we can work in virtual time to achieve testability or to have the ability to replay some real-world (in production) execution because of testing needs, diagnostic needs, or production needs.

 To execute the following examples, import the `Microsoft.Reactive.Testing` and `System.Reactive.Concurrency` namespaces.

The concept is very easy. We can create a scheduler specific for testing purposes, `TestScheduler` (import the NuGet `Rx-Testing` package). Then, we can use it as usual by scheduling jobs. We can advance the virtual clock by letting the scheduler execute as in the real world. Here's a short example to understand it easily:

```
//a scheduler for testing purposes
var scheduler = new TestScheduler();

//records to schedule an immediate action
scheduler.Schedule(() => Console.WriteLine("Hi"));

//advance the virtual clock to let execute the recorded actions
scheduler.AdvanceBy(TimeSpan.FromSeconds(1).Ticks);
```

The preceding example shows how to use `TestScheduler`. `Scheduler` will record each scheduled job we ask it to execute. It never executes jobs as usual schedulers; it only records jobs. Bear in mind that we always need to manually play the recorded job schedule to actually execute jobs.

Alternatively, to manually move the virtual clock forward with the `AdvanceBy` method, we can simply play the record by invoking the `Start` method. Here's an example:

```
////advance the virtual clock to let execute the recorded actions
//scheduler.AdvanceBy(TimeSpan.FromSeconds(1).Ticks);

//play the recorded scheduled jobs at normal speed
scheduler.Start();
```

The `Start` method will let the scheduler immediately output all the outputs regardless of the job's absolute timings while respecting the sequence order. Here's a more complete example:

```
//output the virtual clock
Console.WriteLine("-> {0}", scheduler.Now);

//schedule a future job
scheduler.Schedule(TimeSpan.FromDays(22), () => Console.WriteLine("2
seconds now"));
Console.WriteLine("-> {0}", scheduler.Now);

//play the recorded scheduled jobs at normal speed
scheduler.Start();
Console.WriteLine("-> {0}", scheduler.Now);
```

In the preceding example, we created a future job that will start with a 22 days delay. However, by invoking the `Start` method, the scheduler will immediately advance the virtual clock (available with the `Now` property) to the next job time, causing the related action's execution. This will leave the internal virtual clock to the last job time (in this example, 22 days).

We can register other jobs even after we invoke the `Start` method. These jobs will not fire until we invoke the `Start` method again.

> If multiple jobs are scheduled at the same identical virtual time, `Scheduler` will execute these jobs according to the registration time.

We can advance to a specific virtual time by using the `AdvanceTo` method. Here's an example:

```
//schedule a future job at 1 minute
scheduler.Schedule(TimeSpan.FromMinutes(1), () => Console.WriteLine("2
seconds now"));
Console.WriteLine("-> {0}", scheduler.Now);

//advance to 00:00:30
scheduler.AdvanceTo(TimeSpan.FromSeconds(30).Ticks);
Console.WriteLine("-> {0}", scheduler.Now);

//advance to 00:01:00
scheduler.AdvanceTo(TimeSpan.FromSeconds(60).Ticks);
Console.WriteLine("-> {0}", scheduler.Now);
```

By invoking the `AdvanceTo` method of the `Scheduler` class, we can advance the virtual time as we wish. Obviously, we cannot advance back in time! `Scheduler` is a forward-only virtual time clock.

Another interesting feature is the ability to schedule a `Stop` execution on the scheduler itself. This will pause the scheduler (another `Start` will let the scheduler start again, playing newly recorded jobs eventually) at a specified time. Here's a complete example:

```
//schedule a periodic job and output the virtual time
scheduler.SchedulePeriodic(TimeSpan.FromSeconds(1), () =>
Console.WriteLine("{0} -> Periodic", scheduler.Now));

//this would produce an infinite output
//scheduler.Start();

//to avoid the infinite output, we will need to schedule a Stop request
scheduler.Schedule(TimeSpan.FromSeconds(60), () => scheduler.Stop());

//play the whole record
scheduler.Start();

//append immediately
scheduler.Schedule(TimeSpan.FromTicks(1), () => Console.WriteLine("Running
again"));

//schedule another Stop
scheduler.Schedule(TimeSpan.FromSeconds(60), () => scheduler.Stop());
//start again the scheduler
scheduler.Start();

Console.ReadLine();
```

In the preceding example, we can see the `Stop` usage. Bear in mind that after the first `Start` method executes, the whole record will play until `Stop` fires. This will pause the scheduler setting in its `IsEnabled` property to `False`. Then, we will enqueue the other two jobs, an immediate output and another `Stop`. This second `Stop` method will prevent `Scheduler` from running indefinitely after the second `Start` request. This would happen because the virtual clock can only advance, meaning that after the first `Stop`, it will never go back to running the same (first) `Stop` method again. In other words, invoking multiple times the `Start` method will not restart the `Scheduler` object from the beginning. It will simply start again from its last virtual clock time.

Testing schedulers

Now that we know how to start/stop virtual `Schedulers`, we need to look at how to test `TestScheduler` in an automated way, as we may do in nonreactive coding with unit testing.

To test scheduler and sequences, we need to create the mock version of a sequence and of an observer. They are available as a helper method using the `TestScheduler` class. We can create a mock observer with the `CreateObserver<T>` method and mock sequences with the `CreateColdObservable` or `CreateHotObservable` methods. Bear in mind that a `Cold` sequence produces the same message flow at each subscription while a `Hot` sequence fires its message regardless of the live subscriptions.

Here's a short example regarding a cold sequence:

```
var scheduler = new TestScheduler();

//a cold sequence
var sequence = scheduler.CreateColdObservable<int>(
    //some recorded message
    new Recorded<Notification<int>>(TimeSpan.FromSeconds(1).Ticks,
    Notification.CreateOnNext(10)),
    new Recorded<Notification<int>>(TimeSpan.FromSeconds(2).Ticks,
    Notification.CreateOnNext(20)),
    new Recorded<Notification<int>>(TimeSpan.FromSeconds(3).Ticks,
    Notification.CreateOnNext(30)),
    new Recorded<Notification<int>>(TimeSpan.FromSeconds(4).Ticks,
    Notification.CreateOnNext(40)),
    new Recorded<Notification<int>>(TimeSpan.FromSeconds(5).Ticks,
    Notification.CreateOnNext(50)),
    new Recorded<Notification<int>>(TimeSpan.FromSeconds(6).Ticks,
    Notification.CreateOnNext(60)),
    new Recorded<Notification<int>>(TimeSpan.FromSeconds(7).Ticks,
    Notification.CreateOnCompleted<int>())
);

//a new testable observer
var observer1 = scheduler.CreateObserver<int>();

//subscribe the observer at a given virtual time
scheduler.Schedule(TimeSpan.FromSeconds(2), () =>
sequence.Subscribe(observer1));

//play the record
scheduler.Start();
```

As visible in the preceding example, we can simply create a sequence with the `TestScheduler.CreateColdObservable` method by specifying the message record list to be produced when playing. To produce recorded messages, we will wrap our values (integer values in this example or none for the `OnCompleted` message) into a `Notification` object. Then, we will wrap the notification into a `Recorded` object by providing the relative time defer to use to flow the specified message.

We will subscribe the observer to the sequence within another job in virtual time (after 2 seconds in the example). This will let the observer receive 7 messages regardless of the delay of 2 seconds of the subscription. This happens because we're using a `Cold` observable sequence.

 We can substitute `CreateColdObservable` with `CreateHotObservable`. With a `Hot` observable sequence, we will receive only 5 messages into the observer because the hot observer will produce messages regardless of whether the subscriber exists.

To verify message flowing at the observer's point of view, we can evaluate its `Messages` property after the `TestScheduler.Start` is complete. Here's an example:

```
foreach (var m in observer1.Messages)
{
    var time = m.Time;
    //available only for OnNext messages
    //var value = m.Value.Value;
    //var exception = m.Value.Exception;
    //var kind = m.Value.Kind;
    //var hasValue = m.Value.HasValue;

    Console.WriteLine("{0}", m);
}
```

As visible, there are a lot of interesting properties available in the `Notification` object that details the flowing message. This object is the same as we had while using the `Materialize` method to produce a tracing sequence, as we have already seen in Chapter 5, `Debugging Reactive Extension`.

Now, it is time to make some assertions to check whether messages within the observer behave as expected. The next example will use `AssertEquals` of the `Messages` property of the mock observer. Here's the short code:

```
observer1.Messages.AssertEqual(
    //same messages
    new Recorded<Notification<int>>(TimeSpan.FromSeconds(1).Ticks +
```

```
            TimeSpan.FromSeconds(2).Ticks, Notification.CreateOnNext(10)),
        new Recorded<Notification<int>>(TimeSpan.FromSeconds(2).Ticks +
            TimeSpan.FromSeconds(2).Ticks, Notification.CreateOnNext(20)),
        new Recorded<Notification<int>>(TimeSpan.FromSeconds(3).Ticks +
            TimeSpan.FromSeconds(2).Ticks, Notification.CreateOnNext(30)),
        new Recorded<Notification<int>>(TimeSpan.FromSeconds(4).Ticks +
            TimeSpan.FromSeconds(2).Ticks, Notification.CreateOnNext(40)),
        new Recorded<Notification<int>>(TimeSpan.FromSeconds(5).Ticks +
            TimeSpan.FromSeconds(2).Ticks, Notification.CreateOnNext(50)),
        new Recorded<Notification<int>>(TimeSpan.FromSeconds(6).Ticks +
            TimeSpan.FromSeconds(2).Ticks, Notification.CreateOnNext(60)),
        new Recorded<Notification<int>>(TimeSpan.FromSeconds(7).Ticks +
            TimeSpan.FromSeconds(2).Ticks, Notification.CreateOnCompleted<int>())
);
```

Kindly focus on the need for adding 2 seconds (observer subscription virtual time) to the virtual time value of the messages we're testing.

An in-depth explanation of the Rx scheduler testing (by Rx team) is available at:

```
https://blogs.msdn.microsoft.com/rxteam/2012/06/14/testing-rx-queries-u
sing-virtual-time-scheduling/.
```

Historical records

Another class similar to `TestScheduler` is available to produce a real-life replay of messages flowing from usual sequences, `HistoricalScheduler`. This class is almost identical to `TestScheduler` with the difference that we can use it to replay dumped messages. To dump messages from a sequence, we need to store the physical time together with the value message by using the `Timestamp` extension method. Once we have this time-stamped sequence, we need to move back from a continuous (reactive) programming to a state-driven programming by dumping messages into a finite collection by using the `ToList` extension method. Then, we need to use the `Wait` extension method to pause the sequence completion and produce the required collection.

Now, we're ready to use this collection in the `Observable.Generate` method that will recreate a sequence from a timestamped finite message collection. This method will need `HistoricalScheduler` as a parameter to handle virtual time advancement, as we have already seen with the usual virtual time of `TestScheduler`. Here's a complete example:

```
Console.WriteLine("{0} -> Playing...", DateTime.Now);

//a sourcing sequence
var sequence = Observable.Interval(TimeSpan.FromSeconds(1)).Take(5);
```

```
var trace = sequence
    //marks each message with a timestamp
    .Timestamp()
    //route messages into a list of timestamped messages
    .ToList()
    //materialize the list when the sequence completes
    //and return only the list
    .Wait();

//a scheduler for historical records
var scheduler = new HistoricalScheduler();

Console.WriteLine("{0} -> Replaying...", DateTime.Now);

//generate a new sequence from a collection
var replay = Observable.Generate(
    //the enumerator to read values from
    trace.GetEnumerator(),
    //the condition to check until False
    x => x.MoveNext(),
    //the item
    x => x,
    //the item's value
    x => x.Current.Value,
    //the item's virtual time
    x => x.Current.Timestamp,
    //the scheduler
    scheduler);

//some output
replay.Subscribe(x => Console.WriteLine("{0} -> {1}", scheduler.Now, x));

//play the record
scheduler.Start();

Console.ReadLine();
```

By running the preceding example, we will see the replay producing with the same real-time progression. Similar to `TestScheduler`, `HistoricalScheduler` will flatten virtual time by outputting all the messages immediately after the invocation of the `Start` method.

Downloading the example code

You can download the example code files for this book from your account at `http://www.packtpub.com`. If you purchased this book elsewhere, you can visit `http://www.packtpub.com/support` and register to have the files e-mailed directly to you.
You can download the code files by following these steps:

1. Log in or register to our website using your e-mail address and password.
2. Hover the mouse pointer on the **SUPPORT** tab at the top.
3. Click on **Code Downloads & Errata**.
4. Enter the name of the book in the **Search** box.
5. Select the book for which you're looking to download the code files.
6. Choose from the drop-down menu where you purchased this book from.
7. Click on **Code Download**.

You can also download the code files by clicking on the **Code Files** button on the book's webpage at the Packt Publishing website. This page can be accessed by entering the book's name in the **Search** box. Please note that you need to be logged in to your Packt account.
Once the file is downloaded, please make sure that you unzip or extract the folder using the latest version of:

- WinRAR / 7-Zip for Windows
- Zipeg / iZip / UnRarX for Mac
- 7-Zip / PeaZip for Linux

The code bundle for the book is also hosted on GitHub at `https://githu b.com/PacktPublishing/Reactive-Programming-for-.NET-Devel opers`. We also have other code bundles from our rich catalog of books and videos available at `https://github.com/PacktPublishing/`. Check them out!

Summary

In this chapter, we had the ability to see the most critical Rx internal component: the schedulers. Understanding scheduling and using scheduling allows applications to get the best from Rx. Together, the ability to interact with classic CLR events extends the power of Rx to classic .NET application integration.

In the next chapter, we will see more of CLR integration and custom Rx component creation with multiple case studies on real-world Rx applications.

7
Advanced Techniques

This chapter will show us how to create custom operators and custom schedulers. We will cover some advanced techniques, such as **Interactive Extensions (Ix)** and event sourcing with Reactive Extension (Rx).

Here is a short list:

- Designing a custom operator
- Designing a custom scheduler
- Creating `Pattern<T>`
- Event sourcing with Rx
- Interactive Extensions (Ix)

Designing a custom operator

In the Rx framework, there are multiple extension methods that help us transform a sequence into another one, subscribe to a sequence, or create a new sequence from other objects or from scratch.

In classic .NET development, all these methods are simply functions, because they almost always provide a result. In Reactive Programming, any function that returns an observable sequence is an operator. There are transforming operators, creational operators, diagnostic operators, and so on.

Usually, we use operators from the `Observable` helper class or by using other helper classes from the official Rx library set available throughout the NuGet package explorer. When we cannot find the right operator, or when we want to improve an operator already available, maybe, by adding new overloads or changing its implementation, we can create a new operator by creating an extension method that supports the generic pattern. With this design, we will be able to reuse our operators in the future in all our projects or redistribute them within libraries or components.

Another great usage of custom operators is composing other operators to behave as desired. Usually, the goal of adding an overload to an already available operator or adding a new composite operator or other operators is to make it easier to use.

As the last choice, we may create a custom operator from scratch using LINQ or other features of the CLR together with the low level Rx elements, such as `IObservable`, `IObserver`, or `Subject`.

Usually, making use of operator composition reduces the chances of releasing bugs and unwanted behaviors.

Designing the AsObservable operator

In the following example, we will create an operator to source from a generic `IEnumerable<T>` variable.

To create a similar operator, we will use a `Create` operator. Here is the code:

```
static void Main(string[] args)
    {
        //1000 items to source from
        var items = Enumerable.Range(0, 1000)
            .Select(x =>
            {
                //raise an exception on item #400
                //within VS the debugger will stop the execution as the
                  exception bubbles
                //simply press F5 again to continue bubble the
exception to Rx
                  sequence
                if (x == 400)
                    throw new ArgumentException("The item #400 has been
                    sourcing");

                return x;
            });
```

```
            //invoke our custom operator
            var sequence = items.AsObservable();

            //output value and metadata
            sequence.Materialize().Subscribe(x => Console.WriteLine("->
{0}", x));

            Console.ReadLine();
        }
    }

    public static class RxOperators
    {
        public static IObservable<T> AsObservable<T>(this IEnumerable<T>
source)
        {
            return Observable.Create<T>(observer =>
            {
                foreach (var item in source)
                    try
                    {
                        observer.OnNext(item);
                    }
                    catch (Exception ex)
                    {
                        observer.OnError(ex);
                        break;
                    }

                observer.OnCompleted();
                return Disposable.Empty;
            });
        }
    }
```

The `AsObservable` operator we created in the preceding example sources data from a generic enumerable with the `for-each` clause. This means that we will never materialize the whole collection in the memory. Instead, we will stream data, as this is available at the enumerator, routing data into the messages available to the returning sequence. Together, we will eventually handle generated exceptions by routing these as error messages. At the end, we will signal the completion by routing the proper message. Regarding this implementation, we don't need to implement the disposal of the observer. Wherever we implement this feature, we can use the `Disposable.Create` method to write an action to stop flowing useless messages to an observer that has just been disposed.

Consider that when raising an exception in the `Observer` implementation instead of the sourcing sequence implementation, the behavior is different. In the preceding example, we handled errors from the source. This means that we will route properly only these kind of errors. Otherwise, by raising an exception within the `observer` implementation, `observer` will simply cause the exit from the underlying `Create` implementation, stopping its execution immediately. Carefully, let this happen because this is an error hiding (anti-pattern) case.

Designing the AcceptObservableClient operator

When network programming, there are multiple high-level systems that may help us create amazing applications. Web services (WCF or ASMX), binary remote services (WCF, Remoting), Enterprise Services (COM+), RESTful services and API (WebApi, WCF, MVC), OData services, queues (MSMQ, Azure Service Bus Queue, Storage Queue), and so on use it. Often, when dealing with IoT devices, we need work at a lower level acting as a network socket server.

Consider that, within Microsoft Azure, we can deal with IoT devices with the IotHub that already supports a lot of standard IoT protocols, such as MQTT. When a protocol is not yet implemented, we can still develop a custom protocol for the IotHub gateway. This lets the hub work with our protocol without having to redefine the whole system's architecture.

In this case, we can use the CLR `TcpListener` class that helps us create a socket server with a few code lines with a good level of scalability and reliability (if properly used). Obviously, this choice is available in Rx programming too, but we need to change the application's design a bit to work in the reactive way.

When programming `TcpListener` in a reactive programming way, we need to route something from the listener. At the lowest level, we can only route the client connection as a message; we will route any `TcpClient` connecting to our listener. To route the `TcpClient` messages, we will write a reusable operator named `AcceptObservableClient`.

Here is the code:

```
//the extension method must be put in a static class
public static IObservable<TcpClient> AcceptObservableClient(this
TcpListener listener)
{
    //start listening with a 4 clients buffer backlog
    listener.Start(4);
```

```
            return Observable.Create<TcpClient>(observer =>
            {
                while (true)
                {
                    //accept newly clients from the listener
                    var client = listener.AcceptTcpClient();
                    //route the client to the observer
                    //into an asynchronous task to let multiple clients connect
                        altogether
                    Task.Factory.StartNew(() => observer.OnNext(client),
                    TaskCreationOptions.LongRunning);
                }

                //mandatory to comply with the .Create action signature
                return Disposable.Empty;
            });
        }
```

The operator will start listening for a remote connection with the help of a `TcpListener`
object. Then, each client will flow out as a message within a sequence executing into an
asynchronous `Task`, letting other clients connect to the same listener.

Now, we will see how to use this operator. Here is the code:

```
    //convert a TcpListener into an observable sequence on port 23 (telnet)
    var tcpClientsSequence = TcpListener.Create(23)
        .AcceptObservableClient();

    //subscribe to newly remote clients
    var observer = tcpClientsSequence.Subscribe(client =>
    {
        //remote endpoint (IP:PORT)
        var endpoint = client.Client.RemoteEndPoint as IPEndPoint;
        Console.Write("{0} -> ", endpoint);
        //get the remote stream
        using (var stream = client.GetStream())
            while (true)
            {
                //read bytes until available
                var b = stream.ReadByte();
                if (b < 0)
                    break;
                else
                    Console.Write((char)b);
            }
        Console.WriteLine();
        Console.WriteLine("{0} -> END", endpoint);
        Console.WriteLine();
```

```
    });
```

The preceding code is pretty easy. We will create a new `TcpListener` variable on `port 23`, and with the help of our newly created operator, we will obtain a sequence of `TcpClients`.

Now, we can subscribe to the remote client connection in the usual way. In this implementation, we will simply get access to the remote stream (we're using the stream as a read-only stream, but it accepts writes too) and we will wait until the end of the stream by evaluating the read byte value.

Case study – writing a reactive socket server

Now, that we created the `AcceptObservableClient` operator, to create a complete socket server in Reactive Programming, we simply have to go a bit higher in the level of our design. `AcceptObservableClient` flows out very low level network programming objects (`TcpClient`), while we need an operator that flows out data messages. As a general choice, we will use `Byte`, as it is the only reusable data message that can contains any kind of other messages. In real world implementations, we will use specific business messages instead of general purpose `Byte` type messages.

We need to create another operator, the `AsNetworkByteSource`, which will route messages from the underlying `TcpClient` sequence into another sequence (of `Byte`) with a different granularity, because a single `TcpClient` variable flows out multiple or no `bytes`. This means that routing 10 `TcpClients` means not routing 10 `bytes` (usually more).

The operator will route the `KeyValuePair<IPEndPoint, byte>` messages to give us the ability to correlate multiple bytes of the same source.

Here is the code:

```
public static IObservable<KeyValuePair<IPEndPoint, byte>>
AsNetworkByteSource(this IObservable<TcpClient> source)
{
    return Observable.Create<KeyValuePair<IPEndPoint, byte>>(observer =>
    {
        using (var innerObserver = source.Subscribe(client =>
            {
                using (var stream = client.GetStream())
                    while (true)
                    {
                        var b = stream.ReadByte();
                        if (b < 0)
                            break;
```

```
                    else
                         observer.OnNext(new KeyValuePair<IPEndPoint,
                         byte>(client.Client.RemoteEndPoint
                         as IPEndPoint, (byte)b));

                    }
            }))
    {
        //dispose the innerObserver when completes
    }

    observer.OnCompleted();

    //mandatory to comply with the .Create action signature
    return Disposable.Empty;
    });
}
```

The code is similar to the one that we have already seen in the previous operator usage. The difference is that, here, we wrapped the `TcpClient` usage within a `Create` operator to flow out different messages.

Here is the usage code:

```
//convert a TcpListener into an observable sequence on port 23 (telnet)
var tcpClientsSequence = TcpListener.Create(23)
    .AcceptObservableClient()
    .AsNetworkByteSource();

Console.WriteLine("Subscribing...");
var bytesObserver = tcpClientsSequence.Subscribe(x =>
{
    Console.WriteLine("{0} -> {1} ({2})", x.Key, x.Value, (char)x.Value);
});
```

With this example, we can see that the usage complexity has been heavily reduced. We don't have to deal with low level `TcpClient` objects because we have already received bytes within our sequence together with the source IP and port detail.

Now, we need to abstract more of our code to deal with higher level messages. In the next example, we will consider a text row as a single message. This means that we need to move from per-byte messaging to per-row messaging without losing the client session isolation. To accomplish this task, we need the following flowchart:

1. Flow messaging of remote clients from `TcpListener`.
2. Convert `TcpClient` messaging into byte messaging.
3. Shape single byte messages into single-byte buffered messages to have the ability

to manipulate byte buffers later.
4. Group byte buffers' messages per client session.
5. Within the single group subscription, create a client sequence of bytes.
6. Scan the client sequence to accumulate byte buffers until a CR and LF flows out.
7. Let flow out-only buffers that are correctly terminated.

For a better understanding, here is the simplified flowchart:

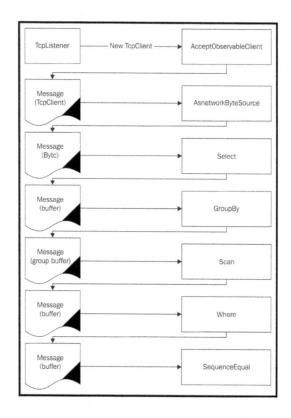

The flow chart of the TcpListener demo

Here is the complete example:

```
//convert a TcpListener into an observable sequence on port 23 (telnet)
var tcpClientsSequence = TcpListener.Create(23)
    .AcceptObservableClient()
    .AsNetworkByteSource();

//map the source message into another with a byte buffer of a single byte
```

```
var bufferUntileCRLFSequence = tcpClientsSequence
    .Select(x => new { x.Key, buffer = new[] { x.Value }.AsEnumerable() })
    //group by client session IPEndPoint (IP/Port)
    .GroupBy(x => x.Key);

//a crlf byte buffer
var crlf = new byte[] { 0x000d, 0x000a };

//subscribe to all nested sequence groups per remote endpoint
bufferUntileCRLFSequence.Subscribe(endpoint =>
{
    var clientSequence = endpoint
        //apply an accumulator function to obtain the byte buffer per
client
        //the function will check if the buffer terminates with the CRLF
then in the case will create a new buffer otherwise it will concat the
previous buffer with the new byte
        .Scan((last, i) => new { last.Key, buffer =
last.buffer.Skip(last.buffer.Count() - 2).SequenceEqual(crlf) ? i.buffer :
last.buffer.Concat(i.buffer) })
        //wait the CR+LF message to read per row
        .Where(x => x.buffer.Skip(x.buffer.Count() -
2).SequenceEqual(crlf));

    //subscribe to the client sequence
    clientSequence.Subscribe(row =>
        Console.WriteLine("{0} -> {1}", row.Key,
Encoding.ASCII.GetString(row.buffer.ToArray())));
});
```

Disposing Create<T>

In the previous examples, we often saw the use of the `Create` operator to start flowing messages based on our needs without the right implementation of the `IDisposable` interface to handle multithreaded code because of editorial needs (shortness and readability). In a real-world application, mostly, it is a good idea to provide the right cancellation support to our sequences, although created with a low level `Create` operator.

Here is the complete example:

```
var sequence = Observable.Create<int>(observer =>
{
    //a task is required for all time consuming activities
    Task.Factory.StartNew(() =>
    {
        for (int i = 0; i < 100; i++)
```

```
    {
        //lot of CPU time
        Thread.SpinWait(10000000);
        //diagnostic output
        Debug.WriteLine(string.Format("Flowing value: {0}", i));
        //flow out a message
        observer.OnNext(i);
    }

    observer.OnCompleted();
});

    return Disposable.Empty;
});


var subscription = sequence.Subscribe(x => Console.WriteLine(x));

//wait 5 seconds
Thread.Sleep(1000);
//kill the subscription
subscription.Dispose();

Console.ReadLine();
```

The preceding example shows that although we can stop the subscription as we wish (effectively the observer stops receiving messages), the inner loop will continue wasting our resources. In the case of the usage of Task in the Create inner implementation, we can use the Task cancellation to gracefully stop the loop.

Here is an example:

```
var sequence = Observable.Create<int>(observer =>
{
    var cts = new CancellationTokenSource();
    var token = cts.Token;

    var task = Task.Factory.StartNew(() =>
    {
        for (int i = 0; i < 100; i++)
        {
            //raise an exception to stop thread's execution on task
cancellation
             request
            token.ThrowIfCancellationRequested();

            //lot of CPU time
            Thread.SpinWait(10000000);
```

```
            //diagnostic output
            Debug.WriteLine(string.Format("Flowing value: {0}", i));
            //flow out a message
            observer.OnNext(i);
        }
    }, token);

    //executes the following action at the subscription disposal
    return Disposable.Create(() => cts.Cancel());
});
```

This other implementation of the `Create` operator will correctly handle the subscription's disposal by stopping the inner loop from wasting resources.

If we are lazy, we can avoid implementing the `Disposable.Create` method by using a `Disposable` object from the `System.Reactive.Disposable` namespace. The direct substitute to raise a `Task` cancellation is `CancellationDisposable`:

```
//raise the token cancellation at the disposal
return new CancellationDisposable(cts);
```

Other usable disposables are as follows:

- `BooleanDisposable`: We can check for the dispose status with a Boolean flag
- `ContextDisposable`: Routes the disposal to `SynchronizationContext`
- `SerialDisposable`: We can change the underlying disposable object with a new one causing the old one's disposal
- `CompositeDisposable`: Disposes multiple resources
- `ScheduledDisposable`: We can schedule the disposal within our scheduler
- `RefCountDisposable`: Waits for referred disposables that are already disposed before triggering the disposal of their inner disposable resources
- `SingleAssignmentDisposable`: The underlying disposable resource can never change
- `MultipleAssignmentDisposable`: We can reuse the inner disposable resource in other `MultipleAssignmentDisposable` objects

In the rare case where we have still not found our right disposing design, as in the case where we don't have a loop that lets us check for the `Task` cancellation, we can still make a low-level `Thread` kill with the usage of the `Thread.Abort` method.

Here is an example:

```
var sequence = Observable.Create<int>(observer =>
{
    var thread = new Thread(new ThreadStart(() =>
    {
        for (int i = 0; i < 100; i++)
        {
            //lot of CPU time
            Thread.SpinWait(10000000);
            //diagnostic output
            Debug.WriteLine(string.Format("Flowing value: {0}", i));

            Thread.BeginCriticalRegion();
            //don't kill me here
            Thread.EndCriticalRegion();

            //flow out a message
            observer.OnNext(i);
        }
    }));

    thread.Start();

    //executes the following action at the subscription disposal
    return Disposable.Create(() => thread.Abort());
});
```

As is evident in the previous example, there is the ability to specify a `Critical` section to avoid killing `Thread` in a potentially dangerous code block. Although we have the ability to specify a `Critical` section, killing `Thread` is always something potentially dangerous because it may lead to state-drive systems in unwanted states or with data inconsistency that is usually difficult to diagnose.

Designing a custom provider

When designing a custom operator is not enough for our needs, we can write a custom provider similar to what happens with LINQ.

Within the Rx world, we can write a custom provider by implementing the `IQbservable` interface. This interface acts in a similar way as the `IQueryable` interface of LINQ that exposes a query made by `Expression` that may contain any composition of `Linq.Expression` in a hierarchical structure that names the `Expression` tree.

The creation of a custom provider is outside the scope of this book because it needs deep LINQ knowledge and requires a lot of pages. As a suggestion to anyone wanting to try writing their own custom provider, there are valid examples and already made providers that can behave as a starting point to design the wanted provider.

A custom provider overview (MSDN) with a downloadable example can be found at the following link:

```
https://msdn.microsoft.com/en-us/library/hh242971(v=vs.103).aspx
```

The `IQbservable` interface (MSDN) is available at:

```
https://msdn.microsoft.com/en-us/library/system.reactive.linq.iqbservab
leprovider(v=vs.103).aspx
```

The `IQbservable` over wire (Dave Sexton) can be found at the following link:

```
http://davesexton.com/blog/post/LINQ-to-Cloud-IQbservable-Over-the-Wire
.aspx
```

Designing a custom scheduler

Usually, all the needed schedulers already exists. Although, sometimes, it may happen that we may need a custom scheduler because we may need to choose how to schedule our jobs by ourselves. In the next example, we will see how to create a scheduler to throttle message flowing based on the CPU time. The `CpuThrottlingScheduler` method will verify each message flowing if the CPU time is at the desired level. Then, eventually, the obscrver's implementation will receive the message in the context thread of the `ThreadPool` thread to achieve multithreading if multiple subscribers exist.

Here is the scheduler code:

```
/// <summary>
/// Enqueues unit of works only if the current CPU time is lower than the
/// specified limit.
/// </summary>
public class CpuThrottlingScheduler : IScheduler, IDisposable
{
    public int CpuLimitPercentage { get; set; } = 80;
    public DateTimeOffset Now { get; private set; }

    private static PerformanceCounter cpuTimeCounter = new
```

```csharp
PerformanceCounter("Processor Information", "% Processor Time", "_Total");
    public IDisposable Schedule<TState>(TState state, Func<IScheduler,
TState, IDisposable> action)
    {
        while (true)
        {
            //checks the CPU time
            var cpu = cpuTimeCounter.NextValue();
            if (cpu >= CpuLimitPercentage)
                Thread.Sleep(200);
            else
                break;
        }

        //once the CPU time is lower than the limit
        //enqueue the job on the thread pool
        new Thread(new ThreadStart(() => action(this, state))).Start();
        Now += TimeSpan.FromTicks(1);

        return Disposable.Empty;
    }

    /// <summary>
    /// Not supported! Will be scheduled immediately
    /// </summary>
    public IDisposable Schedule<TState>(TState state, DateTimeOffset
dueTime, Func<IScheduler, TState, IDisposable> action)
    {
        return Schedule<TState>(state, action);
    }

    /// <summary>
    /// Not supported! Will be scheduled immediately
    /// </summary>
    public IDisposable Schedule<TState>(TState state, TimeSpan dueTime,
Func<IScheduler, TState, IDisposable> action)
    {
        return Schedule<TState>(state, action);
    }

    public void Dispose()
    {
        cpuTimeCounter.Dispose();
    }
}
```

As can be seen, the class `CpuThrottlingScheduler` implements the `IScheduler` interface. In this implementation, we're not dealing with future scheduling because this kind of `scheduler` works best for immediate scheduling. The `Schedule` method body executes a check against the CPU time performance counter, waiting until the value is within the limit. Then, the job is sent to `ThreadPool` for execution.

Here is the usage code:

```
var scheduler = new CpuThrottlingScheduler() { CpuLimitPercentage = 50 };

//a simple looping sequence
var sequence = Observable.Range(0, 50, scheduler);

//a huge observer list
for (int i = 0; i < 10; i++)
    sequence.Subscribe(x=>
    {
        Thread.SpinWait(100000000);
        Console.WriteLine("{0} -> {1}",
Thread.CurrentThread.ManagedThreadId, x);
    });

Console.ReadLine();
```

As we have already seen in `Chapter 6`, *CLR Integration and Event Scheduling*, we're specifying the `scheduler` class as a parameter of the `Range` operator. Later, multiple observers will subscribe to the sequence by inheriting the same `scheduler` class of the underlying sequence. The scheduler configuration set a 50% time limit to the CPU usage; this means that wherever our other applications use the CPU time more than the limit, the `scheduler` class will continue throttling requests until the CPU time is lower than specified.

Although this implementation is too simplified for editorial needs, it shows us the powerfulness of the scheduling that supports complete customization.

Dealing with the scheduler state

In the previous example about `IScheduler` implementation, we had the opportunity to see that the `scheduler` class supports a state value. Although in a reactive world, it is something odd to deal with, sometimes, we need the help of some external variables to complete our task.

Anytime we use external variables, an unintentional behavior may happen. Although a `Scheduler` schedules the execution of its jobs in the virtual time following its own order (the virtual time and then the registration time of jobs), this doesn't means that other involved CLR objects will do the same, eventually causing unwanted inconsistent data states. Take a look at `Thread` from `ThreadPool` or `Task` that will execute the inner job action; although `Scheduler` will follow the right order in firing these jobs, the CLR object may alter the right execution order by some milliseconds. This is why immediate scheduling may produce unpredictable behaviors that we should avoid. In case we cannot avoid this design, we could be in a situation like the following example:

```
int value = 0;

//a scheduler
var scheduler = Scheduler.Default;

//multiple immediate jobs
scheduler.Schedule(x => { value = 14; });
scheduler.Schedule(x => { Console.WriteLine(value); });
scheduler.Schedule(x => { value = 15; });
scheduler.Schedule(x => { Console.WriteLine(value); });
scheduler.Schedule(x => { value = 16; });
scheduler.Schedule(x => { Console.WriteLine(value); });
```

Although, usually, the result is correct, often, there is a repetition of the same value in the console output of this code.

> Respecting reactive jobs, this behavior of using the same external (and distant talking about layers) variable creates `Action` at a distance anti-pattern. More information on `Action` at a distance anti-pattern is available here:
> `https://en.wikipedia.org/wiki/Action_at_a_distance_(compu ter_programming)`

To avoid this unwanted behavior, we can pass the state variable within the `Schedule` method instead of letting the `Lambda` function embed it into the `Lambda` scope itself. Here is an example:

```
value = 14;
scheduler.Schedule<int>(value, (_scheduler, state) =>
{
    Console.WriteLine(state);
    return Disposable.Empty;
});

value = 15;
```

```
scheduler.Schedule<int>(value, (_scheduler, state) =>
{
    Console.WriteLine(state);
    return Disposable.Empty;
});

value = 16;
scheduler.Schedule<int>(value, (_scheduler, state) =>
{
    Console.WriteLine(state);
    return Disposable.Empty;
});
```

This overload of the Schedule method accepts a state parameter and Action that contains Scheduler itself and the state parameter, as it was valued when the job was scheduled. A great difference from the previous example is that, although we cannot guarantee the execution order of CLR objects (Threads) involved in the execution, we can now guarantee that all the three values will output correctly.

Creating Pattern<T>

The Pattern<T> is an odd kind of message that we can use to create flattened sequences of values sourcing from multiple sources.

As we have already seen in the *Combining operators* section of Chapter 3, *Reactive Extension Programming,* we can use the Zip operator to create a single output from multiple sources:

```
var values2 = Observable.Range(0, 100).Where(x => x % 2 == 0);
var values3 = Observable.Range(0, 100).Where(x => x % 3 == 0);
var values5 = Observable.Range(0, 100).Where(x => x % 5 == 0);

//flatten sourcing sequences into a new sequence
//based on the sourcing message index
var zip = values2.Zip(values3, values5, (a, b, c) => new { a, b, c });

Console.WriteLine("Zip:");
zip.Subscribe(x => Console.WriteLine(x));
```

Other than the Zip operator, the Rx library give us the ability to create Pattern, a group of messages sourcing from different sequences at the same speed by correlating messages with their index in the sourcing sequence.

Here is an example:

```
//create a pattern by grouping messages based on their index
var pattern = values2.And(values3).And(values5)
    //then produce a single output
    .Then((a, b, c) => new { a, b, c });

//creates a sequence from the pattern
var then = Observable.When(pattern);

Console.WriteLine("Then:");
then.Subscribe(x => Console.WriteLine(x));
```

The key operators of the preceding example are And, Then, and When. The And operator creates the pattern from the sourcing sequences. Multiple uses of the And operator will increase the sourcing sequence's availability, making it later available to the Then operator. The Then operator will shape all the sourcing messages into a single message similar to what happens with the selector Action of the Zip operator. The difference is that the And operator produces an output we can store somewhere, flow somehow, or schedule in time, while the selector Action of the Zip operator offers less programmability.

At the end of the example, the Observable.When operator will flatten the pattern into an observable sequence usable as we're now used to. Just to be clear, the Pattern class is unable to directly interact with the core Rx interfaces.

Another interesting feature is the ability to flatten multiple patterns within the When operator.

Here is an example:

```
//multiple patterns
var values7 = Observable.Range(0, 100).Where(x => x % 7 == 0);
var values9 = Observable.Range(0, 100).Where(x => x % 9 == 0);
var values11 = Observable.Range(0, 100).Where(x => x % 11 == 0);

var pattern79 = values7.And(values9).And(values11).Then((a, b, c) => new {
a, b, c, });

//flatten multiple sourcing pattern into a new sequence
var then79 = Observable.When(pattern, pattern79);

//the message order will follow the sourcing patterns message index
Console.WriteLine("Then79:");
then79.Subscribe(x => Console.WriteLine(x));
```

As is evident in this last example, although the `Zip` operator is very powerful, the implementation based on `Pattern` made with the `And/Then/When` operators may give a higher programmability level and a great flexibility to use in our applications.

Implementing event sourcing with Rx

Event Sourcing (**ES**) is a software design that requires the persistence of events instead of results. In the *Programming experience* section of `Chapter 1`, *First Steps Toward Reactive Programming*, we had the opportunity to understand how to persist data in a reactive way. Even though this is not mandatory using ES when programming reactive, this is the most natural way of dealing with data persistence from an observable sequence.

> Talking exhaustively about ES is outside the scope of this book. We will assume the reader already has some knowledge about ES. Otherwise, here are some details:
> ES:
> https://msdn.microsoft.com/en-us/library/jj591559.aspx
> CQRS with Event Sourcing:
> https://msdn.microsoft.com/en-us/library/jj591577.aspx
> Further reading:
> *Microsoft .NET: Architecting Applications for the Enterprise, 2nd Edition, Microsoft.*

By implementing the ES design instead of persisting results at specific dates, we persist data exactly as we receive it from an external system or a user. This means that if a user creates an invoice on a web application, we will persist what the user changes, not the result of any change.

Usually, when working with Rx and ES, we are already working with **Command/Query Responsibility Segregation** (**CQRS**). This design asks the subdivision of business object retrieval (`query`) and business object persistence (`command`) from a unique global business domain. In other words, we will divide a classic domain into two specialized domains with the need of dealing, persistence, or retrieval.

Within this design, Rx fits perfectly into the `Command` side. We can create commands as Rx messages that can flow throughout multiple sequence operators to apply all the required transformations, validations, and business logic. At the end, these messages will flow to a persistence observer that will be in charge of storing these messages into a dedicated database. To persist this kind of data, the best fitting choice is using a NoSQL database that is able to persist documents without having to deal with external languages as SQL or different data layouts as what happens within a relational database. Obviously, this doesn't mean that we cannot use a relational database. We can. In the real world, we should, because together with an event persistence, usually, we need to persist an updated state to address the future needs of data retrieval of the huge amounts of events to compute the right ending state. Different from what happens in normal state persistence, this is only a data cache.

When dealing with data persistence messages, the ES behaves excellently with CQRS because when we create a specific object to model any single event or action our system may receive, this mapping will be pretty perfect. Differently, think of a classic object model that tries to model in the same classes the needs of data reading for the UI, data validations for user input, data consistency checks for business needs, and so on. At best it is difficult, at worst we're left with a nightmare to maintain.

Creating and validating an invoice

The following example will show how to create an invoice, validate an invoice, update an invoice detail, and add multiple validated items to get all the resulting calculations immediately. The example will not store data in a real persistence store. We will only take a look at the overall application's design. As already mentioned, any NoSQL database is the most fitting choice of doing such persistences, such as Microsoft DocumentDB, RavenDB, MongoDB, and so on.

Let's have some code. A simple validation framework is available to our application to make all the messages `validable` required within the observable sequence pipeline:

```
public interface IValidable { }

public interface IValidableObjectResult<T>
        where T : IValidable
{
    bool IsValid { get; }
    IEnumerable<ValidationResult> Result { get; }
    T Instance { get; }
}

public sealed class ValidableObjectResult<T> : IValidableObjectResult<T>
        where T : IValidable
{
    public bool IsValid { get; set; }
    public IEnumerable<ValidationResult> Result { get; set; }
    public T Instance { get; set; }
}

public static class ValidableObjectHelper
```

```
{
    /// <summary>
    /// Validates the argument
    /// </summary>
    public static IValidableObjectResult<T> Validate<T>(T arg)
        where T : IValidable
    {
        var context = new ValidationContext(arg);
        var errors = new List<ValidationResult>();

        if (Validator.TryValidateObject(arg, context, errors))
            return new ValidableObjectResult<T>()
            {
                Instance = arg,
                IsValid = true,
                Result = Enumerable.Empty<ValidationResult>(),
            };
        else
            return new ValidableObjectResult<T>()
            {
                Instance = arg,
                IsValid = false,
                Result = errors.AsEnumerable(),
            };
    }
}
```

Now that we're ready to validate messages, we can create all the basic message types to flow invoice events. We will only map the invoice creation, update, and item addition events that act as commands regarding the event sourcing:

```
/// <summary>
/// Represents a command message
/// </summary>
public interface ICommand { }

public class CreateNewInvoice : ICommand, IValidable
{
    [Required, Range(1, 100000)]
    public int InvoiceNumber { get; set; }

    [Required]
    public DateTime Date { get; set; }

    [Required(AllowEmptyStrings = false), StringLength(50)]
    public string CustomerName { get; set; }

    [Required(AllowEmptyStrings = false), StringLength(50)]
```

```csharp
    public string CustomerAddress { get; set; }

    //apply updates
    public static CreateNewInvoice operator +(CreateNewInvoice invoice,
UpdateInvoiceCustomerAddress updater)
    {
        if (!invoice.InvoiceNumber.Equals(updater.InvoiceNumber))
            throw new ArgumentException();

            return new CreateNewInvoice
            {
                InvoiceNumber = invoice.InvoiceNumber,
                Date = invoice.Date,
                CustomerName = invoice.CustomerName,
                CustomerAddress = updater.CustomerAddress,
            };
    }
}

public class UpdateInvoiceCustomerAddress : ICommand, IValidable
{
    [Required]
    public int InvoiceNumber { get; set; }

    [Required(AllowEmptyStrings = false), StringLength(50)]
    public string CustomerAddress { get; set; }
}

public class AddInvoiceItem : ICommand, IValidable
{
    [Required]
    public int InvoiceNumber { get; set; }

    [Required]
    public string ItemCode { get; set; }

    [Required(AllowEmptyStrings = false), StringLength(50)]
    public string Description { get; set; }

    [Required, Range(1, 10000)]
    public int Amount { get; set; }

    [Required, Range(-10000, 10000)]
    public decimal Price { get; set; }

    public decimal TotalPrice { get { return Amount * Price; } }
}
```

In the preceding code, there is an interesting method, the operator + that specifies the result of the addition of a `CreateNewInvoice` object with an `UpdateInvoiceCustomerAddresss` object. This lets multiple updating objects create newly running (updated) totals regarding the invoice's details. Later, we will see the usage.

Now, all the requirements are already set. The first step is having a subject to deal with that acts as a sequence for messages and targets for user inputs:

```
//the root sequence of all user input messages
var commandSource = new Subject<ICommand>();

//register the diagnostic output of all messages
commandSource.Materialize().Subscribe(Console.WriteLine);
```

Now that we have the sourcing sequence and a useful live logging system, we will create a reusable validation result sequence to route validation results from the commands flowing within our sequence:

```
//register validation error output
var validables = commandSource
    //routes only validable messages
    .OfType<IValidable>()
    //convert messages into validation results
    .Select(x => ValidableObjectHelper.Validate(x));

//filter in search of invalid messages
validables.Where(x => !x.IsValid)
    //notify the error on the output
    .Subscribe(x => Console.WriteLine("Validation errors: {0}",
string.Join(",", x.Result)));
```

With this sequence, we can easily evaluate invalid messages and produce outputs, as we saw in the preceding example. The same sequence is useful for producing results against valid messages. Mainly, there are two different types of valid messages we can see flowing: invoice detail messages and invoice item messages. To get the running total amount of the invoice, we need to filter the desired messages from other messages (with the `OfType` operator). Then, we need to group per invoice number and get the running total by applying an accumulator function:

```
//filter in search of valid messages
validables.Where(x => x.IsValid)
    //get back the command message
    .Select(x => x.Instance as ICommand)
    //routes only invoice item messages
    .OfType<AddInvoiceItem>()
    //group items per invoice
```

```
.GroupBy(x => x.InvoiceNumber)
.Subscribe(group => group
    //project the message to a new shape for getting the result
    .Select(x => new { NewItem = x, TotalPrice = x.TotalPrice })
    //apply the accumulator function to get the result
    .Scan((old, x) => new { NewItem = x.NewItem, TotalPrice =
old.TotalPrice +
    x.TotalPrice })
    //output the result
    .Subscribe(x => Console.WriteLine("Current total amount: {0:N2}",
    x.TotalPrice))
);
```

Similarly, we will filter, group, shape, and accumulate values regarding the invoice detail messages. But here, we will use the operator we've just created to add invoice detail and invoice detail update messages to get a new message with the last state:

```
//filter in search of valid messages
validables.Where(x => x.IsValid)
    //get back the command message
    .Select(x => x.Instance as ICommand)
    //routes only new invoices or invoice updates messages
    .Where(x => x is CreateNewInvoice || x is UpdateInvoiceCustomerAddress)
    //group items per invoice
    .GroupBy(x => x is CreateNewInvoice ? (x as
CreateNewInvoice).InvoiceNumber :
    (x as UpdateInvoiceCustomerAddress).InvoiceNumber)
    .Subscribe(group => group
        //apply the updates to get the last state
        //a custom "+" operator to apply updates to the original invoice
        //is available into the CreateNewInvoice class
        .Scan((old, x) => x is CreateNewInvoice ? x as CreateNewInvoice :
(old as
        CreateNewInvoice) + (x as UpdateInvoiceCustomerAddress))
        //change type
        .OfType<CreateNewInvoice>()
        //output the new invoice details
        .Subscribe(x => Console.WriteLine("Available an invoice nr: {0} to
{1}
        living in {2}", x.InvoiceNumber, x.CustomerName,
x.CustomerAddress))
    );
```

Event sourcing an invoice creation

Now, we're ready to execute a simple test to check the usage of all the commands:

```
Console.WriteLine("Return to start saving an invoice");
Console.ReadLine();

var invoicenr = new Random(DateTime.Now.GetHashCode()).Next(0, 1000);
//create a new invoice

commandSource.OnNext(new CreateNewInvoice { InvoiceNumber = invoicenr, Date
= DateTime.Now });
//now a validation error will flow out the sequence
Console.WriteLine("Return to continue");
Console.ReadLine();

//create a valid invoice
commandSource.OnNext(new CreateNewInvoice { InvoiceNumber = invoicenr, Date
= DateTime.Now.Date, CustomerName = "Mr. Red", CustomerAddress = "1234,
London Road, Milan, Italy" });
Console.WriteLine("Return to continue");
Console.ReadLine();

//updates the invoice customer address
commandSource.OnNext(new UpdateInvoiceCustomerAddress { InvoiceNumber =
invoicenr, CustomerAddress = "1234, Milan Road, London, UK" });
Console.WriteLine("Return to continue");
Console.ReadLine();

//adds some item
commandSource.OnNext(new AddInvoiceItem { InvoiceNumber = invoicenr,
ItemCode = "WMOUSE", Price = 44.40m, Amount = 10, Description = "Wireless
Mouse" });
Console.WriteLine("Return to continue");
Console.ReadLine();

commandSource.OnNext(new AddInvoiceItem { InvoiceNumber = invoicenr,
ItemCode = "DMOUSE", Price = 17.32m, Amount = 5, Description = "Wired
Mouse" });
Console.WriteLine("Return to continue");
Console.ReadLine();

commandSource.OnNext(new AddInvoiceItem { InvoiceNumber = invoicenr,
ItemCode = "USBC1MT", Price = 2.00m, Amount = 100, Description = "Usb cable
1mt" });

Console.WriteLine("END");
Console.ReadLine();
```

The overall result is an application to flow commands to subscribers that will inform users of the eventually available validation errors or will flow messages to the right accumulator functions to inform the user of the last invoice status.

Although the example is very simple and lacks in any kind of UI, it should show the difference with state-driven programming when dealing with invoice creation. An activity that usually any developer will be familiar with. To store messages into a database, simply save valid messages. Nothing more. We simply store commands without any transformation. Later, when we need to read back these messages from the database, we can get them back into another (or the same) sequence and they will be available to the application with the same behavior of the new messages. This is the difference with the state-driven system. Here, we can review whole command history read from a database instead of getting the only the final result.

Creating Interactive Extensions (Ix) operators

Ix is the LINQ-based operator library that contains operators similar to the ones available within Rx. The design goal of developing a library like Ix is reusing designs and solutions from reactive programming to state-driven programming.

The following examples require referencing the NuGet package `Ix-Main`.

This library is powerful to help developers get access operators reactive, like into classic state-drive **Programming with LINQ (PLINQ)**, without having to convert in sequences and back all enumerables. The usage is almost identical to the one with real Rx operators; the difference is that within Ix, there is the support of only a short list of operators. Let's see some operators in action:

```
var buffer = Enumerable.Range(0, 1000)
    //split enumerable into multiple buffers
    .Buffer(100);

//enumerate from the first enumerable
//in case of exception continue enumerating
//from the second enumerable
//similarly there is the OnErrorResumeNext operator
var catched = Enumerable.Range(0, 1000).Catch(Enumerable.Range(0, 1000));
```

```
//returns a list from a single instance
var returned = EnumerableEx.Return(10);

//retry if an error occurs
var retry = Enumerable.Range(0, 1000).Retry(10);

//creates an enumerable from a yielder
var enumerable = EnumerableEx.Create<int>(async yielder =>
{
    for (int i = 0; i < 1000; i++)
        await yielder.Return(i);
});

//start yelding values
var enumerableValues = enumerable.ToArray();

//opposite of Any
enumerable.IsEmpty();

//create a finite buffer of values
//materializing values only on usage
//instead ToArray/ToList always materialize
//act as a cache of elements from the source enumerable
var memoized = enumerable.Memoize();

//cause memoize to materialize the internal collection
var firstValue = memoized.FirstOrDefault();

//accumulator function
var runningTotal = enumerable.Scan((old, x) => old + x);
```

This is only a short list, even though there are very interesting operators, such as `Memoize` (caches enumerable data), `Scan` (accumulate running totals), `Catch/OnErrorResumeNext` for exception handling, and so on.

Another useful list is available here:

```
https://www.infoq.com/news/2011/07/Ix
```

Summary

In this chapter, you have seen Rx internals at work with the ability to create custom implementations or operators and schedulers. You even have an idea of how to create custom providers. Together, we had the opportunity to look at some case studies that help to illustrate more realistic implementations of Rx-based applications.

In the next chapter, we will see how to deal with classic functional F# programming and how to use F# in FRP.

F# and Functional Reactive Programming

8

F# (pronounced as F sharp) is an open source programming multiparadigm language introduced for the first time by Microsoft in Visual Studio 2010. F# is a first class member of the .NET Framework languages and derives from the ML family of functional languages. F# supports the functional paradigm in addition to the traditional object-oriented and imperative paradigm of the Microsoft .NET Framework. Microsoft Visual F# is the real language implementation of Visual Studio. In the previous chapters, we have already seen some examples of functional programming (the *Functional programming* section of `Chapter 1`, *First Steps Toward Reactive Programming*) written in C# using Reactive Programming concepts.

In the next two chapters, we will extend the information combining F# and Rx to introduce and understand **Functional Reactive Programming** (**FRP**).

In particular, in this chapter, we will see the following topics:

- The F# language and its syntax as an introduction to Functional Programming
- The key points to differentiate object-oriented and functional paradigm
- Functional design pattern (**Active Pattern**, **Pattern Matching**, choice result, and so on) and the types to implement them
- Asynchronous programming in F#
- Introduction to F# for Reactive Programming
- A few examples based on collections and the F# Rx functions
- The concepts of asynchronous data flow and push-pull bases through a real scenario

F# – first time

When we use .NET Framework, the first thought goes to languages such as C# and VB.NET. If you want to write a program or services using a functional paradigm, probably your choice would include other languages, for example, Erlang, Haskell, Scala, Wolframe Language (Mathematica), and so on.

This occurs for a variety of reasons, such as the following:

- The .NET Framework and its principal languages are related to object-oriented programming
- The syntax of F# and the applications in the functional paradigm are totally different from any other .NET language
- F# was born in Microsoft research and later used in specific sectors and environments
- More functional languages, some of which were created many years before, were thought of exclusively for this paradigm

Contrary to the reasons just written, F# is a very interesting language, because it combines the potential of the .NET Framework with a simple syntax and the functional paradigm.

Introduction to F# and FRP

F# is different from the C# and VB.NET languages. This is mainly due to the basic paradigm.

The principal features of F# are as follows:

- The types are immutable
- The concept of null values does not exist
- The concurrence never occurs if the context is purely functional
- The intrinsically multiprocessor approach for the reasons listed above

Moreover, writing functions in F# is very simple and advantageous because the syntax is very concise:

```
let sum a b = a + b
let add5 = sum 5
let result = add5 2 // the result value is 7
let result2 = add5 3 // the result value is 8
```

As you can see in the first row of the previous example, a `sum` function is declared between two values (a, b). In the second row, the function `add5` is equivalent to `sum 5`, where 5 is the value of the parameter a. The `add5` variable is a partial function because we have to declare the second parameter if we want to execute `sum`, as we can see in `result` and `result2`:

```
[0..100] |> List.map (fun x -> x * x)
    |> List.iter (fun y -> printfn "the value is: %i " y)
```

Instead, in the preceding example, you have more instructions concatenated with the `|>` (pipe forward) operator. In particular, declare a list of `int`. After this, for each value, it is applied to the square and it returns a new list. In the end, through `List.iter`, print a visual result value.

By using C# and **object-oriented programming** (**OOP**), the code to write these functions will be bigger than in F#. Instead, by using the functional paradigm with C#, the result would be more or less the same.

The functions `iter` and `map` are also a useful example to introduce the FRP.

The immutable and deduce type

One of the most important features of F# is the immutability. This is fundamental to writing a function that respects the algebraic principles:

```
//C# code
int x = 5;
x = x + 1;
```

In mathematics, no value attributed to x could solve the function `x = x + 1`. In F#, writing this code directly, without using the keyword `mutable`, would generate the following error:

```
//F# code:
let x = 5
x <- x + 1

error FS0027: This value is not mutable
```

 The operator `<-` indicates the allocation of the value to the right on the left-hand side (called variable). It is conceptually equal to the `=` operator in C# or VB.NET.

To execute this code correctly, it will be sufficient to change the declaration of x in the following way:

```
let mutable x = 6
```

The result of the operation using F# Interactive is as follows:

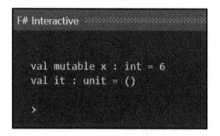

 F# Interactive is a tool available in Microsoft Visual Studio used to run F# directly. It also exists in another version called Fsi.exe and you can find it in the path c:\Program Files (x86)\Microsoft SDKs\F#\ <version>\Framework\ <version>\.

They both allow you to run F # code and the file .fsx (F# script).

 Performing the code is simple: you just have to select rows of interest and press Alt + Enter or right-click and use the command Execute In Interactive. The selected text will be executed by generating a result or an exception.
Instead, if you want to run script files, it's preferable to use Fsi.exe from the windows console by specifying the file path; in this way, you will get the result in real time in the output window.

Type inference

Another important feature of the language is its ability to *interpret the types*. In reality, this is not a real characteristic, but a technique for the system to deduce the type.

Indeed, F# has a powerful type inference system. Take a look at the following code:

```
//declare a tuple
let tupleValues = 1, "one"

//unpack values
```

```
let v1, v2 = tupleValues

let sumfloat values = List.reduce (+) values
printfn "The sum is: %A" (sumfloat [4.6; 10.3])
```

List.reduce is a function applicable to a list of values and reduces two elements of a collection to a single one. In the preceding example, the function List.reduce (+) values adds the first two elements of the collection. Then, the result is processed with the third element and so on, until the final result is obtained.

The same operation could be written using the operator pipe forward:

values |> List.reduce (fun x y -> x + y) or

values |> List.reduce (+)

In this example, in the first four lines, we have declared a tuple from which individual values are extracted. The result in the console F # Interactive is the following:

```
val tupleValues : int * string = (1, "one")
val v2 : string = "one"
val v1 : int = 1
```

Due to the inherent ability to infer the type, the compiler links v1 and v2 with the correct type, respectively, int and string. Similarly, for the subsequent lines, the first use of the function sumfloat is deduced by the declaration of the float type items of the list [4.6; 10.3]. The result is as follows:

```
The sum is: 14.9
val sumfloat : values:float list -> float
```

Functions as first class values

The title of this section is not easy to understand. It is true that the functions are the basis of F# and its paradigm, but first class values does not mean anything.

However, to make sense of these words, you need to think in functional programming sense.

The key to understand this is much easier than you might think.

F# is a functional language and, as such, it is functional-oriented.

This is one main difference compared to the other .NET languages, which are object-oriented.

Moreover, if one considers the functions in F#, they are everywhere. All of the examples, even the rows, done so far are functions!

Even the simplest of instructions, `let x = 5`, is a function.

For correctness, it is good to talk about identities and not pure values. In fact, when you declare an identifier assigning a value, it can no longer be changed.

Being functional-oriented forces F# to comply with certain rules and to have some benefits and drawbacks.

The rules are as follows:

- A function cannot change the status of the program
- The result of the function cannot be influenced from the outside
- Regarding immutability, each identifier is considered as a value and then it can be passed as a parameter or simply be the result of a function itself

The benefits are as follows:

- The factoring and refactoring is a plus with F# and its functions. Refactoring in F# does not require significant time and does not impact the entire project as in C#. This is true only if we apply functional paradigm.
- The pattern of composition is the basis of functional programming. In this way, you can interpret and solve any problem, from the most complex one to the simplest. Any function can be divided into simpler functions.
- The functional programming and, in particular, the syntax of functions make the code more concise and thus easier to maintain.

The drawbacks are as follows:

- F# is a functional programming language; consequently, it is mathematics-oriented, and writing functional code could take much more time than writing object-oriented code.
- It is not convenient to develop a whole application using F#, because both the development tools and some aspects of the project, such as the GUI, are not optimized for this language.

Naturally, these features are valid only in a functional context. By declaring an identifier using the keyword mutable, as seen previously, you can change the value of the identifier itself.

In mathematics, a function can be represented in this way: $y = f(x)$. Also, given a function, the same input value will give the same output value. This rule is one of the reasons why, in F#, it's easier to code and avoid concurrency.

Using the Type function for object-oriented programming

F# is *not only a* functional programming language. This is a fundamental principle to remember. By definition, F# is a programming language that provides support for functional programming in addition to traditional object-oriented and imperative (procedural) programming.

If you want object-oriented programming in F#, the language makes all the necessary constructs available. One of the main types of object-oriented programming is *classes*.

The syntax to declare a class is as follows:

```
type CustomerName(firstName : string, middleName, lastName) =
    member __.FirstName = firstName
    member __.MiddleName = middleName
    member __.LastName = lastName
```

The keyword __ is the equivalent of the keyword `this` in C#.

In the first row of the previous example, the keyword type suggests that `CustomerName` is a class. Unlike C#, you can see that the constructor signature is declared in the same row.

Instead, the keyword member indicates all the class members. In this particular case, members are properties, but they could be also methods.

It is very important to point out that let declarations in the classes have the same meaning as a private member in C#.

In the following example, you can observe how the signature of the `member` method is declared and one of these `this.SetMutable` method allows us to change the mutable value of the private member:

```
type MyClass(intParam : int, strParam : string) =
    let mutable mutableValue = 42
    member this.SetMutable x = mutableValue <- x
    member this.CurriedAdd x y = x + y
    member this.TupleAdd(x,y) = x + y
```

Like in C# and VB, in these functional languages, derivate and abstract class concepts exist:

```
type DerivedClass(param1, param2) =
    inherit BaseClass(param1)

[<AbstractClass>]
type GeometricBaseClass() =
    abstract member Add: int -> int -> int  // abstract method
    abstract member Pi : float // abstract immutable property
    abstract member Area : float with get,set // abstract read/write
property
```

TIP

It is interesting to see how the signature of the `add` method is written. Regarding `int -> int -> int`, the first two stand for parameters, and the last one is the result.

The code to declare `interface` is similar to the abstract class signature, as you can see in the following example:

```
type IGeometricBase =
    abstract member Add: int -> int -> int  // abstract method
    abstract member Pi : float // abstract immutable property
    abstract member Area : float with get,set // abstract read/write
property
```

The main syntax difference between the `abstract` class and `interface` is the signature. In the first one, the parenthesis must be written straight after the name, contrary to the other one.

Collection – The heart of F#

In the .NET Framework, when it comes to collections, the first thing that comes to mind is the **Language Integrated Query** (**LINQ**). It is a revolutionary component, included for the first time in .NET version 3.5, which provides a set of instructions and keywords to query objects, in particular, collections.

 The peculiarity of LINQ is its origin with functional nature. LINQ implements the functional paradigm through the use of query expressions, through extension methods, and the lambda expression related to the collections of the namespace `System.Collection.Generic`.

It is easy to see at this point how important the collections and all that concerns them are.

In F#, there are three major types of collection: `array`, `list`, and n. Each of them exhibits a set of functions and properties to elaborate the collection themselves.

`Array`, by definition, is fixed-size, zero-based, mutable collection of consecutive data elements that are all of the same type:

```
let myArr1 = [| 'a'; 'b'; 'c' |]
```

The `myArr1` variable identifies an array of chars. The keywords `[| |]` are used to declare `array` and, in this case, the values are entered by separating them with a semicolon(`;`).

There are many other ways to create `array`, and `array` of different dimension exist. Some of them are shown in the following examples:

```
let myArr2 = [| 1 .. 5 |]
let myArr3 - [| for i in 1 .. 5 -> i * i |]
let arrayOfZeroes : int array = Array.zeroCreate 5
let multiArr = [| [|0,0|]; [|1,1|] |]
```

 The keyword `..` specifies an interval of values and is an abbreviation of `for .. in`. Moreover, there is a variant that allows us to insert an increment value, as follows:

```
let arr = [|0..4..16|]
//val arr : int [] = [|0; 2; 4; 6; 8; 10; 12; 14; 16|]
```

 The function `Array.zeroCreate` creates an array with five values set to . There are many different ways to enter the items. It is important to remember that the value between square brackets refers to the position in zero-based.

```
let a = myArr2.[1] // 2
let b = myArr2.[2..] // 3,4,5
let c = myArr2.[..2] // 1,2,3
let d = multiArr.[1] // [|(1, 1)|]

myArr2.[1 ] <- 3 // to change a value
```

List, in F#, is an ordered and immutable series of elements of the same type. The syntax is not very different other than the keywords used for declaration; list uses [ ] and array uses [| |]:

```
let myList2 = [ 1 .. 5 ]
let myList3 = [ for i in 1 .. 5 -> i * i ]
let list = [0..2..16]
let a = myList2.[1] // 2
let b = myList2.[2..] // 3,4,5
let c = myList2.[..2] // 1,2,3
```

A sequence can be easily confused with list because both the collections are used to represent an ordered and huge series of elements, all of the same type. However, sequences, unlike lists, are useful if you do not want to use all the elements of the collection.

Elements can represent numerous data structures and can be managed in many different ways, for example, through some operations, such as grouping, counting, and extracting functions.

In F#, sequences are defined with the syntax seq<T> also known as IEnumerable<T>, as you can see in the following example:

```
let myseq1 = seq { 0 .. 10 .. 100 }
let myseq2 = seq { for i in 1 .. 5 do yield i * i }
let myList3 = Seq.init 5 (fun n -> n * 5)
```

The real power of arrays, lists, and sequences is their ability to manipulate data using their methods and the possibility to concatenate methods through the pipe operator or others.

In the following example, you can notice how simple it is to transform data and type collection only with a few instructions using the type array, sequence, and list. In the end, values are printed:

```
[| 1 .. 100 |]
    |> Seq.ofArray
    |> Seq.map (fun x -> x * x)
    |> List.ofSeq
    |> List.iter (fun y -> printfn "the value is: %i " y)
```

The code also suggests how essential it is to know collections and their methods. As you can see in the following table, there are so many methods and overloads of them that could be useful having on hand the table with all the possibilities (refer to complete table MSDN link `https://msdn.microsoft.com/en-us/library/hh967652.aspx`). Take a look at the following table:

Function	Array	List	Seq	Description
append	●	●	●	Returns a new collection that contains the elements of the first collection, followed by elements of the second collection.
add	–	–	–	Returns a new collection with the element added.
average	●	●	●	Returns the average of the elements in the collection.
averageBy	●	●	●	Returns the average of the results of the provided function applied to each element.
blit	●	–	–	Copies a section of an array.
cache	–	–	●	Computes and stores elements of a sequence.
cast	–	–	●	Converts the elements to the specified type.
choose	●	●	●	Applies the given function f to each element x of the list. Returns the list that contains the results for each element where the function returns Some(f(x)).
collect	●	●	●	Applies the given function to each element of the collection, concatenates all the results, and returns the combined list.
compareWith	–	–	●	Compares two sequences by using the given comparison function element by element.
concat	●	●	●	Combines the given enumeration-of-enumerations as a single concatenated enumeration.
contains	–	–	–	Returns true if the set contains the specified element.
containsKey	–	–	–	Tests whether an element is in the domain of a map.
count		–	–	Returns the number of elements in the set.
countBy	–	–	●	Applies a key generating function to each element of a sequence, and returns a sequence that yields unique keys and their number of occurrences in the original sequence.

copy	●	–	●	Copies the collection.
create	●	–	–	Creates an array of whole elements that are all initially the given value.
delay	–	–	●	Returns a sequence that's built from the given delayed specification of a sequence.
difference	–	–	–	Returns a new set with the elements of the second set removed from the first set.
distinct			●	Returns a sequence that contains no duplicate entries according to generic hash and equality comparisons on the entries. If an element occurs multiple times in the sequence, later occurrences are discarded.
distinctBy			●	Returns a sequence that contains no duplicate entries according to the generic hash and equality comparisons on the keys that the given key generating function returns. If an element occurs multiple times in the sequence, later occurrences are discarded.
empty	●	●	●	Creates an empty collection.
exists	●	●	●	Tests whether any element of the sequence satisfies the given predicate.
exists2	●	–	●	Tests whether any pair of corresponding elements of the input sequences satisfies the given predicate.
fill	●			Sets a range of elements of the array to the given value.
filter	●	●	●	Returns a new collection that contains only the elements of the collection for which the given predicate returns `true`.
find	●	●	●	Returns the first element for which the given function returns true. Returns `KeyNotFoundException` if no such element exists.
findIndex	●	●	●	Returns the index of the first element in the array that satisfies the given predicate. Raises `KeyNotFoundException` if no element satisfies the predicate.

findKey	–	–	–	Evaluates the function on each mapping in the collection, and returns the key for the first mapping where the function returns true. If no such element exists, this function raises `KeyNotFoundException`.
fold	•	•	•	Applies a function to each element of the collection, threading an accumulator argument through the computation. If the input function is `f` and the elements are `i0...iN`, this function will compute `f (...(f s i0)...) iN`.
fold2	•	•	–	Applies a function to the corresponding elements of two collections, threading an accumulator argument through the computation. The collections must have identical sizes. If the input function is `f` and the elements are `i0...iN` and `j0...jN`, this function will compute `f (...(f s i0 j0)...) iN jN`.
foldBack	•	•	–	Applies a function to each element of the collection, threading an accumulator argument through the computation. If the input function is `f` and the elements are `i0...iN`, this function will compute `f i0 (...(f iN s))`.
foldBack2	•	•	–	Applies a function to the corresponding elements of two collections, threading an accumulator argument through the computation. The collections must have identical sizes. If the input function is f and the elements are `i0...iN` and `j0...jN`, this function will compute `f i0 j0 (...(f iN jN s))`.
forall	•	•	•	Tests whether all the elements of the collection satisfy the given predicate.
forall2	•	•	•	Tests whether all the corresponding elements of the collection satisfy the given predicate pairwise.
get / nth	•	•	•	Returns an element from the collection given its index.
head	–	•	•	Returns the first element of the collection.
init	•	•	•	Creates a collection given the dimension and a `generator` function to compute the elements.

`initInfinite`	–	–	•	Generates a sequence that, when iterated, returns successive elements by calling the given function.
`intersect`	–	–	–	Computes the intersection of two sets.
`intersectMany`	–	–	–	Computes the intersection of a sequence of sets. The sequence must not be empty.
`isEmpty`	•	•	•	Returns `true` if the collection is empty.
`isProperSubset`	–	–	–	Returns `true` if all the elements of the first set are in the second set, and at least one element of the second set isn't in the first set.
`isProperSuperset`	–	–	–	Returns `true` if all the elements of the second set are in the first set, and at least one element of the first set isn't in the second set.
`isSubset`	–	–	–	Returns `true` if all the elements of the first set are in the second set.
`isSuperset`	–	–	–	Returns `true` if all the elements of the second set are in the first set.
`iter`	•	•	•	Applies the given function to each element of the collection.
`iteri`	•	•	•	Applies the given function to each element of the collection. The integer that's passed to the function indicates the index of the element.
`iteri2`	•	•	–	Applies the given function to a pair of elements that are drawn from matching indices in two arrays. The integer that's passed to the function indicates the index of the elements. The two arrays must have the same length.
`iter2`	•	•	•	Applies the given function to a pair of elements that are drawn from matching indices in two arrays. The two arrays must have the same length.
`length`	•	•	•	Returns the number of elements in the collection.
`map`	•	•	•	Builds a collection whose elements are the results of applying the given function to each element of the array.

map2	●	●	●	Builds a collection whose elements are the results of applying the given function to the corresponding elements of the two collections pairwise. The two input arrays must have the same length.
map3	–	●	–	Builds a collection whose elements are the results of applying the given function to the corresponding elements of the three collections simultaneously.
mapi	●	●	●	Builds an array whose elements are the results of applying the given function to each element of the array. The integer index that's passed to the function indicates the index of the element that's being transformed.
mapi2	●	●	–	Builds a collection whose elements are the results of applying the given function to the corresponding elements of the two collections pairwise, also passing the index of the elements. The two input arrays must have the same length.
max	●	●	●	Returns the greatest element in the collection, compared by using the max operator.
maxBy	●	●	●	Returns the greatest element in the collection, compared by using max on the function result.
maxElement	–	–	–	Returns the greatest element in the set according to the ordering that's used for the set.
min	●	●	●	Returns the least element in the collection, compared by using the min operator.
minBy	●	●	●	Returns the least element in the collection, compared by using the min operator on the function result.
minElement	–	–	–	Returns the lowest element in the set according to the ordering that's used for the set.
ofArray	–	●	●	Creates collection that contains the same elements as the given array.
ofList	●	–	●	Creates collection that contains the same elements as the given list.
ofSeq	●	●	–	Creates collection that contains the same elements as the given sequence.

pairwise	–	–	●	Returns a sequence of each element in the input sequence and its predecessor except for the first element, which is returned only as the predecessor of the second element.
partition	●	●	–	Splits the collection into two collections. The first collection contains the elements for which the given predicate returns `true`, and the second collection contains the elements for which the given predicate returns `false`.
permute	●	●	–	Returns an array with all the elements permuted according to the specified permutation.
pick	●	●	●	Applies the given function to successive elements, returning the first result where the function returns `Some`. If the function never returns `Some`, `KeyNotFoundException` will be raised.
readonly	–	–	●	Creates a sequence object that delegates to the given sequence object. This operation ensures that a type cast can't rediscover and mutate the original sequence. For example, if given an array, the returned sequence will return the elements of the array, but you can't cast the returned sequence object to an array.
reduce	●	●	●	Applies a function to each element of the collection, threading an accumulator argument through the computation. This function starts by applying the function to the first two elements, passes this result into the function along with the third element, and so on. The function returns the final result.
reduceBack	●	●	–	Applies a function to each element of the collection, threading an accumulator argument through the computation. If the input function is `f` and the elements are `i0...iN`, this function will compute `f i0 (...(f iN-1 iN))`.
remove	–	–	–	Removes an element from the domain of the map. No exception is raised if the element isn't present.
replicate	–	●	–	Creates a list of a specified length with every element set to the given value.

rev	●	●	–	Returns a new list with the elements in reverse order.
scan	●	●	●	Applies a function to each element of the collection, threading an accumulator argument through the computation. This operation applies the function to the second argument and the first element of the list. The operation then passes this result into the function along with the second element and so on. Finally, the operation returns the list of intermediate results and the final result.
scanBack	●	●	–	Resembles the foldBack operation but returns both the intermediate and final results.
singleton	–	–	●	Returns a sequence that yields only one item.
set	●	–	–	Sets an element of an array to the specified value.
skip	–	–	●	Returns a sequence that skips N elements of the underlying sequence and then yields the remaining elements of the sequence.
skipWhile	–	–	●	Returns a sequence that, when iterated, skips elements of the underlying sequence while the given predicate returns true and then yields the remaining elements of the sequence.
sort	●	●	●	Sorts the collection by element value. Elements are compared using compare.
sortBy	●	●	●	Sorts the given list by using keys that the given projection provides. Keys are compared using compare.
sortInPlace	●	–	–	Sorts the elements of an array by mutating it in place and using the given comparison function. Elements are compared by using compare.
sortInPlaceBy	●	–	–	Sorts the elements of an array by mutating it in place and using the given projection for the keys. Elements are compared by using compare.
sortInPlaceWith	●	–	–	Sorts the elements of an array by mutating it in place and using the given comparison function as the order.

sortWith	●	●	–	Sorts the elements of `collection` using the given `comparison` function as the order and returning a new collection.
sub	●	–	–	Builds an array that contains the given subrange that's specified by starting `index` and `length`.
sum	●	●	●	Returns the sum of the elements in the collection.
sumBy	●	●	●	Returns the sum of the results that are generated by applying the function to each element of the collection.
tail	–	●	–	Returns the list without its first element.
take	–	–	●	Returns the elements of the sequence up to a specified count.
takeWhile	–	–	●	Returns a sequence that, when iterated, yields the elements of the underlying sequence while the given predicate returns true and then returns no more elements.
toArray	–	●	●	Creates an array from the given `collection`.
toList	●	–	●	Creates a list from the given `collection`.
toSeq	●	●	–	Creates a sequence from the given `collection`.
truncate	–	–	●	Returns a sequence that, when enumerated, returns no more than *N* elements.
tryFind	●	●	●	Searches for an element that satisfies a given predicate.
tryFindIndex	●	●	●	Searches for the first element that satisfies a given predicate and returns the index of the matching element or `None` if no such element exists.
tryFindKey	–	–	–	Returns the key of the first mapping in the collection that satisfies the given predicate or returns `None` if no such element exists.
tryPick	●	●	●	Applies the given function to successive elements, returning the first result where the function returns something for some value. If no such element exists, the operation will return `None`.

unfold	–	–	●	Returns a sequence that contains the elements that the given computation generates.
union	–	–	–	Computes the union of the two sets.
unionMany	–	–	–	Computes the union of a sequence of sets.
unzip	●	●	●	Splits a list of pairs into two lists.
unzip3	●	●	●	Splits a list of triples into three lists.
windowed	–	–	●	Returns a sequence that yields the sliding windows of containing elements that are drawn from the input sequence. Each window is returned as a fresh array.
zip	●	●	●	Combines the two collections into a list of pairs. The two lists must have equal lengths.
zip3	●	●	●	Combines the three collections into a list of triples. The lists must have equal lengths.

In addition, in the next paragraph, you will see how to apply a case condition for each possibility of interrogation, manipulation, or extrapolation data.

F# – how to use it

Up to this point, we have been discussing the general characteristics of F# without even taking into consideration FRP. In addition, we have seen some of the theoretical aspects of the language. They detailed the general nature of the programming that is functional through simple examples.

Through this section, we will show how you can leverage the features of F#: both syntactic and technical. We will precisely discuss this in the various sections of some constructors required to exploit the full potential of the language. In this way, it will be easier to introduce and above all understand FRP, which will be addressed later.

In detail, you will see the following:

- Pattern Matching and pipeline for very concise code and functions
- **Record** type and **Discriminate Union** to represent and query simple types in F#
- Active Pattern to customize the code used in Pattern Matching

Pattern Matching and pipe forward

Pattern Matching is a very important model for comparison. In particular, through Pattern Matching, you can write input data conditions and output actions to transform data from the condition to the right action. Pattern Matching can be a constructor, or a model, or perhaps, even better called a *syntax to compare*.

It is easy; refer to the following code:

```
let v1 = 3
let v2 = 2

let printEvenOdd x =
    match x % 2 with
    | 0 -> printfn "The value is odd"
    | _ -> printfn "The value is even"

printEvenOdd v1
printEvenOdd v2
```

The result for v1 and v2 will be even and odd, respectively.

The composition of this pattern requires an expression of control to indicate the keywords match <expression> with =. Then, it should include a set of models of the condition and the result to be obtained. The expected syntax is the following: | pattern [when condition] -> result-expression.

All of this is similar to the switch case of C#, but in fact, Pattern Matching is much more powerful.

 The heart of this matching is the pattern of the condition. The model can be any constant or identifier, any Boolean condition, list, array, tuple, record, type, wildcard, and much more.

In the example, you can see precisely the use of the wildcard (_). This is a jolly character and represents a *placeholder* for any input value that does not match a specific case of a result or simply groups all the other values in a single output. The wildcard can be seen as the default keyword in the C# switch construct.

In the syntax of the pattern condition | `pattern [when condition] -> result-expression,` when is an optional keyword to indicate or compare, for example, group-specific cases. For example, the following code is used to compare the first value to the second:

```
let compareTwoValue x =
    match x with
    | (v1, v2) when v1 > v2 -> printfn "%d is greater than %d" v1 v2
    | (v1, v2) when v1 < v2 -> printfn "%d is less than %d" v1 v2
    | (v1, v2) -> printfn "%d equals %d" v1 v2

compareTwoValue (0, 1)
compareTwoValue (1, 0)
compareTwoValue (0, 0)
```

Once you understand the operation of Pattern Matching, it is easy to see that, in the functional-oriented context, writing code using Pattern Matching instead of the usual comparison conditions, such as `if <..> then <..> else`, is a best practice. In fact, the design of the code turns out to be cleaner and certainly more concise.

Pipeline and composition

Pipe forward is one of the most commonly used operators in F#. It is so common that it has been used since the earliest examples of the chapter. The operation is very simple and it involves the passage of the result of the one work to the next one.

There are two types of operator. They are as follows:

- The classic pipe forward (|>) passes the result of the operation to the left toward the right function. Refer to the following example:

```
[ 0..10 ] |> List.iter (fun x -> printfn "the value is %d" x)
```

- The pipe backward (<|) inversely passes the result of the operation to the right toward the left function. Refer to the following example:

```
List.iter (fun x -> printfn "the value is %d" x) <| [ 0..10]
```

The `Composition` operator (forward is `>>` and backward is `<<`) is similar to pipeline, but it is used to concatenate the n functions with a single result, as shown in the following example:

```
let add1 x = x + 1
let times2 x = 2 * x

let Compose2 = add1 >> times2 //Forward
let Compose1 = add1 << times2 //Backward

Compose2 1 //The result is 4
Compose1 1 //The result is 4
```

> The main difference between `pipeline` and `composition` is the signature and the use. The `pipeline` operator takes functions and arguments, while `composition` combines the functions.

Even through these two operators, it is known when the syntax of F# favors a concise code writing and, especially in this case, with the possibility of making it very readable. Nothing prevents you from writing multiple lines respecting the rules of indentation, or just one:

```
[ 0..10 ]
|> List.map (fun x -> x * x)
|> List.iter (fun y -> printfn "the value is: %i " y)

//or

[ 0..10 ] |> List.map (fun x -> x * x) |> List.iter (fun y -> printfn "the
value is: %i " y)
```

Discriminated Unions and the Record type

Discriminated Unions and Union types represent for the first time since the beginning of the chapter constructs not necessarily related to functional programming. They are essential to simplify the development of libraries and applications in F#.

The Record type is a set of simple values that are named and can optionally have members.

Their syntax is as follows:

```
[ attributes ]
type [accessibility-modifier] typename = {
    [ mutable ] label1 : type1;
    [ mutable ] label2 : type2;
    ...
    }
    member-list
```

Take a look at the following example:

```
//Record Type
type Point = { x : float; y: float; z: float option; }

let point2D = { x = 1.0; y = 1.0; z = None}
let point3D = { point2D with z = Some(-1.0)}
```

In this example, you can see some of the syntactic features of the Record type.

The keyword option declared during the type definition indicates that value can be inserted or not. None and Some (<value>) are used precisely to indicate in the first variable not assigned a value and in the second such award, respectively.

The keyword with preceded by an identifier already valued permits passing all the values of the first variable to the declaration of the new variable. In this way, we don't have to change the values every time, but we have the advantage to replace only the values that you want to change.

The Record type might seem like a class of C #, but in reality, there are some important differences. They are as follows:

- The fields come directly exposed as properties: in read-only by default and read-write with the keyword mutable
- In a Record type, you cannot define a constructor
- Importantly, the Record type, unlike classes, are compared as value types (similar to the structures of the C#) and not as reference types

Instead, Discriminated Unions provide support for *tagged* values with a label, forming a casuistic. In addition, each of them can have completely different values and types.

The syntax is as follows:

```
type type-name =
    | case-identifier1 [of [ fieldname1 : ] type1 [ * [ fieldname2 : ] type2
...]
    | case-identifier2 [of [fieldname3 : ]type3 [ * [ fieldname4 : ]type4
...]
```

An example is as follows:

```
//Discriminated unions
type Shape =
    | Rectangle of width : float * length : float
    | Circle of radius : float
    | Prism of width : float * float * height : float

let rect = Rectangle(length = 1.3, width = 10.0)
let circ = Circle (1.0)
let prism = Prism(5., 2.0, height = 3.0)
```

The `labelable` type can be anything. If there are no values, discriminated unions are similar to the enumeration of .NET. Instead, if there are values, each of them can be a primitive type or `tuple` or just one Record type.

One particular development of discriminated unions is the possibility to insert them into another through the association with a label. These discriminated recursive unions are used to represent the tree structures.

In Microsoft Visual Studio, by creating a new F# project called `Tutorial`, you can see the sample code of most language constructs.

Here, we will report a good example of Record and Discriminated Unions type. In addition, this code portion allows us to understand the concepts discussed previously with regard to the good design and conciseness of F#. Take a look at the following example:

```
type Suit = | Hearts | Club | Diamonds| Spades
    // Represents the rank of a playing card
    type Rank =
        | Value of int // Represents the rank of cards 2 .. 10
        | Ace
        | King
        | Queen
        | Jack
        static member GetAllRanks () =
            [ yield Ace
              for i in 2 .. 10 do yield Value i
              yield Jack
```

```
            yield Queen
            yield King ]
    type Card =  { Suit: Suit; Rank: Rank }
    // Returns a list representing all the cards in the deck
    let fullDeck =
        [ for suit in [ Hearts; Diamonds; Clubs; Spades] do
            for rank in Rank.GetAllRanks() do
                yield { Suit=suit; Rank=rank } ]
```

Active Patterns

Active Patterns are conceptually similar to discriminated unions. What really changes is how they are used, not the syntax.

By definition, it can be said that an active pattern is a set of called partitions used to compare the input data. Also, these partitions (labels) can be used in `expression`.

This is the syntax:

```
let (|identifer1|identifier2|...|) [ arguments ] = expression
let (|identifier|_|) [ arguments ] = expression
```

As we can see in the preceding code lines, there are two different implementations. They are as follows:

- **Complete Active Patterns**: They are described in the first row and all the labels are explicitly denominated. They must be a maximum of seven and each one must have a result return.
- **Partial Active Patterns**: It is similar, but one's choice must be the wildcard operator |_| seen previously. This operator is used to define all the cases in which the input must not be partitioned.

The main example to understand how to use the action pattern is as follows:

```
let (|Even|Odd|) input = if input % 2 = 0 then Even else Odd
```

Placing more than seven items in Visual Studio at write-compiled time phase would generate an exception. In this case, you might rethink the logic using the Record type.

Instead, an easy example of the partial Active Pattern is as follows:

```
let (|BooleanValue|_|) input =
    match input with
        | 0 -> Some true
        | 1 -> Some false
        | _ -> None

let IntBoolIdentification value =
    match value with
        |BooleanValue a -> printfn "The bool value is %b" a
        |_ -> printfn "The value is invalid"

IntBoolIdentification 0 //The bool value is true
IntBoolIdentification 1 //The bool value is false
IntBoolIdentification 2 //The value is invalid
```

It defines a partial Active Pattern that allows us to understand and extrapolate a Boolean value by an integer. For any value greater than one, nothing is returned (the keyword None).

A partial implementation must be composed exclusively of a single label and a single operator wildcard; otherwise, it will generate an exception.

Asynchronous pattern in F#

In the previous sections, we first discussed functional programming. Then, we introduced F# and its main features. Finally, we described how to use the most important constructs in the F# language. The meaning of all this is to be able to deal with the main topic: FRP.

An important element is missing in order to introduce FRP. This is required because without it, you cannot fully understand reactive programming.

F#, like any other language of the .NET Framework, supports asynchronous programming. It is crucial to perform portions of code in a separate thread.

The syntax for applying asynchronous code is really simple. The following is the syntax:

```
async { <expression> }
```

The code inserted in place of <expression> will be withdrawn in various ways through the use of specific types and their methods of asynchronous invocation. For example, the async class provides several methods that allow you to run this code on different threads.

A very important concept is surely to understand why asynchronous programming is crucial, especially in recent years.

The main task of `async` is to offer the ability to run code on different threads. In this way, the application will not have delays or even worse blocks during execution This will prove to be much more fluid to the end user.

In the next sections, we will show in detail all the features and keywords to be used in asynchronous programming.

The concept of asynchronous workflow

In .NET Framework, there are several ways to implement a workflow asynchronously. First of all, the workflow represents the complete management of our code asynchronously. That is, in addition to implementing the code, it will run the results returning any exceptions thrown in the threads and synchronization.

In F#, to do this, there are the syntax rules to be followed:

```
open System.IO

let fileContent (path : string) =
    async {
        use stream = new StreamReader(path)
        return stream.ReadToEnd()
    }

Async.RunSynchronously(fileContent "<filepath>")
```

The `use` keyword is used instead of `let` for all those objects that inherit from `IDisposable`. However, with `return`, it indicates what must be returned.

The behavior of `use-return` is analogous to C#'s `using`.

In addition, in the sample code, you can see how you can instantiate the object `StreamReader` belonging to the .NET Framework. The keyword `open` indicates the module or the namespace of the elements that you want to see without using the full name.

In this first example, you can see a function that returns the content of a file through its path. Inside the core of the function, the `async` keyword followed by a set of statements enclosed in brackets braces indicates the code to be executed in a context asynchronous.

Trying to run the code of the first two instructions into the `F# Interactive` console, the result would be `val fileStr : path:string -> Async<string>`. This is because any asynchronous method returns `Async <'T>`: an asynchronous operation, where `'T` stands for the return type. `'T`, in the example, is a string.

With the instruction `Async.RunSynchronously`, you can run the code in the current thread. In this way, it will be possible to extract the contents of the method.

The `Async` class is the heart of the asynchronous programming in F#. In the next section, we will see many of its features.

Asynchronous code and examples

In the previous example, it is shown how to extract from an `Async <'T>` type its generic through the method `Async.RunSynchronously`. But in some cases, it is necessary to wait for the execution of some asynchronous instructions and get their result.

Naturally, all of this must take place in an asynchronous context:

```
let tupleByteArray =
    async {
        use stream = new System.IO.StreamReader("<filepath>")
        let result1 = stream.BaseStream.AsyncRead(10)
        let! result2 = stream.BaseStream.AsyncRead(10)
        return (Async.RunSynchronously result1), result2
    }

let item1, item2 = Async.RunSynchronously tupleByteArray
```

In the last line of code, there is a special initialization syntax identifier. `letitem1, item2` allows you to extract the values of a `tuple` for each variable according to the internal sorting.

In the example, there are two identifiers: `result1` and `result2`. Both of them have an equal function core. However, they differ in the case of the keyword header identifier.

The keyword let! (unlike let) allows you to extract directly the generic types from an object Async <'T>, executing the following code synchronously. To be used, it must be inserted in an asynchronous expression. It will be used in the same way you use the use! keyword for the types that inherit from IDisposable.

The function tupleByteArray returns a tuple with two equal type items (byte[]). This is possible because, before returning the value, the call to the identifier result1 runs Async.RunSynchronously to extract the byte array.

Basically, it writes the following command:

```
let! result2 = stream.BaseStream.AsyncRead(10)
```

The preceding code is similar to the following:

```
let result1 = Async.RunSynchronously (stream.BaseStream.AsyncRead(10))
```

The Async object also provides a number of additional methods to run code in parallel. A very interesting example of how you can exploit parallelism with many other features of the class is by declaring a list of links that is calculated by the number of characters in the web page:

```
Open System.Net

let urlList =
    [ "Microsoft.com", "http://www.microsoft.com/"
      "MSDN", "http://msdn.microsoft.com/"
      "Bing", "http://www.bing.com" ]

let fetchAsync (name, url : string) =
    async {
        try
            let uri = new System.Uri(url)
            let webClient = new WebClient()
            let! html = webClient.AsyncDownloadString(uri)
            printfn "Read %d chars for %s" html.Length name
        with ex -> printfn "%s" (ex.Message)
    }

let runAll() =
    urlList
    |> Seq.map fetchAsync
    |> Async.Parallel
    |> Async.RunSynchronously
    |> ignore

runAll()
```

Using the pipe forward in this example shows the enormous potential of F#. Thinking about function-oriented code combinations, you can write functions that are structurally complex, but simple. All these have the ability to break up into simple functions.

The expression try...with is used to manage a possible exception that occurs within the statements enclosed between the two keywords. It is similar to the try...catch statement in C#.

One interesting feature is the syntax with which they have differentiated behaviors depending on the type of exception:

```
let divide2 x y =
  try
     Some ( x / y )
  with
     | :? System.DivideByZeroException as ex -> printfn
  "Exception! %s " (ex.Message); None
```

Finally, in this last example, it is shown how to simulate a kind of complex computational task:

```
// Simulate CPU calc.
let child() =
    for i in [ 1..4000 ] do
        for i in [ 1..400 ] do
            do "Fsharp".Contains("F") |> ignore

let parentTask =
    child
    |> List.replicate 30
    |> List.reduce (>>)

let asyncChild = async { return child() }

let asyncParentTask =
    asyncChild
    |> List.replicate 30
    |> Async.Parallel

//test single
#time
parentTask()
#time

//test async with parallel
#time
asyncParentTask |> Async.RunSynchronously
#time
```

In the previous code, there is a method that simulates an operation (`child()`) for calculation. Then, there are two other instructions through the function `List.replicate` that replicates the code of calculation *n* times.

One of the main key points in this code is how we can obtain some benefits (or not) if we run code in parallel. The preprocessor directive `#time` allows you to see inside the console `F# Interactive` some useful counters. Take a look at the following screenshot:

```
F# Interactive

--> Timing now on

Real: 00:00:05.988, CPU: 00:00:05.984, GC gen0: 124, gen1: 1, gen2: 0
val it : unit = ()

--> Timing now off


--> Timing now on

Real: 00:00:01.641, CPU: 00:00:10.593, GC gen0: 123, gen1: 1, gen2: 0
val it : unit [] =
  [|null; null; null; null; null; null; null; null; null; null; null; null;
    null; null; null; null; null; null; null; null|]

--> Timing now off

>
```

The screenshot shows that running in parallel is much more powerful than running it synchronously. In addition, the directive `#time` shows a series of useful counters. It is activated at the beginning and deactivated at the end of counting.

The counters are represented as follows:

- `Real`: This is the real-time execution expressed in `hh:mm:ss:fff`
- `CPU`: This is the sum of the calculation time of the CPU in `hh:mm:ss:fff`
- `GC`, `gen0`, `gen` and `gen2`: These are counters, `,1`, and `2` collections of `Garbage Collection`

F# Interactive (FSI) is a very powerful tool.

 The FSI tool is very useful, not only for F# developers, but also for those developing in C# or VB.NET. Having full access to the .NET Framework, you can query (in real-time) each library with a little knowledge of the basic syntax of F#.

In the following table taken from the website of Microsoft MSDN (https://msdn.microsoft.com/en-us/library/dd233175.aspx), you can see the main FSI directives of the preprocessor:

Directive	Description
#help	Displays information about available directives.
#I	Specifies an assembly search path in quotation marks.
#load	Reads a source file, compiles it, and runs it.
#quit	Terminates an F# Interactive session.
#r	References an assembly.
#time ["on"|"off"]	By itself, #time toggles whether to display performance information. When it is enabled, F# Interactive measures real time, CPU time, and garbage collection information for each section of code that is interpreted and executed.

Functional Reactive Programming

FRP, the central theme of the second half of the chapter, may be considered by definition as a programming paradigm. In fact, this paradigm is different from the more common ones, such as imperative, object-oriented and functional, because it applies only to Reactive Programming. The context of use is much smaller.

In the previous chapters, we understood how the library Rx represents all these data sequences as observable sequences and how it can be used to compose asynchronous and event-based programs.

Similarly, we will now introduce FRP exploiting objects and, in general, all the features of F# and functional programming. This is possible due to the inherent ability of the language to make almost every instruction in a function block.

In the following sections, we will see in detail the following points:

- What is FRP and how can you represent it?
- What are the main features and applicable scenarios?
- The concept of asynchronous data flow
- The types on push-based and pull-based

What is FRP and how is it represented?

We previously introduced FRP (acronym for Functional Reactive Programming) as a type of paradigm. Actually, it is not a real paradigm because it can be described using simple functions, similar to many other functional patterns.

To better understand this concept, we should take a little step back and discuss object-oriented programming, especially events. Events are everywhere and are the basis to understand FRP. Managing them individually is a very simple procedure, but if we want to develop more advanced functionalities, such as event handling, then it will become more complex.

Observer is a kind of design pattern based on events and it is one of the most common patterns in object-oriented programming. Furthermore, it is the basis of *Reactive Extensions* and *event flow*, as mentioned in the previous chapters.

 Instead, in functional programming with F#, Reactive Programming is supported natively through the functions themselves.

Reactive programming together with the functional paradigm explains the concept of FRP. This simplification is a starting point to better understand basic concepts up to more complicated ones.

Since FRP is based on functions, will it be possible to understand or simply represent it in .NET Framework and F#? Actually, we have already seen numerous examples.

 Consider the following code:
```
let numberList = [ 2.0; 4.0; 6.0]
let result = numberList |> List.map (fun x -> x**2.0)
```
The symbol ** is the mathematical operator that represents the mathematical function *power*. It is recommended in particular that the elements are of the double type.

The `map` method is a suitable example of FRP. In the same way, almost all the members of the type method of collections are appropriate examples, such as `filter`, `reduce`, `zip`, and many others.

In functional programming, one of the main features is immutability. Consequently, the methods that operate on the elements of collections don't modify the list itself, but instead they process a function event on every single element creating a new object.

In particular, in FRP, there are two different fundamental types of data: `Event` and behavior.

A value of the behavior type is characterized by the ability to continuously change over time. A classic example of behavior is all the time objects, but it could also be an `int` type or a constant (object color).

A value of the event type is instead a sequence of the occurrence of the `Event` itself with a value for each occurrence of the value type.

In the preceding example, both the types are represented: a flow of events that change the values in every element of the list by adopting the function `power` and returning a new sequence with different values.

 In other words, it is possible to combine different behaviors and events (`combinators`) together to create new ones, as seen in the example.

This introduces concept of *time flows*, which will be described in detail in the following chapters.

Introduction to functional reactive programming

FRP is defined as a programming paradigm for Reactive Programming. It is actually much more than that.

When we program in .NET, events are everywhere. Many of these events are based on the delegate called `EventHandler` and the base class called `EventArgs`. Along with object-oriented programming, they are used for the technique called event programming.

In Visual Studio, if you create a WinForm project, it will be clearly seen as it is set to work on events. Not only this, even the newest template **Windows Presentation Framework** (**WPF**) fully supports the programming events. Though, with the latter, it is more appropriate to use the **Model View ViewModel** (**MVVM**) pattern for a series of structural advantages and more.

With the expansion of asynchronous programming, the event-based model has evolved as well. As a consequence, in the .NET Framework, a standard called **Event-based Asynchronous Programming** (**EAP**) was developed. It will only make available the asynchronous methods that run on a different thread of the same operation as the corresponding synchronous method. Also, some of these classes exhibit events for flow control as asynchronous, such as `methodCompleted` or `methodCancel`.

FRP extends a host programming language with the notion of time flow. In this way, it will be possible to obtain powerful control over the flow of data through a model of observation (the `Observable` pattern).

Collections and functions in a flow

In the previous chapters dedicated to LINQ and C#, it has been shown that collections are at the heart of reactive programming. We will explain an example of FRP in F# that includes all the main features:

- The concept of time flow
- The intrinsic characteristics of the event flow
- The concept of asynchronous data flow and the `Observable` pattern

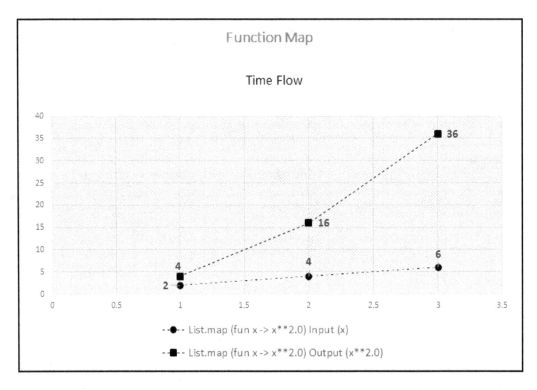

In the preceding graphic, the line with circular points shows the three input values of the list, while the line with square points, shows three output values to which the function `List.map` is adopted. It is important to notice how the function is gradually applied to every single value, respecting exactly the input time flow.

It means that the event of execution of the function is processed for each value added in the list. Furthermore, thanks to functional programming (in this case, to F# and the .NET Framework that provides this method by default) and its intrinsic features, this execution is completely thread safe. So, as a consequence, in terms of reactive programming, it is possible to obtain an asynchronous data flow.

FRP and its scenarios

We briefly introduced FRP and how we can use it in software applications. Actually, FRP is applicable not only to basic implementations as a synchronous or asynchronous event flow handling. We also can introduce a set of features able to solve different problems in a very simple way.

 Thanks to FRP, we can have a full-scale supervision of the entire event flow introducing the concept of continuous time, where events and behaviors are stream transformers.

So, we can see which possible scenarios are appropriate for FRP.

As previously described, given an event flow, we can execute some functions maintaining time flow control in a particular domain.

Therefore, there are particular domains suitablefor the reactive system. They are as follows:

- Interactive computer animation
- Robotics
- Control and real-time systems
- GUIs

Event data flow

We assumed so far, especially in the examples in the previous chapters, that in FRP, there is a flow of events and that these events can be defined as signals. Moreover, we understood that the workflow is well defined and it is processed in a synchronous way. Nevertheless, signals change continuously, so it could be necessary to interrupt or modify the flow. It could be essential having an asynchronous data flow.

Graphic applications better related to GUI are definitely some of the most interesting cases where we can verify how synchronous event data flows work.

For example, we can imagine the change of position or color of a graphic object inside an application.

It is essential to understand the following three concepts:

- Changes always occur through an event. For example, in the color type, a ValueChanged event related to any control that supports it can modify one or more of the three RGB channels.
- Changes can occur regularly, but in a completely discontinuous way. Once again, in the case of a change of the color type, it is not possible to predict neither how many times nor when an event originating from the user will occur.
- It could be necessary to filter or add some events. As an example, we could think of a user that frantically keeps changing the contrast value of an image. It is very expensive in terms of performance, and useless to reprocess the image if the new image is already elaborated.

Fortunately, F# and the assembly Fsharp.Core.dll in particular, can help us, and it makes available the Event type to manage the functions of the events themselves:

```
type Event<'T> =
 class
  new Event : unit -> Event<'T>
  member this.Trigger : 'T -> unit
  member this.Publish :   IEvent<'T>
 end
```

<'T> is the syntax that identifies generic type. Moreover, the Event type is also called FSharpEvent. It is important to know to use the object through reflection.

IEvent<'T> represents the interface every single event should have. It does nothing but combine the other two interfaces, IObservable<T> and IDelegateEvent.

In this way, an F# event through IDelegateEvent has at its disposal all the features of delegates of the event type of the .NET Framework. Thanks to the IObservable interface, it also acquires the ability to apply functions to events, such as filtering or mapping, as well as using the lambda expression. This is possible thanks to the Event module of F#, which exhibits all these member functions.

A very interesting example of how powerful it is to use the IObservable interface is the following example. It demonstrates how powerful the IObservable interface is. The code is taken from the Microsoft MSDN website (https://msdn.microsoft.com/en-us/library/dd233189.aspx) and it is slightly modified to avoid a runtime error:

```
open System.Windows.Forms
let form = new Form(Text = "F# Windows Form",
                    Visible = true,
                    TopMost = true)
form.MouseMove
```

```
|> Event.filter ( fun evArgs ->
    evArgs.X > 0 && evArgs.Y > 0 &&
    evArgs.X < 255 && evArgs.Y < 255)
|> Event.add ( fun evArgs ->
    form.BackColor <- System.Drawing.Color.FromArgb(
        evArgs.X, evArgs.Y, evArgs.X ^^^ evArgs.Y))
```

Interestingly, here we can see how, in three simple blocks of instructions, we created a form with the relative namespace. The form is composed of two different events, each of them with a specific behavior.

In the preceding code, we can see how the `Event.filter` function acts as a predicate. In fact, it also requires a lambda expression with the argument of the event (in this specific case, `MouseEventsArgs`) as a parameter and the results of a condition as a result value.

Consequently, if the condition is respected, the `callbackEvent.add` function will be processed and run the body function. For this reason, the background color of the window changes to the movement of the mouse through the coordinate positions of the mouse itself.

Given that the `Event` module is one of the F# first-class, it exposes a wide set of functions, as in most cases. You can refer to the following link on the Microsoft MSDN website `https://msdn.microsoft.com/en-us/library/ee340422.aspx`.

Some of the main functions are provided in the following table:

Value	Description
`add:('T -> unit) -> Event<'Del,'T> -> unit`	Runs the given function each time the given event is triggered.
`filter:('T -> bool) -> IEvent<'Del,'T> > IEvont<'T>`	Returns a new event that listens to the original event and triggers the resulting event only when the argument to the event passes the given function.
`choose:('T -> 'U option) -> IEvent<'Del,'T> -> IEvent<'U>`	Returns a new event that fires on a selection of messages from the original event. The selection function takes an original message to an optional new message.

Push and pull-based domains

In the previous chapter, we analyzed how it is possible to implement and use a synchronous data flow using F#. However, it represents only a part of FRP. In fact, we ignored the asynchronous world.

When discussing FRP, it is important to distinguish the two scenarios because they have two *different conceptual domains*. The synchronous and asynchronous domains reflect their different characteristics also in the strategy of implementation that is respectively push-based and pull-based.

So, we can better identify the two scenarios:

- When we refer to **synchrony**, we are in a push-based oriented context, which is a data-driven context typically used in reactive systems
- When we refer to **asynchrony**, we are in a pull-based oriented context, which is a demand-driven context, for example, any kind of behavior

If we think about the example mentioned in the previous section, it is easy to understand that we discussed a synchronous push-based oriented context, so we are in a reactive system.

 Usually, when the user or even an automation system generates events in graphical interface of software, we are using a reactive system.
In our specific case, in the .NET Framework, **Windows Presentation Foundation (WPF)** could be projects that implement events. Moreover, WPF can also implement `ObservableCollection`.

Let's see the main differences between these scenarios.

For push-based scenarios:

- Synchronous context
- Data-driven implementation
- No control creation
- An example of the representation interface in F# is `IObervable<T'>`
- Events change continuously and randomly, for example, `ButtonClick`

For pull-based scenarios:

- Asynchronous context.
- Demand-driven implementation.
- How rapidly the events are generated doesn't count; in fact, they are all elaborated because it is an asynchronous context.
- An example of the representation interface in F# is `AsyncSeq<T'>`.
- In this case, it doesn't matter when events change, but rather how they occur. In fact, the term behavior. As an example, usually, the parameter passed by reference is a `Time object` type.

It is useful knowing that there are particular scenarios in which it is possible to have both a push-based context and a pull-based context.

In the next section, we will find an example of a pull-based scenario.

Examples of scenarios with AsyncSeq

When we introduced the main features that distinguish the two different scenarios and pull-based in particular, we used the `AsyncSeq<T'>` representation as an example.

 `AsyncSeq` is a sequence in which individual elements are retrieved using an `Async` computation. It is similar to `seq<'a>`, where subsequent elements are demand-driven.

The assembly `FSharp.Control.AsyncSeq.dll` is not a part of the F# libraries natively, so this type of assembly must be downloaded using the NuGet console and referenced into the project:

```
#r
"../packages/FSharp.Control.AsyncSeq.2.0.8/lib/net45/FSharp.Control.AsyncSe
q.dll"
open FSharp.Control

let asyncSeq = asyncSeq {
    do! Async.Sleep(100)
    yield 1
    do! Async.Sleep(100)
    yield 2 }

let two = asyncSeq |> AsyncSeq.filter (fun x -> x = 2)
let res = two |> Async.RunSynchronously //result is 2
```

To download `FSharp.Control.AsyncSeq` from NuGet, we just have to select the right project in **Package Manager Console** and select **Install-Package** `FSharp.Control.AsyncSeq`.

The key word `do!` indicates the asynchronous execution of an instruction without any assignment (corresponding to `let! () = istr`).

Similarly, concerning the `Observable` interface mentioned in the preceding lines, another possibility is to filter the elements of the list using the specific method `AsyncSeq.filter`. The module `AsyncSeq`, indeed, exposes all the required functionalities of interrogation and modification together with the possibility of using the lambda expression.

The following lines show us how to create a sequence in a completely asynchronous context using the keywords `asyncSeq` and yield.

> On the other hand, if we tried to create a similar sequence with no asynchrony, then the access to static `Sleep` method of the `Thread` class would stop the execution of the thread itself:
>
> ```
> let syncSeq = seq {
>
>     System.Threading.Thread.Sleep(100)
>
>     yield 1
>
>     System.Threading.Thread.Sleep(100)
>
>     yield 2
>
> }
> ```

Summary

In this chapter, we introduced the F# language and the functional paradigm. This is essential if we want to understand how functional programming works. Furthermore, it is a necessary step if we want to apply and implement FRP. In particular, we discussed event data flow and the two kinds of FRP: pull-based and push-based.

In the next chapter, you will learn about FRP in depth, starting from the basic theoretical concepts to the practical examples of real scenarios. Afterward, we will enter the second part of FRP, where we will discuss advanced concepts such as discrete-continuous components and time-flow with dynamic change. Finally, we will look at different examples of the scenarios (pull- based and pull-based) using F# and FRP.

9
Advanced FRP and Best Practices

In the previous chapter, we introduced a 360-degree description of FRP. We discussed the main features related to this type of programming, passing from a theoretical introduction to the concrete examples of the scenarios. We also described how the `Event` module of the F# language exposes functionalities to manage the `Event` type delegate in the .NET Framework and how this module amplifies its capabilities, adding also a set of functionalities to manage events, such as collection (the `IObservable` interface). Finally, we conclude the chapter showing the main differences between *push-based* and *pull-based* scenarios.

FRP is not a simple subject to understand; in fact, it is frequently considered very difficult to assimilate. This problem depends on the complexity of the concepts; anyway, once you understand their meaning, it is not so straightforward to put them into practice. In other words, the only relatively simple aspect is the presence of objects that can create a more complete description of FRP.

This chapter aims to examine in depth the previous introduction of FRP, implementing the description with other information in order to have a general and complete overview of FRP.

In particular, we will discuss the following:

- Differences between the *discrete* and *continuous* components with related examples of scenarios
- Concepts of *time flow* and *dynamic change*, in detail, through a synchronous data flow
- Interoperability between the F# observable and FRP from a comparison to an example in the .NET multiparadigm

Discrete and continuous components

Discrete and continuous components are fundamental to better understand FRP. From the first introduction, one of the main axes is exactly the distinction between discrete and continuous. In the previous chapter, we analyzed many aspects related to these two components, but we never mentioned them. If we had so, then the argument could have been too complicated and theoretical.

By definition, discrete and continuous components can be described as the two main characteristics which FRP provides. In other words, they are the basics to apply time flow in our application or to improve our scenario of use.

We previously discussed the execution of the following function:

```
List.map (fun x -> x ** x)
```

While doing so, we introduced the concept of time flow to underline that every execution of the mathematical function *power* occurs step by step.

In the example, it seems that this scenario is continuous, because for every input value of the list, a new output value is generated.

Actually, with a more in-depth analysis, List.map could be seen as a *hybrid scenario*. In fact, the exponentiation of every single value shall be made according to the order of the elements, which is a prerogative of discrete scenarios.

As a consequence, we will obtain combinators made up of behavior and Event.

Most of the concrete applications of FRP adopt a hybrid scenario. This is because, given a time flow, it is highly probable using both the *time-varying* and *time-ordered* implementations.

In the next sections, we will discuss in more detail about discrete components, while continuous components will be treated later.

Discrete components

The Event module is the basis of discrete components. They are the milestones of FRP in an event-driven context.

In the previous chapter, we introduced the concept of signals.

 Events are a collection of particular signals that can be separated from one another as *discrete occurrences*.

In other words, each event is able to modify a reactive system independently from other signals. We will consider the following graphic:

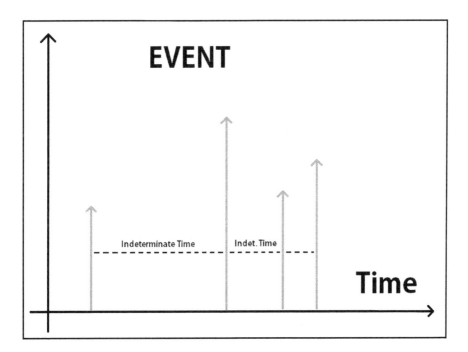

Each orange arrow shows the occurrence of an event. We can easily understand that it is *impossible* to determine when an occurrence happens between a signal and the next one.

In a discrete component, events are considered as a set and they are called `Event Stream`. This *event flow* is nothing but the scenario called *push-based* in the previous chapter:

```
open System.Windows.Forms
let form = new Form(Text = "F# Windows Form",
                    Visible = true,
                    TopMost = true)
form.MouseMove
    |> Event.filter ( fun evArgs ->
        evArgs.X > 100 && evArgs.Y > 100 &&          evArgs.X < 255 &&
evArgs.Y < 255)
    |> Event.add ( fun evArgs ->
        form.BackColor <- System.Drawing.Color.FromArgb(
            evArgs.X, evArgs.Y, evArgs.X ^^^ evArgs.Y))
```

It is interesting to notice that we can decide how to act once the occurrence happened. We can't stop the event, but only filter or ignore it.

This leads us to question ourselves that a discrete implementation is always possible in counting the number of occurrences, whether the count is finite or infinite.

For example, the graphical representation of the function $y=x^2$ is discrete if the axis domain is composed only of integers. As a result, we will obtain a set of separated points, but in a countable range.

In the next example, the `Charting` library using NuGet is used to represent data. Notice that it is necessary to install the library if you want to run the code and pay attention to the current version of the library.

We will start with the following F# code:

```
#r @"../packages/FSharp.Charting.0.90.14/lib/net40/FSharp.Charting.dll"
#load @"..\packages\FSharp.Charting.0.90.14\FSharp.Charting.fsx"

open System
open System.Drawing
open System.Windows.Forms
open FSharp.Charting

let list = [for x in -10 .. 10 -> (x, x * x)]
Chart.Point(list,Name="Integer")
```

We will obtain this graphic:

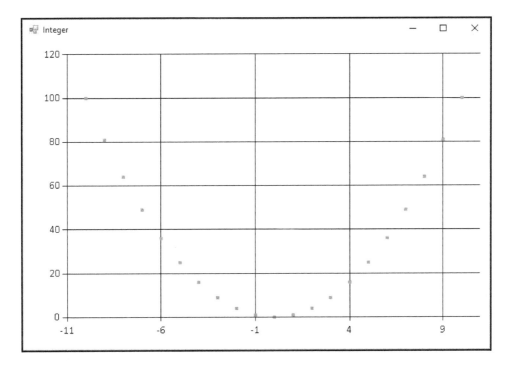

To sum up, a discrete component has the following features:

- Event-driven (or data-driven) context
- Push-based scenario
- Events are *streams of event occurrences*
- Time domain is of the type discrete
- We can always count the number of signals

The discrete event example with the discriminated union

It is very important to remember that, when we discuss about events in F#, we are dealing with the type Event of the module in the assembly Fsharp.Core.dll with the namespace Microsoft.FSharp.Control, not with DelegateEvent of the .NET framework.

In fact, this particular type of events offers many more functionalities, as previously seen.

When we presented an example of code related to the events, we confined ourselves to filter the stream of occurrences by using the position of the mouse. However, thanks to F#, now it is possible to apply more powerful flow controls:

```
open System
open System.Windows.Forms

let form = new Form(Text = "F# Windows Form",
                    Visible = true,
                    TopMost = true)
form.MouseMove
    |> Event.choose(fun evArgs ->
        match evArgs.Button with
            | MouseButtons.None -> None
            | _ -> Some( evArgs.X, evArgs.Y))

    |> Event.filter (fun (x, y) ->
        x > 0 && y > 0 && x < 255 && y < 255)

    |> Event.add (fun (x, y) ->
        form.BackColor <- System.Drawing.Color.FromArgb(
            x, y, x ^^^ y))
```

The `Event.choose` function is similar to `Event.filter`; however, it creates a selection of messages from the original event, so it creates a new message.

Notice that through *Pattern Matching* and *Built-In Discriminate union (option-choice)*, we can pass values with different types using `Some` and we can also stop the execution using `None` when `MouseButtons` is in the status none.

Continuous components

Continuous components differ from discrete ones in many aspects. Anyway, together, they represent one of the main axes of FRP.

In this specific case, signals are called *behavior* and they change continuously over time. In other words, a continuous component is composed of a constant value (signals) that can become any value during the time flow in a set of definite or indefinite values.

The following graphic shows how the time flow of a behavior works over time:

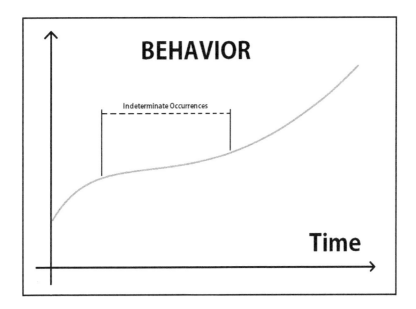

Unlike a discrete scenario, there are no events in a continuous component, but a continuous change flow. Therefore, if a signal changes continuously, the calculation performed at each modification will be *greater*, since it will occur *many more times*.

When working with continuous components, we can find a *latency state* and the scenario will be different because it will be pull-based. Regardless of how many times signals change, every new state of these signals will be elaborated, almost exclusively, in an *asynchronous* context.

In a continuous implementation, it is not possible to count the number of occurences (changes), but every change will certainly be elaborated.

We can see the mathematical example and the related F# code again.

If we consider the function $y = x^2$ and we move the axis domain from integer to real, we will obtain *a continuous line, not a set of different points*. This will happen because the scenario will move *from discrete to continuous*, since any value will be included in the set of real numbers.

As a consequence, the representative F# code will be as follows:

```
#r @"../packages/FSharp.Charting.0.90.14/lib/net40/FSharp.Charting.dll"
#load @"..\packages\FSharp.Charting.0.90.14\FSharp.Charting.fsx"

open System
open System.Drawing
open System.Windows.Forms
open FSharp.Charting

let list = [for x in -10.0 .. 10.0 -> (x, x ** 2.0)]
Chart.Line(list,Name="Float")
```

We will get the following graphical output:

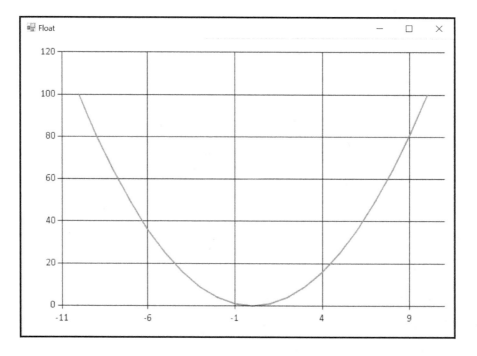

In conclusion, a continuous component has the following features:

- Demand-driven context
- As a consequence, the scenario will be pull-based
- Behaviors are *indefinite occurrences of the change of scenario*
- Time domain is of the type continuous
- There is a *reactive system*

- Often, we cannot count the number of occurred changes, but we know that they all are certainly processed

Changing continuous value and event stream

In F#, if we want to represent a discrete scenario, we have the module `Event` at our disposal, which expresses the `Event Stream` concept in detail.

However, in a continuous component, we do not find the type `Event`; in fact, it is more correct to talk about values and constants.

A good example of behavior is any `object Time` that continuously changes values over time. This modification can be negative or positive, but it certainly has different values in two different moments of the time flow.

It is not easy to find other cases in which it is simple to imagine an object that changes over time. Actually, in the example of the code used in the previous chapter, there is a kind of value that frequently changes:

```
form.MouseMove
    |> Event.filter( fun evArgs ->
        evArgs.X > 0 && evArgs.Y > 0 &&
        evArgs.X < 255 && evArgs.Y < 255)
```

We have already defined a value that changes over time. The example shows how the position of the mouse (struct point) updates at every movement of the mouse with the value of the position of the absolute coordinates in the application window.

This is another good example of behavior. So, why did we previously consider it as an example of `Event Stream`?

In FRP, `Event` and behavior, such as discrete and continuous, *are conceptually similar* and together they represent one of the main fundamentals.

By definition, we can state that:

Event a ~ Behavior (Maybe a) => Signals

Symbol ≈ means *circa* or *approximately the same*.

Now that we understand the main object of FRP, we can go further and analyze the common use scenario that includes both the concepts discussed up to this point.

Hybrid system

The use of the signals is almost always essential in cases in which the system has to respond in realtime. Usually, these scenarios have as their objective the need to respond to incentives and they have to occur in a definite period of time. As a consequence, an essential aspect that comes to light is the fact that, in a *reactive system*, it's very important to consider all the costs related to *execution time* and *used memory*. Imagine how much it could cost to not analyze these aspects in depth. It might result in memory leak or infinite cycles.

When referring to hybrid system or simply the **Real Time FRP** (**RT-FRP**) in FRP, a reactive system is made up mainly of two parts:

- The *Reactive part*, which contains everything that has to be technically developed, such as FRP
- A *base language part*, developed in any language and paradigm of programming on which it is always possible to stop the execution and use definite resources

Scenarios where it is possible to apply RT-FRP and create a hybrid system are numerous, for example, animations and **Graphical User Interface** (**GUI**) seen in the code in the previous chapter.

Otherwise, it is very interesting, considering the application in robotics where responding to incentives in a reactive way is fundamental and it is important to accurately manage all data and the memory used.

Moreover, it is also important to notice that the evolution of technology in the last few years, such as the Cloud and **Internet of Things** (**IoT**), opens the way for new possibilities concerning the application of FRP and also the reactive system, or more aptly called the hybrid system, in particular. In fact, thanks to FRP and F#, it is possible to simplify the development of technologies by using the lambda architecture, composite functions, and actors.

In the following section, we will explain in detail how to interact with and integrate RT-FRP with some examples.

Time flow and dynamic change

Time flow and dynamic change are now clear concepts of FRP. In the previous chapter, we discussed over and over again what they are. They represent one of the main axes of FRP together with discrete and continuous semantics.

Concerning reactive systems (hybrid systems), we immediately understood how much important the concepts of execution time and used memory are. These two features may have some problems that could make the system nonreactive. The title of this section suggests a solution for them both. The following are the methods which can be used:

- A good approach to avoid prolonged execution time or, even worse, the inability to manage the time flow; this results in having control on information flow (data or events)
- Instead, if we want to control used memory, for example, useless information or instances, it would be interesting to use a dynamically changing system according to the information obtained
- and architecture that already support these two features

F# and any other language based on functional paradigm exposes and uses functions and architecture that already support these two features This is one of main reasons why languages that allow a functional approach are usually used for reactive scenarios

Time flow in asynchronous data flow

In FRP and also in real time scenarios, it is very likely that data flow and its manipulation happens in an asynchronous way.

Anyway, we know that in an asynchronous context it is not possible to establish with certainty the execution time of any operation. We can analyze the following code taken from MSDN (https://msdn.microsoft.com/en-us/library/ee370262.aspx):

```
let bufferData (number:int) =
    [| for count in 1 .. 10 -> byte (count % 256) |]
    |> Array.permute (fun index -> index)

let writeFile fileName bufferData =
    async {
      use outputFile = System.IO.File.Create(fileName)
      do! outputFile.AsyncWrite(bufferData)
    }

Seq.init 10 (fun num -> bufferData num)
|> Seq.mapi (fun num value -> writeFile ("file" + num.ToString() + ".dat")
value)
|> Async.Parallel
|> Async.RunSynchronously
|> ignore
```

The function `Array.permute` performs the mapping from the input index to the output index.

The keyword `do!` and the asynchronous counterpart of the keyword `do` is the equivalent of the instruction `let () = expr.`, that is, the execution of an expression that returns a value unit type.

If we try to perform the function in `Interactive Console` of F#, in the Windows `Temp` folder, the following code will generate `10` files with `1000` chars in each one.

Anyway, if instead of `10` files, there are thousands or even worse infinite files, then it would not be possible to determine the time flow. In this case, it would be pointless to add a timeout to control the flow. Take a look at the following code:

```
let bufferData (number:int) =
    [| for i in 1 .. 1000 -> byte (i % 256) |]
    |> Array.permute (fun index -> index)

let counter = ref 0

let writeFileInner (stream:System.IO.Stream) data =
    let result = stream.AsyncWrite(data)
    lock counter (fun () -> counter := !counter + 1)
    result

let writeFile fileName bufferData =
    async {
      use outputFile = System.IO.File.Create(fileName)
      do! writeFileInner outputFile bufferData
    }

let async1 = Seq.init 1000 (fun num -> bufferData num)
                |> Seq.mapi (fun num value ->
                    writeFile ("file_timeout" + num.ToString() + ".dat")
value)
                |> Async.Parallel
try
    Async.RunSynchronously(async1, 200) |> ignore
with
    | exc -> printfn "%s" exc.Message
             printfn "%d write operations completed successfully." !counter
```

Through the second parameter of the method `Async.RunSynchronously(async1, 200)`, we can set up the maximum execution time value in order to be able to control the time flow.

In this specific case, it will stop the flow that generates files when the countdown hits zero. In fact, if we look into the `Temp` folder or simply read the output message in `Interactive Console`, we can find a number of generated *N* files that can change slightly at every execution, according to CPU work.

 You should take into account that the number of generated files depends very much on your personal computer configuration and performance.

Using F# and collection function for dynamic changing

When we presented F# and FRP in particular, we introduced the following set of essential concepts:

- Everything can be considered as a stream of data or events
- A reactive system is dynamic and flexible, and allows the management of a time flow

Now, if we try to put together these features, we can obtain an evolution of FRP, or better, a chance to organize our code and logical architecture through a *flow of choices*.

To be able to handle a set of choices, such as a set of objects or functions, first of all we should have a common denominator which represents them, otherwise it won't be possible. In informatics term, we could say *switch from a concrete implementation to an abstract one*.

In particular, functional programming has a strict connection with mathematics, so we should create **Computation Expressions**. These expressions are inspired by the **Monads** of the functional language Haskell, which in turn are inspired by the Monads concept in mathematics.

Computation Expressions are merely expressions that execute a function given an input and return a result (output). Otherwise, in terms more similar to programming, they are interfaces with rules for the execution of their own methods. For example, this allows us to connect more Monads and handle a workflow.

In F#, one of the simplest representations of Computation Expression during the flow of choices is the following:

```
type Result<'TSuccess,'TFailure> =
    | Success of 'TSuccess
    | Failure of 'TFailure
```

This code represents a general discriminate union that has as a possible result Success or Failure of the type 'TSuccess or 'Tfailure, respectively.

The next code shows how we can take full advantage of Monads, connecting more functions that return always the same output:

```
type Result<'TSuccess,'TFailure> =
    | Success of 'TSuccess
    | Failure of 'TFailure

let bind inputFunc =
    function
    | Success s -> inputFunc s
    | Failure f -> Failure f


type Account = { UserName : string; IsLogged : bool; Email : string  }

let validateAccount account =
    match account with
    | account when account.UserName = "" -> Failure "UserName is not valid"
    | account when account.Email = "" -> Failure " Email is not empty"
    | _ -> Success account


let checkLogin account =
    if(account.IsLogged) then
        Success account
    else
        Failure "User is not logged"

let LogIn account =
    if(account.IsLogged) then
        Failure "User has already Logged"
    else
        Success {account with IsLogged = true}

let LogOut account =
    if(account.IsLogged) then
        Success {account with IsLogged = false}
    else
        Failure "User has already Logged"

let ProcessNewAccount =
    let checkLogin = bind checkLogin
    let login = bind LogIn
    validateAccount >> login >> checkLogin
```

```
let NewFakeAccount = { UserName = ""; Email = ""; IsLogged = false }
let AccountLogged = { UserName = "User"; Email = "user@user.net"; IsLogged
= true }
let NewAccount = { UserName = "User1"; Email = " user1@user.net "; IsLogged
= false }

ProcessNewAccount NewFakeAccount |> printfn "Result = %A"
ProcessNewAccount AccountLogged |> printfn "Result = %A"
ProcessNewAccount NewAccount |> printfn "Result = %A"
```

As you can see, we created different Monads: `validateAccount`, `checkLogin`, and `LogIn`, which return a type `Result<Account, string>` as a result. Later, we created a function called `ProcessNewAccount` that, through the use of the composition operator, (>>) connects each Monads in a definite flow. It is important to note how, for every function, it is necessary to use the method `bind` to avoid cast and anonymous type errors.

In the last row, three different accounts are defined, which are processed with the function `ProcessNewAccount`.

The result obtained through `Interactive Console` is as follows:

```
Result = Failure "UserName is not valid"
Result = Failure "User has already Logged"
Result = Success {UserName = "User1";
                  IsLogged = true;
                  Email = " user1@user.net ";}
```

Even more on FRP and F#

The second half of the chapter shows how we can make the best use of F# and what the Microsoft .NET Framework makes available to enjoy and adopt FRP.

In the last few years, technology has evolved at an increasing rate. Nowadays, everything is connected and, in the future, each and every device will be able to receive and send data to and from each other. This will certainly lead to a technical evolution about the way we write the code. Let's think, only for a minute, about the notification messages that appear in our smartphone, our personal computer, and even in our smartwatch. All these need is a *reactive system that is able to send millions if not billions of these messages simultaneously* on multiple devices.

This is why functional programming and (Functional) Reactive Programming in particular play a key role in this evolution.

Social networks, e-commerce servers dedicated in sending information from and to IoT devices, are already using hybrid systems that complement part of their architecture as a reactive system.

They communicate through *signals* that are constantly processed in a time flow, sometimes well defined and sometimes indefinite. In the past, FRP was applied only to a specific domain, such as image elaboration or military terms. Now, even front end-web framework in JavaScript is designed for a reactive use (see Bacon.js `https://baconjs.github.io/`).

In this introduction, we summarized most of the concepts detailed in the previous chapters. Now, we will examine in depth some of the possibilities offered by the F# language and .NET Framework, particularly the following:

- We will see the last example on Computation Expression defining effectively what we will apply in that context
- We will analyze the F# `Obeservable` module

Railway-oriented Programming

We know that F# and functional paradigms can be recognized, in the previous example regarding Monads, as a particular programming technique. We are talking indeed about **Railway-oriented Programming**, so let's figure out what it is. Railway-oriented Programming refers to a programming technique that connects different functions in a *composition function* (called `path`), which has the task of sending the output of a single request to the following function in case of the success or failure of the management of the exception, prematurely ending the execution of the composition function itself.

The following image represents an execution path using this technique and is based on the function `ProcessNewAccount` of the previous example:

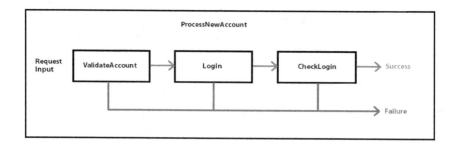

As you can see, the diagram depicts three functions held in the Computation Expression that return **Success** or **Failure**. In case of failure, we can notice how the flow stops without passing to the next Monad and, in this specific case, it returns a string:

```
let ProcessNewAccount =
    let checkLogin = bind checkLogin
    let login = bind LogIn
    validateAccount >> login >> checkLogin

//OutPut in interactive
//val ProcessNewAccount : (Account -> Result<Account,string>)
```

It becomes clear that one of the aims of Railway-oriented Programming is the unified management of errors in a process. However, this kind of programming can be used in other domains provided that they can all be translated in a choice.

F# helps us in implementing this technique, presenting a general type that has whatever is necessary to manage a Monad without having to create a custom interface.

In the assembly FSharp.Core, there are a lot of types called Choice that contain a set of overloads for the type Choice varying from 2 to 8 in the multiple implementations. Actually, we are interested in the following one that has two choices:

```
[<StructuralEquality>]
[<StructuralComparison>]
type Choice<'T1,'T2> =
| Choice1Of2 of 'T1
| Choice2Of2 of 'T2
 with
   interface IStructuralEquatable
   interface IComparable
   interface IComparable
   interface IStructuralComparable
 end
```

If we change the previous code with the implementation of the type Choice, the code in the example would be easier and concise, eliminating the general type Result<'TSuccess, 'TFailure>, as you can see in the following code:

```
let bind inputFunc =
    function
    | Choice1Of2 s -> inputFunc s
    | Choice2Of2 f -> Choice2Of2 f

type Account = { UserName : string; IsLogged : bool; Email : string }

let validateAccount account =
```

```
        match account with
            | account when account.UserName = "" -> Choice2Of2 "UserName is not
    valid"
            | account when account.Email = "" -> Choice2Of2 " Email is not empty"
            | _ -> Choice1Of2 account


    let checkLogin account =
        if(account.IsLogged) then
            Choice1Of2 account
        else
            Choice2Of2 "User is not logged"

    let LogIn account =
        if(account.IsLogged) then
            Choice2Of2 "User has already Logged"
        else
            Choice1Of2 {account with IsLogged = true}

    let LogOut account =
        if(account.IsLogged) then
            Choice1Of2 {account with IsLogged = false}
        else
            Choice2Of2 "User has already Logged"

    let ProcessNewAccount =
        validateAccount >> (bind LogIn) >> (bind checkLogin)

    let NewFakeAccount = { UserName = ""; Email = ""; IsLogged = false }
    let AccountLogged = { UserName = "User"; Email = "user@user.net"; IsLogged
    = true }
    let NewAccount = { UserName = "User1"; Email = " user1@user.net "; IsLogged
    = false }

    ProcessNewAccount NewFakeAccount |> printfn "Result = %A"
    ProcessNewAccount AccountLogged |> printfn "Result = %A"
    ProcessNewAccount NewAccount |> printfn "Result = %A"
```

It is important to notice how much Railway-oriented Programming is strictly connected to FRP. In fact, thanks to these composed functions, it is possible to manage the personalized Monads flow in a reactive way. For example, we can create one for `LogOut`:

```
    let ProcessLogOutAccount =
        validateAccount >> (bind LogOut) >> (bind checkLogin)
```

We can also create another one for the validation and the login state:

```
let ControlAccount =
    validateAccount >> (bind checkLogin)
```

Finally, we could even connect the composed functions to each other:

```
let ControlAndLoginAccount =
    ProcessNewAccount >> (bind ControlAccount)
```

Making an Observable in FRP

In the previous chapter, we presented how the type `FsharpEvent` from the assembly `Fsharp.Core` includes a set of methods for event management:

```
type Event<'T> =
 class
  new Event : unit -> Event<'T>
  member this.Trigger : 'T -> unit
  member this.Publish :   IEvent<'T>
 end
```

The interface `IEvent` inherits in turn `IObservable` and `IdelegateEvent` from two other interfaces.

The first one defines an agreement for the shipping of push-based notifications. In other words, we are talking about the same type used in .NET. In fact, its counterpart is the interface `IObserver`, which represents the agreement of notification reception.

Such as for the module `Event`, also for the type `IObservable` there exists a module called `Observable` that exposes a set of functions useful for the management and registration of observer.

Also, in this case, by using the guideline MSDN at the link `https://msdn.microsoft.com/en-us/library/ee370313(v=VS.100).aspx`, we can find a table that summarizes the functions of the module.

In this short extract, we report single methods with their signatures:

Function	Value
add	('T -> unit) -> IObservable<'T> -> unit
choose	('T -> 'U option) -> IObservable<'T> -> IObservable<'U>
filter	('T -> bool) -> IObservable<'T> -> IObservable<'T>
map	('T -> 'U) -> IObservable<'T> -> IObservable<'U>
merge	IObservable<'T> -> IObservable<'T> -> IObservable<'T>
pairwise	IObservable<'T> -> IObservable<'T * 'T>
partition	('T -> bool) -> IObservable<'T> -> IObservable<'T> * IObservable<'T>
scan	('U -> 'T -> 'U) -> 'U -> IObservable<'T> -> IObservable<'T>
split	('T -> Choice<'U1,'U2>) -> IObservable<'T> -> IObservable<'U1> * IObservable<'U2>
subscribe	('T -> unit) -> IObservable<'T> -> IDisposable

Through these functions, it is possible to create a subscriber, such as in C#. Then, we can use it to manage notifications:

```
module Observable =
   open System
   let ofSeq (values:'T seq) : IObservable<'T> =
      {
      new IObservable<'T> with
         member __.Subscribe(obs) =
            for x in values do obs.OnNext(x)
            {
            new IDisposable with
               member __.Dispose() = ()
            }
      }
   let inline print (observable:IObservable< ^T >) : IObservable< ^T > =
      {
      new IObservable<'T> with
         member this.Subscribe(observer:IObserver<'T>) =
            let value = ref (Unchecked.defaultof<'T>)
            let iterator =
               {
               new IObserver<'T> with
                  member __.OnNext(x) = printfn "%A" x
                  member __.OnCompleted() = observer.OnNext(!value)
                  member __.OnError(_) = failwith "Error"
               }
```

```
        observable.Subscribe(iterator)
    }
let first (obs:IObservable<'T>) : 'T =
    let value = ref (Unchecked.defaultof<'T>)
    let _ = obs.Subscribe(fun x -> value := x)
    !value


let obsValue =
    {0.0..100.0}
    |> Observable.ofSeq
    |> Observable.filter (fun x -> x % 2.0 = 0.0)
    |> Observable.map (fun x -> x ** 3.0)
    |> Observable.print
      |> Observable.first
```

In the preceding example, the module F# has been extended with the following functions:

- first to return the first subscribed element
- print to process all the elements one by one and display their values
- ofSeq to cast a sequence in a observable list

Summary

In this chapter, we further deepened the main concepts of FRP.

In the first part, we presented the main differences between the discrete and continuous components, showing both theoretical analysis and examples of code. Afterward, we discussed the time flow and the asynchronous data flow. Then, we introduced Computation Expressions and also the concept of Monad.

In the second and last half of the chapter, we discussed the flow of choices, Railway-oriented Programming, and finally, the module Observable.

On reaching this point, we acquired all theoretical basic information to apply Reactive Programming and Functional Reactive Programming.

It is fundamental to understand how much these two paradigms are continuously intertwined. In fact, talking about Linq and Rx is almost the same as FRP and vice versa.

On the Web, there are not many concrete examples about using FRP through F# language. However, with little practice and knowledge of functional language Haskell, on the site Microsoft Academic (Link: `https://academic.microsoft.com/`) there are lots of documents you can download that either implement and extend FRP to real cases or simply describe the principles.

To those who develop and program with object-oriented languages, I also suggest to learn to get used to compositional thinking when dealing with functional programming.

In fact, most of everyday architecture and design pattern used in OOP are just simple functions in F# and in functional paradigm languages in general. Therefore, it could be useful to extend the way of thinking to a better subdivision of these functions, so compositional thinking could be the right way.

Index

A

Action
  reference link 180
Active Patterns
  about 217, 218
  Complete 217
  Partial 217
advanced operators
  about 113
  IgnoreElements factory method 114
  Multicast factory method 119
  Publish method 115
  PublishLast method 118
  RefCount method 117
  Repeat factory method 114
  Replay factory method 118, 119
asynchrony 232

B

Base Class Library (BCL) 29

C

C# 10
CLR enumerables
  sourcing from 55
CLR events, used for sourcing
  about 137
  FromEvent method, using 143, 144
  FromEventPattern, using 138
  ToEvent method, using 145
CLR events
  sourcing from 137
CLR streams
  sourcing from 52
combining operators
  about 78

combined latest 78
  Concat 79, 80
  Merge 81
  Sample 82
  StartWith 83
  Zip 84
Command/Query Responsibility Segregation
    (CQRS) 183
Common Language Runtime (CLR) 10
Computation Expressions 247
continuous components
  about 236, 240
  continuous value, changing 243
  event stream, changing 243
  working with 241
custom operator
  AcceptObservableClient operator, designing 168
  AsObservable operator, designing 166
  Create operator, disposing 173
  custom, designing provider 176
  designing 165, 166
  reactive socket server, wiring 170
  SerialDisposable 175
custom provider overview
  reference link 177
custom scheduler
  designing 177, 179
  scheduler state, dealing with 179, 180

D

dataflow programming
  about 11, 12
  data streams 14, 15
  data-driven approach 14
  observer pattern 15
  statelessness 13, 14
default scheduler

about 151
ObserveOn 151
OserveOn method 153
Scheduler.Default scheduler 150
SubscribeOn method 151, 153
discrete components
about 236, 238, 239
discrete event example, with discriminated union
239, 240
Event module 237
Discriminated Unions
about 214, 215
Dispatcher scheduler 150
disposal
ContextDisposable 175
dynamic change 244

E

Elm
reference link 26
Event module
reference link 231
Event Sourcing (ES)
about 183
implementing, with Rx 183
invoice creation 189
invoice, creating 184
invoice, validating 184
reference link 183
events
correlating 47, 48, 50, 51
filtering 44, 46, 47
sourcing 42, 44
exception handling
about 130
Catch method, using 130, 132
Finally method, using 132
OnErrorResumeNext method, using 132
Retry sequence 134, 135
Extract, Transform, and Load (ETL) 12

F

F# collection type
reference link 203
F# Interactive 196

F# Interactive (FSI) directives
#help 224
#l 224
#load 224
#quit 224
#r 224
#time 224
reference link 224
F# Interactive (FSI)
about 224
F#
about 193, 194
and collection function used for dynamic
changing 247, 248
asynchronous pattern 218
benefits 198
collection 201
deduce type 195
drawbacks 198
features 194
functions, as first class values 197
functions, rules 198
immutable type 195
Type function, used for object-oriented
programming 199, 200
type inference 196
using 211
filtering operators
about 85
distinct 86
DistinctUntilChanged 87, 88
ElementAt 88
filter 85
Skip 89
Take 90
functional programming 16
Functional Reactive Programming (FRP)
about 193, 194, 224, 225, 226, 227, 249
event data flow 229, 230
functions 227
pull-based domains 232, 233
push-based domains 232
representing 225
scenario examples, with AsyncSeq 233
scenarios 229

functions
  add 203
  append 203
  average 203
  averageBy 203
  blit 203
  cache 203
  cast 203
  choose 203
  collect 203
  compareWith 203
  concat 203
  contains 203
  containskey 203
  count 203
  countBy 203
  create 204
  difference 204
  distinct 204
  distinctBy 204
  empty 204
  exists 204
  exists2 204
  fill 204
  filter 204
  find 204
  findIndex 204
  findKey 205
  fold 205
  fold2 205
  foldBack 205
  forall 205
  forall2 205
  get/nth 205
  head 205
  init 205
  initInfinite 206
  intersect 206
  intersectMany 206
  isProperSubset 206
  isProperSuperset 206
  isSubset 206
  isSuperset 206
  iter 206
  iter2 206

  iteri 206
  iteri2 206
  length 206
  map 206
  map1 207
  map2 207
  map3 207
  mapi2 207
  max 207
  maxBy 207
  maxElement 207
  min 207
  minBy 207
  minElement 207
  ofArray 207
  ofList 207
  ofSeq 207
  pairwise 208
  partition 208
  permute 208
  pick 208
  readonly 208
  reduce 208
  reduceBack 208
  remove 208
  replicate 208
  rev 209
  scan 209
  scanBack 209
  set 209
  singleton 209
  skip 209
  skipWhile 209
  sort 209
  sortBy 209
  sortInPlace 209
  sortInPlaceBy 209
  sortInPlaceWith 209
  sortWith 210
  sub 210
  sum 210
  sumBy 210
  tail 210
  take 210
  takeWhile 210

toArray 210
toList 210
toSeq 210
truncate 210
tryFind 210
tryFindIndex 210
tryFindkey 210
tryPick 210
unfold 211
union 211
unionMany 211
unzip 211
unzip3 211
windowed 211
zip 211
zip3 211

G

Graphical User Interface (GUI) 244

H

hybrid systems 244

I

imperative programming paradigm 9
Interactive Extension (Ix) operators
  creating 190
  reference link 191
Interactive Extensions (Ix) 165
Internet of Things (IoT) 15, 244
IObservable interface 33, 35, 37
IObserver interface 29, 30, 31
IQbservable interface
  reference link 177
IQbservable over wire
  reference link 177

L

Language Integrated Query (LINQ) 201
logic operators
  about 91
  Every 92
  SequenceEqual 92, 93
  Some 92

M

marble diagram 65
mathematical operators
  about 90
  Avg 91
  Count 91
  Includes 92
  Max 91
  Min 91
Meteor
  reference link 26
Microsoft Excel 7
Model View ViewModel (MVVM)
  about 140
  reference link 141
Monads 247

N

NuGet 64

O

object-oriented programming (OOP) 195
observer patterns
  reference link 94
operator list
  reference link 94
operator
  classic pipe forward 213
  pipe backward 213

P

Pattern Matching 212, 213
pipe forward 213
Programmable Logic Controller (PLC) 69
programming language
  generations 8
Programming with LINQ (PLINQ) 190

Q

Quality of Service (QoS) 148

R

Railway-oriented Programming
  about 250, 251
  Observable, creating in FRP 253
React
  reference link 26
Reactive Extension (Rx) programming
  about 63
Reactive Extensions (Rx)
  about 7
  debugging 121
Reactive Extensions
  reference link 26
reactive programming
  about 20, 21
  approaches 26, 27
  cancellation 24
  change propagation 23
  dataflow programming 11
  frameworks 25
  functional programming 16
  linguistic characteristics 24, 25
  messages 23
  paradigms 8, 9
  programming experience 22
  programming languages 25
  reactive manifesto 21
Reactive.js
  reference link 26
Real Time FRP (RT-FRP) 244
Record type
  differentiating, with C# 215
relative manifesto
  reference link 21
Rx scheduler testing
  reference link 161
Rx scheduling 148
Rx-Main (Reactive Extensions-Main Library) 64
Rx.NET
  setting up 64

S

schedulers
  injecting 153

  testing 159, 160
scheduling
  custom scheduling 154
  default scheduler 150, 151
  future scheduling 155
  HistoricalScheduler class 161
  using 147, 149
  virtual time, working in 156, 157, 158
sequence creation
  about 95, 96
  Create factory method, using 97
  Empty factory method, using 96
  Generate factory method, using 100
  Never factory method, using 96
  Range factory method, using 99
  Return factory method, using 96
  Throw factory method, using 97
sequence manipulation and filtering
  about 105
  If factory method, using 107
  Observable.Join factory method, using 106, 107
  SkipLast factory method, using 109
  SkipWhile operator, using 108
  TakeLast factory method, using 109
  TakeUntil operator, using 108
  TakeWhile operator, using 108
  Where factory method, using 105
sequence partitioning
  about 110
  Aggregate factory method, using 111
  GroupBy extension method, using 110
  MaxBy factory method, using 112
  MinBy factory method, using 112
sequence, inspecting
  about 127
  All method, using 128
  Any method, using 128
  Contains extension method, using 127
  SequenceEqual extension method, using 129
sequence, tracing
  about 121
  Dematerialize method, using 123, 124
  Do extension method, using 125, 126
  Materialize extension method, using 122

TimeInterval operator, using 124
sequence
  delay 204
sourcing, from CLR enumerables
  changeable collections 56, 57
  infinite collections 59
SQL Server Integration Services (SSIS) 12
Subject class
  about 66, 67
  AsyncSubject 69
  BehaviorSubject 68
  creating, from IObservable 72
  creating, with IObserver 72
  custom subjects 69
  ReplaySubject 67
  transforming operators 73
subscription life cycle
  about 38, 39, 41
synchronous pattern, F#
  about 218
  asynchronous code and examples 220
  asynchronous workflow 219, 220
  synchronous codes and examples 221
synchrony 232

T

Task Parallel Library (TPL) 24
thread integration
  about 145
  sourcing, from Task process 146

task cancellation 146
time flow
  about 244
  in asynchronous data flow 245, 246, 247
  methods 245
time-based sequence creation
  about 100
  Interval operator, using 100, 101
  TimeInterval factory method, using 104
  Timeout factory method, using 102
  Timer factory method, using 101
transforming operators
  Amb 77, 78
  debounce 75
  delay 73
  map 74
  scan 74, 75

U

Union types 214
usable disposables
  BooleanDisposable 175
  MultipleAssignmentDisposable 175
  RefCountDisposable 175
  ScheduledDisposable 175
  SingleAssignmentDisposable 175

W

Windows Presentation Foundation (WPF) 139,
  232